Busy Woman's Cookbook

Other cookbooks by Farm Journal

FARM JOURNAL'S COUNTRY COOKBOOK
FREEZING & CANNING COOKBOOK
FARM JOURNAL'S COMPLETE PIE COOKBOOK
LET'S START TO COOK
COOKING FOR COMPANY
HOMEMADE BREAD
AMERICA'S BEST VEGETABLE RECIPES
HOMEMADE CANDY

Busy Woman's Cookbook

Containing **SHORT-CUT COOKING**
and **MAKE-AHEAD COOKING**
by the Food Editors of *Farm Journal*

A Completely Revised and Reorganized
Edition of *Farm Journal's*
TIMESAVING COUNTRY COOKBOOK

DOUBLEDAY & COMPANY, INC.
GARDEN CITY, NEW YORK

Contents

PART II MAKE-AHEAD COOKING

LIST OF COLOR ILLUSTRATIONS

Part I
Short-cut Cooking

Introduction

"Never enough hours in a day" is the story of many a busy home-maker's life today wherever she lives. One busy farm woman's diary substantiates this: "Up at 5 A.M. Dressed and organized four children for a trip to orthodontist. Off to hospital volunteer duty. Home in time to fix supper for the hungry tribe. Then all of us off to a birthday party. . . ."

Such pressure for time seems to be almost universal. And yet most wives and mothers must prepare and serve at least three meals every day—more than one thousand a year! There's concern, too, about feeding your family well, selecting foods and menus that will supply them with good nutrition.

To help you with these problems we've produced this Short-cut Cookbook in our Countryside Test Kitchens. First we browsed through the supermarkets and their exciting collection of ready-to-fix mixes, a tremendous selection of frozen foods and an almost never-ending choice of canned goods. Every one of these modern convenience foods—whether a complete dish or a short-cut ingredient—is a way of buying time. By using them creatively, we believe we can help you whip up perfectly respectable, tasty and nutritious meals in minutes. The emergency shelf of yesterday has become the easy, even elegant meal of today.

Perhaps you are a working wife—perhaps a teacher as well as a homemaker, or a busy woman deeply involved in time-consuming community projects. We have tried to meet your situation by giving you superior recipes that take a minimum of your time and yet bring approval from friends and family.

Section 1
Main Dishes

This section brings you a choice of over 100 main dishes that are speedy and delicious—some even spectacular. The assortment includes hearty casseroles, complete dinners in a skillet and last-minute meals that take less than thirty minutes from cupboard to table.

All these recipes are built around protein-rich meats, chicken, fish, eggs and cheese. There are many stick-to-the-ribs dishes that men will go for—and dig in for seconds.

Many are special enough for company fare but easy enough for everyday menus when you want to give the family a little extra-special treat. And they are kind to a tight budget too.

Everyone will want your recipe when you serve the Bacon-Potato skillet. Our Round Steak Dinner will do you proud every time. When you are looking for a filling and nourishing breakfast, lunch or brunch turn to the recipe for Egg/Corned Beef Stacks. High praise from everyone!

Discover new and exciting ways with ground beef. Try Chili Hash —it's zippy; the Hamburger Pie crowned with cheese-flecked potatoes.

To stretch a stingy budget toss together the Tuna Cornbread casserole (all the makings already likely in your cupboard or freezer). Unexpected company will be delighted with the elegant looking and tasting Salmon Biscuit Roll with Piquant Sauce.

You'll make the Potato Omelet again and again—failproof but looks so pretty. And the Baked Eggs Nestled in Spinach Cups add special character to a meal.

You'll enjoy the imaginative mix of these easy-to-fix main dishes, and most of all you will enjoy the special glow of satisfaction from having fed the family well.

Short-cut Cooking is divided into five sections for easy use. Beginning with Main Dishes, it progresses to Vegetables and Salads, Sandwiches and Breads, Desserts and winds up with Snacks, Nibbles and Beverages, chock full of last minute recipes for impromptu entertaining.

Meats

SIZZLING STEAKS—BROILER-FAST Broiling is a speedy way to cook meat. And almost everyone agrees that a hot, tender steak, browned on the outside, juicy and pink within, has few peers on the platter. When steaks are less than 1″ thick, pan-broiling gives the best results. Here are the directions for broiling beef successfully.

Beef Cuts to Broil Club, porterhouse, rib, sirloin, T-bone and tenderloin (filet mignon). Hamburger patties and liver also may be broiled.

Thickness of Steaks 1″ to 2″.

How to Broil Preheat broiler 10 minutes, or as directed by range manufacturer. Rub heated broiler rack with piece of suet.

To prevent steaks from curling, slash fatty edge of steak with a knife or scissors at 1″ intervals, but do not cut into meat. Lay steak on heated rack 3″ to 5″ from heat—5″ for well-done, 3″ to 5″ for medium to rare. If the distance in your broiler must be less, reduce temperature accordingly.

Broil steak on one side; turn and broil on the other side. Season with salt and pepper and serve at once on warm platter.

How Long to Broil The time depends on many factors like thickness of steak, its size and shape and the amount of bone and fat. All timetables for broiling are an approximate guide. The test for doneness is to cut a slit in the steak near the bone and observe the color—gray for well-done, pink for medium-rare and red for rare. Broil 1″ steak from 5 to 7 minutes, 1½″ steak from 8 to 12 minutes, and a 2″ steak from 15 to 20 minutes on each side.

Seasonings for Broiled Steaks Salt and pepper may be the only seasonings desired. Bottled meat sauces may be sprinkled over the hot steak. Other toppings to add just before serving are: dabs of butter, butter blended with prepared mustard, a squeeze of lemon juice or a little mashed Roquefort or blue cheese mixed with butter or margarine. Or mix ⅛ lb. Roquefort or blue cheese with 1 tblsp. heavy cream and 1 tblsp. Worcestershire sauce. Spread on broiled steak before removing it from rack. Broil close to heat for 2 minutes.

For a barbecued flavor, brush the steak before broiling and as it broils with bottled French dressing. Or brush both sides of the steak before broiling with salad oil; when cooked to desired doneness, sprinkle with garlic salt and seasoning salt.

PAN-BROILED STEAKS

Cuts to Pan-broil Same as for broiling but cut ½″ to ¾″ thick—up to 1½″ if you like steak pink inside.

How to Cook Place in preheated heavy skillet. Rub skillet with a little suet, but do not add fat. Do not cover; do not add water. Brown on both sides. Reduce heat and cook to the desired degree of doneness, pouring off fat as it accumulates in pan. Turn occasionally to insure even cooking. It takes 6 to 12 minutes to pan-broil a rare steak and 18 to 24 minutes for a well-done steak. Season and serve.

Minute Steaks These are thin steaks from the round that are scored by a special machine to cut the connective tissue. Rub a hot, heavy skillet with a little fat. Cook the steaks quickly, about 1 or 2 minutes on each side. Season with salt and pepper.

Tenderized Steaks Chuck, round, rump, flank and any less tender steak may be broiled if tenderizer is used. Sprinkle tenderizer on all surfaces of the steak, ½ tsp. per pound of meat. Do not season tenderized steaks with salt.

After adding the tenderizer, deeply pierce all surfaces of the meat with a sharp-tined fork, at 1″ intervals. Then cover loosely and place in refrigerator in the evening to use the next day. Broil like any other steak. Since tenderized meats tend to cook more quickly than other steaks, be careful not to overcook.

Instead of refrigerating meat after tenderizer has been added, you can let it stand at room temperature. It requires no attention until time for broiling. Let it stand 30 to 40 minutes if the steak is 1″ thick, about an hour for thicker steaks.

OTHER BEEF CUTS TO BROIL

Hamburger Patties Broil 1" patties like steak about 5 minutes on each side.

Liver (calf's and young beef): Brush ½" slices with soft butter or margarine and broil on rack in shallow pan 3" or 4" from heat, 2 to 4 minutes on each side. Broil until delicate pink inside or well-done, but use care not to overcook, for that toughens it.

London Broil Use only top-quality flank steak scored lightly, criss-cross fashion on both sides. Salt both sides of the steak and brush generously with French dressing. Broil 3" from heat 4 to 5 minutes on each side. Slice diagonally in thin slices. For 6 servings, use flank steak weighing 2½ lbs.

California Minute Steaks Pan-fry minute (cube) steaks quickly in a little butter. Sprinkle one side of steaks lightly with a touch of rosemary or oregano; add a thin slice of tomato and one of Cheddar cheese. Run under broiler just long enough to melt cheese.

Variation: For sandwiches, serve California Minute Steaks on slices of toast or French bread, buttered and sprinkled with parsley.

OVEN-ROASTED STEAKS

Place ½" steaks on rack in shallow oven. Place in preheated slow oven (300°) and cook 30 minutes for medium-rare steaks. Steaks 1" to 1¼" take 45 to 60 minutes to reach the medium-rare stage. There's no spattering, no turning and no watching during cooking.

Have you tried skewering poatoes on aluminum nails to bake in half the time? You can put them in the oven with the steak. Otherwise, give the potatoes a head start.

BAKED LEMON STEAK

3 tblsp. butter or margarine, melted
3 lbs. sirloin steak, 1½" thick
1 tsp. salt
¼ tsp. pepper
1 lemon, thinly sliced
2 onions, thinly sliced
1 c. ketchup
1 tblsp. Worcestershire sauce
¼ c. water

Brush butter on both sides of steak; season with salt and pepper. Place on rack in shallow pan. Lay lemon slices on steak and cover with onions.

Mix ketchup, Worcestershire sauce and water. Pour over steak.

Bake in hot oven (425°) 30 to 45 minutes, depending on degree of doneness desired. Makes 6 to 8 servings.

ROUND STEAK DINNER

1½ lbs. round steak, ½" thick	1 (10½ oz.) can tomato soup
¼ tsp. salt	1 whole clove
⅛ tsp. pepper	1 c. water
½ tsp. oregano	1 tblsp. instant minced onion
2 tblsp. shortening	1 (10 oz.) pkg. frozen peas

Cut steak into 1" strips; then cut strips in ½" diagonal pieces. Sprinkle with salt, pepper and oregano; brown in hot fat. Add soup, clove, water and onion; simmer ½ hour.

Cook peas according to package directions; drain and add to stew. Simmer 15 minutes longer. Serve over noodles or rice. Makes 6 servings.

BARBECUED BEEF RIBS

4 lbs. beef ribs	1 tblsp. brown sugar
¼ c. chopped onion	¼ tsp. fennel seed (optional)
¼ c. chopped green pepper	½ bay leaf
1 tsp. salt	2 tblsp. lemon juice
¼ tsp. pepper	1 c. water
1 tsp. celery seed	

Heat pressure cooker. Add ribs a few at a time to hot pan. Brown ribs thoroughly on all sides. Drain off all fat. Combine remaining ingredients and pour over ribs.

Close cover securely. Place over high heat. Bring to 15 lbs. pressure according to manufacturer's directions for your pressure cooker. When pressure is reached (control will begin to jiggle or rock), reduce heat immediately and continue to cook at 15 lbs. pressure for 25 minutes. Remove from heat. Allow pressure to reduce naturally 5 minutes, then place unopened cooker under running faucet or in pan of cold water.

Remove ribs. Skim off excess fat. Thicken sauce with a paste of 1 tblsp. flour and 1 tblsp. water. Pour over ribs. Makes 6 servings.

SUPREME OF LIVER

1 lb. calf's liver	¼ c. cornmeal
½ tsp. salt	3 to 4 tblsp. salad oil
¼ tsp. pepper	Cream Gravy (recipe follows)
¼ tsp. sage	

Slice liver thin.

Mix seasonings and cornmeal. Roll liver in this mixture and brown on both sides in hot oil in skillet. Serve with Cream Gravy. Makes 4 servings.

Cream Gravy Drain all but 1 tblsp. fat from skillet. Add ½ c. heavy or dairy sour cream. Season with salt and pepper. Heat, but do not boil. Pour over hot liver slices.

BROILED HAMBURGER STEAK

2 lbs. ground beef	2 tsp. salt
½ c. milk	⅛ tsp. pepper
1 egg	French salad dressing
1 tblsp. Worcestershire sauce	

Thoroughly mix all ingredients except salad dressing. Spread soft mixture in an oval about 1½" thick. Place on preheated broiler rack. Brush top of meat with bottled French dressing.

Broil 3" from heat source 12 minutes. Turn with broad spatula (or 2 spatulas), brush with salad dressing and broil 12 minutes longer.

Cut in thick slices. Makes 6 servings.

STUFFED HAMBURGER PILLOWS

1 lb. hamburger	⅛ tsp. pepper
1 tblsp. shortening	1 (8 oz.) can refrigerator
3 tblsp. finely chopped	crescent rolls
mushrooms	1 (4 oz.) carton French onion
¼ c. finely chopped green	dip
pepper	1 tblsp. butter
1 tblsp. butter	1 to 3 tblsp. milk
¼ tsp. salt	

Shape hamburger into eight 3½ × 2½" rectangles. Brown each in shortening on both sides; drain and set aside.

Sauté mushrooms and green pepper in butter until tender. Sprinkle with salt and pepper. Spread vegetables evenly on 4 hamburger rectangles; top with remaining patties.

Unroll crescent rolls, leaving each 2 triangles joined to form 4 rectangles; press the perforations to seal. Place a filled pattie in center of each rectangle; fold up sides and ends; press edges to seal well. Place seamside down on ungreased baking sheet. Bake in hot oven (400°) for 12 minutes, until brown. Combine in a 1 qt. saucepan onion dip and butter with enough milk to thin to sauce consistency; heat to simmering. Pour over pillows. Makes 4 servings.

FROSTED MEAT LOAF

1 slightly beaten egg	1 tbsp. instant minced onion
¼ c. milk	1½ c. soft bread crumbs
2 tsp. salt	2 lbs. ground beef
¼ tsp. pepper	½ pkg. instant mashed potatoes
¼ c. ketchup or chili sauce	½ c. shredded Cheddar cheese

Combine egg and milk; stir in salt, pepper, ketchup, onion and bread crumbs. Mix in ground beef. Form into a loaf and place in shallow baking pan (13×9×2″).

Bake in moderate oven (350°) 1 hour.

Prepare mashed potatoes as directed on package. Frost baked meat loaf with potatoes. Sprinkle with cheese. Return to oven until cheese melts. Makes 8 servings.

SAVORY MEAT LOAF

2 lbs. lean ground beef	½ c. milk
1 egg	1 (10½ oz.) can condensed cream
½ c. fresh bread crumbs	of mushroom soup
1 pkg. onion soup mix	1 tsp. prepared mustard

Combine beef, egg, bread crumbs, onion soup and milk. Form into loaf about 3″ high and place on large sheet of aluminum foil. Combine mushroom soup and mustard; spread over top of loaf. Wrap loosely in foil, making a tight seal. Place on baking sheet and bake in moderate oven (350°) for 1½ hours. Makes 8 servings.

BEEF VEGETABLE BAKE

2 lbs. ground beef
1½ c. soft bread crumbs
2 eggs
2 (8 oz.) cans tomato sauce
2 tsp. salt
1½ tsp. chili powder
⅛ tsp. cayenne

1 (10 oz.) pkg. frozen carrots
 and peas
1 (10 oz.) pkg. frozen corn
¼ tsp. garlic salt
½ tsp. salt
¾ c. shredded process
 American cheese

Combine beef, bread crumbs, eggs, 1 can tomato sauce, salt, chili powder and cayenne. Press into a 2 qt. casserole, building up the sides to shape a well in center. Bake in moderate oven (350°) 20 minutes.

Run hot water over vegetables to separate them; drain. Season with garlic salt and salt. Place in center of hot meat. Pour remaining tomato sauce over loaf. Bake in moderate oven (350°) 20 minutes. Sprinkle cheese over top and bake 5 minutes, or until cheese is melted. Makes 6 to 8 servings.

PORCUPINE MEAT BALLS

1½ lbs. ground beef
½ c. uncooked regular rice
⅔ c. milk
1 tblsp. instant minced onion
 (or 1 medium onion,
 chopped)

1½ tsp. salt
¼ tsp. pepper
1 (10½ oz.) can condensed
 tomato soup
¾ c. water

Combine beef, rice, milk, onion, salt and pepper. Drop rounded tablespoonfuls of mixture into shallow baking pan (13×9×2″).

Combine soup and water. Pour over meat.

Cover pan tightly with foil. Bake in moderate oven (350°) 1 hour. Makes 6 to 8 servings.

BAKED MEAT BALLS

2 eggs
½ c. milk
1 tblsp. instant minced onion
3 slices bread, cut in cubes

2 tsp. salt
¼ tsp. pepper
2 lbs. ground beef

Beat together eggs and milk. Stir in onion, bread and seasonings. Add beef and mix well.

For uniformity in size, measure meat mixture in a ¼ c. measure. Turn out and shape into balls.

Place balls in shallow pan. Bake in moderate oven (350°) 30 minutes. Makes approximately 18 balls.

BEEF BALLS WITH RICE

1½ lbs. ground beef	2 beef bouillon cubes
¾ c. fine bread crumbs	1 tsp. sugar
2 eggs	1½ tsp. celery salt
2 tsp. salt	3 c. tomato juice
½ c. ketchup	2 c. precooked rice
2 tblsp. shortening	¼ c. butter or margarine
⅓ c. finely chopped onion	¼ c. chopped parsley

Combine ground beef, bread crumbs, eggs, salt and ketchup; mix well. Form into 12 to 14 (1½″) balls. Heat shortening in a large skillet and cook meat balls, shaking pan to cook them evenly and keep them round.

Add onion and brown lightly. Add bouillon cubes, sugar, celery salt, tomato juice, rice and butter. Bring to a boil. Cover tightly; place over low heat 10 minutes. Garnish with wreath of parsley snipped with scissors. Makes 6 servings.

MORE WAYS WITH GROUND BEEF The Michigan woman who shares this recipe says it's the world's best chili con carne. Taste her version of this sturdy dish and see if you don't agree.

CHILI CON CARNE

1 lb. ground beef	1 small garlic clove
1 (15 oz.) can red beans	2 tblsp. chili powder
1 (1 lb.) can tomatoes	½ tsp. salt
1 (⅕ oz.) pkg. instant onion	¼ tsp. cumin seed

Brown ground beef in skillet. Add beans, tomatoes and onion.

Run toothpick through garlic so it can be removed easily after cooking. Add to meat along with seasonings.

Cover and simmer 15 minutes. Remove garlic. Makes 6 servings.

CHILI WITH HOMINY

1 lb. ground beef
1 medium onion, chopped
  (¾ c.)
1 (1 lb.) can tomatoes

1 (1 lb.) can hominy
2 tblsp. chili powder
1 tsp. salt

Cook ground beef and onion in skillet until beef is browned. Add remaining ingredients. Simmer, covered, 15 minutes. Makes 6 servings.

CHILI HASH

2 c. precooked rice
1 medium onion, chopped
2 tblsp. shortening
1 lb. ground beef
2 (10½ oz.) cans condensed
  tomato soup

1 tsp. chili powder
1 tsp. salt
¼ tsp. pepper
½ c. precooked rice

Prepare 2 c. rice as directed on package. Keep warm.
Sauté onion in shortening; add beef and brown lightly.
Stir in soup and seasonings; heat to boiling. Add ½ c. rice; cover, remove from heat and let stand 5 minutes. Fluff up with fork. Spoon remainder of rice in ring around hash on platter. Makes 6 to 8 servings.

HEARTY ITALIAN SPAGHETTI

1 (½ oz.) pkg. Italian
  spaghetti sauce mix
1 (8 oz.) can tomato sauce
1 lb. ground beef

12 oz. spaghetti
½ c. shredded pizza cheese
1 tsp. instant parsley flakes
(optional)

Prepare sauce as directed on package. Meanwhile brown beef in skillet. Add spaghetti sauce and simmer.
Cook spaghetti as directed on package. Place drained, cooked spaghetti on platter or in large, shallow bowl. Top with sauce. Sprinkle with cheese and parsley. Makes 4 to 6 servings.

BEEF-MACARONI SKILLET

1 lb. ground beef
1 medium onion, chopped
3 c. tomato juice
1 tblsp. Worcestershire sauce
1 tblsp. vinegar
1 tsp. salt
⅛ tsp. pepper
1 tsp. dry mustard
1 c. uncooked elbow macaroni

Brown beef and onion in skillet. Add remaining ingredients and cook, covered, until macaroni is done, about 20 minutes. Stir occasionally while cooking. Makes 6 servings.

HAMBURGER/CHEESE BISCUIT RING

2 lbs. ground beef
⅓ c. chopped onion
1 (10½ oz.) can condensed
  cream of celery soup
½ c. tomato juice
¾ c. beef bouillon
¼ c. ketchup
1 tsp. chili powder
¼ c. sliced olives
Cheese Biscuits (recipe
  follows)

Brown ground beef and onion in large skillet; pour off excess fat. Add all ingredients except biscuits; simmer until slightly thickened.

To serve, spoon meat into center of platter and surround with hot Cheese Biscuits. Garnish with sliced stuffed olives. Makes 6 servings.

Cheese Biscuits

¼ c. shortening
⅓ c. shredded Cheddar cheese
2 c. biscuit mix
⅔ c. milk

Cut shortening and cheese into biscuit mix. Add milk; stir with fork to make a soft dough, beating 15 strokes. Drop dough by tablespoons onto a greased baking sheet. Bake in hot oven (425°) for 12 to 15 minutes or until golden. Makes 12 large biscuits.

DOUBLE CORN BAKE

1 lb. hamburger
1 tsp. salt
¼ tsp. oregano
½ tsp. chili powder
⅓ c. chopped onion
⅓ c. ketchup
1 (12 oz.) can whole kernel
  corn
1 (10 oz.) pkg. corn bread mix
2 tblsp. melted butter
Tomato Sauce (recipe follows)

Combine meat and next 5 ingredients in a skillet. Cook, stirring until meat is browned. Press against sides and rim of a 10″ greased pie plate. Drain corn; pour into center of pie plate.

Use package directions to prepare corn bread, adding melted butter. Spread evenly over meat and corn. Bake in hot oven (425°) for 20 minutes. Let stand 10 minutes; then invert onto serving plate. Accompany with Tomato Sauce. Makes 6 to 8 servings.

Tomato Sauce

1 (1 lb.) can stewed tomatoes
1 tblsp. butter
½ bay leaf

1 tsp. cornstarch
1 tblsp. water

Combine stewed tomatoes, butter and bay leaf in a 1 qt. saucepan. Simmer for 10 to 15 minutes. Dissolve cornstarch in water. Gradually stir into hot mixture. Stir and cook until thick.

HAMBURGER PIE

1 lb. ground beef
1 medium onion, chopped
  (about ¾ c.)
½ tsp. salt
Dash pepper

1 (10½ oz.) can condensed
  tomato soup
1 (1 lb.) can green lima beans
½ pkg. instant mashed potatoes
½ c. shredded Cheddar cheese

Cook meat and onion in heavy skillet until meat is browned. Add salt, pepper, tomato soup and beans with their liquid. Simmer 5 minutes. Place in a greased 2 qt. casserole.

Prepare potatoes as directed on package. Drop in mounds over hot meat mixture. Sprinkle with cheese.

Bake in moderate oven (350°) 20 minutes. Makes 6 servings.

MEAT-VEGETABLE PIE

1 lb. ground beef
1 medium onion, chopped
  (about ¾ c.)
1 tsp. salt
⅛ tsp. pepper

2 (10½ oz.) cans condensed
  vegetable soup
2 c. biscuit mix
½ c. milk

Brown beef and onion in skillet. Add seasonings and soup; simmer 5 minutes. Pour into a greased 2 qt. casserole.

Combine biscuit mix with milk as directed on package to make biscuits. Drop by spoonfuls over the hot meat.

Bake in hot oven (425°) until biscuits are browned, 15 to 20 minutes. Makes 8 servings.

BAKED PORK CHOPS

4 pork chops
1 tblsp. onion soup mix

2 tblsp. French salad dressing
¼ c. water

Place pork chops in skillet. Top with soup mix and pour in the salad dressing and the water. Bake covered in moderate oven (350°) 1 hour. Makes 4 servings.

COMPANY PORK CHOPS

6 pork chops, ½″ thick
¼ tsp. salt
¼ tsp. pepper
2 tblsp. shortening

1 (10½ oz.) can condensed
    chicken with rice soup
¼ tsp. fennel seed
1 bay leaf

Sprinkle pork chops with salt and pepper and brown on both sides in shortening in a large skillet. Drain off excess fat. Combine soup, fennel and bay leaf and pour over chops. Cover and simmer over low heat until chops are tender, about 45 minutes. Makes 6 servings.

PORK NOODLE CASSEROLE

2 lb. pork steak, cubed
2 tblsp. shortening
1 c. chopped celery
1 c. chopped onion
1 (10½ oz.) can condensed
    cream of chicken soup
1 (10½ oz.) can condensed
    cream of mushroom soup

1 (4 oz.) can sliced mushrooms,
    drained
2 c. water
⅛ tsp. pepper
⅛ tsp. ground sage
1 tblsp. Worcestershire sauce
1 (10 oz.) pkg. frozen peas
1½ c. cooked wide egg noodles

Brown pork in shortening in a large skillet. Push pork to one side. Sauté celery and onion until tender. Add soups, mushrooms, water and seasonings; simmer 20 minutes, covered. Add frozen peas and noodles; cook 15 minutes longer. Makes 8 servings.

Broiled Ham Slash fatty edge of 1″ ham slice in several places. Broil 2″ from heat, about 8 minutes per side, if the ham is ready-to-eat or cooked, and 12 minutes per side if ham is uncooked.

Spicy Broiled Ham Place center-cut, ready-to-eat or cooked slice of ham in shallow pan. (A center cut weighs around 2 lbs. and makes 4 servings.) Mix ¼ c. brown sugar, 2 tblsp. cider vinegar and

1½ tsp. dry mustard and spread over top of ham. Broil under moderate heat until lightly browned, baste with drippings, turn and brown other side.

Company Broiled Ham   Broil or pan-fry a slice of ham. Spread top to within ½″ of outer edge with mixture made by combining ⅓ c. mayonnaise, 3 tblsp. grated Parmesan cheese and ½ tsp. prepared mustard. Broil until bubbly and tinged with brown.

Supper Ham and Eggs   Lay thin slices of cooked ham on warm platter. Top with sliced hard-cooked eggs and heated cooked or canned asparagus spears or broccoli. Pour warm Nobby Cheese Sauce (see Index) over eggs.

CANDIED HAM SLICE

½ c. dark corn syrup	1 (1 lb. 7 oz.) can yams or
¼ c. brown sugar	sweet potatoes, drained
¼ c. butter	2 oranges, peeled and cut into
1 tblsp. grated orange rind	4 slices each
¼ tsp. cinnamon	2 ham slices, ½″ thick
⅛ tsp. ground cloves	

Combine corn syrup, brown sugar, butter, orange rind, cinnamon and cloves in a skillet. Bring to a boil; simmer 5 minutes. Add yams; cook over low heat, basting occasionally, 8 to 10 minutes. Add orange slices; continue basting for 5 minutes or until well glazed.

Meanwhile, place ham slices in preheated broiler about 3″ from source of heat. Broil about 4 minutes on each side or until browned.

Garnish ham with glazed yams and orange slices. Makes 4 servings.

EASY BAKED HAM

1 (5 to 6 lb.) canned ham	1 tblsp. horse-radish
Whole cloves	1 tsp. dry mustard
1 c. red currant jelly	

Place ham, fat side up, on rack in shallow roasting pan.

Heat in slow oven (325°) 15 minutes per pound. One half hour before end of heating time, score and stud with cloves.

Soften jelly over low heat. Stir in horse-radish and mustard.

Spread ham with glaze; continue heating ½ hour longer, basting 3 times.

Let stand 15 minutes. Slice and serve. Makes 15 to 20 servings.

HAM BALLS WITH GLAZED PEACHES

1 (1 lb. 13 oz.) can peach halves
1 egg, beaten
½ c. fine bread crumbs
1 tsp. prepared mustard
2 tsp. Worcestershire sauce
¼ tsp. pepper

1 lb. ground ham
¼ c. chopped green pepper
Nutmeg
2 tblsp. flour
2 tblsp. melted butter
2 tblsp. brown sugar

Drain peaches, reserving ¼ c. syrup. Combine reserved syrup, egg, bread crumbs, mustard, Worcestershire sauce, and pepper. Stir in ham and green pepper. Shape in 18 balls.

Broil in preheated broiler until browned, about 7 minutes. Turn ham balls. Place peach halves in broiler with ham balls. Sprinkle peaches with nutmeg and broil 4 minutes. Combine flour, butter and brown sugar. Brush over peaches and broil until topping is bubbly and browned, about 1 minute. Remove ham balls and peaches from broiler. Serve a peach half with 3 ham balls. Makes 6 servings.

HAM-ASPARAGUS CASSEROLE

1 (10½ oz.) can condensed cream of mushroom soup
⅓ c. light cream
2 c. diced cooked ham

1 c. cooked or canned cut asparagus
Buttered bread crumbs

Blend soup with cream; add ham and asparagus. Pour into 4 individual ramekins, or a small, shallow baking dish. Top with crumbs.

Bake in moderate oven (375°) about 20 minutes. Makes 4 servings.

Variation: Use 1 c. diced ham and 2 c. asparagus pieces.

MUSHROOM BREADED VEAL

2 lbs. veal steak, ½" thick
1 (1½ oz.) pkg. mushroom soup mix
1 c. cracker crumbs

2 eggs, slightly beaten
2 tblsp. water
⅓ c. hot fat
½ c. water

Cut veal in serving pieces.

Roll mushroom soup mix in unopened package with rolling pin to crush large pieces. Combine with cracker crumbs.

Dip veal in crumbs, then in egg mixed with water, then in crumbs again. Brown on both sides in hot fat until golden. (Do not over-brown.)

Add water, cover and bake in moderate oven (350°) 45 minutes. Uncover during last 10 minutes of cooking. Makes 6 to 8 servings.

Variation: Substitute pieces of broiler-fryer chickens for the veal steaks. An easy way to fix Mushroom Fried Chicken.

VEAL IN SOUR CREAM

1½ lbs. cubed veal steaks, cut
   in serving-size pieces
2 tblsp. fat
1 (10 oz.) can mushroom
   gravy

½ c. water
½ c. dairy sour cream
Parsley

Cook veal over medium heat in hot fat about 5 minutes on each side, or until tender. Lift to warm platter and keep warm.

Pour fat from skillet. Add gravy and water and stir, heating to boiling and simmering 3 minutes.

Stir in sour cream, but do not cook. Pour around veal, garnish with parsley and serve. Makes 5 to 6 servings.

VEAL PATTIES

1½ lbs. ground veal
½ c. melted fat (chicken fat
   if available)
½ tsp. lemon juice
Salt

Pepper
1 egg, beaten
2 tblsp. water
1 c. cracker crumbs

Combine meat, fat, lemon juice, salt and pepper. Shape into 6 patties.

Mix egg with water.

Dip patties in egg mixture and then into cracker crumbs. Brown on both sides in hot fat. Cook about 15 minutes. Makes 6 servings.

Note: Gravy may be made with drippings and light cream or milk. Season delicately with nutmeg if desired.

Variations: Brush patties with French dressing before dipping them in the egg mixture and cracker crumbs. Heat dairy sour cream (do not let come to a boil) and serve over veal patties.

BROILED LAMB

Cuts to Use Loin, rib or shoulder chops and leg steaks, cut 1" thick.

How to Broil Place on rack in preheated broiler 3" from heat. Brown on one side, 6 to 7 minutes. Season with salt and pepper and turn. Brown on the other side another 6 to 7 minutes. To test for doneness, cut a slit along the bone and note if color is that of rare, medium-rare or well-done meat. Serve at once on a hot platter.

Seasonings Rub the lamb before broiling with a cut garlic clove. Or sprinkle broiled lamb with a little dry salad mix, garlic flavor. Or serve broiled lamb topped with lemon juice and butter, mixed. Cream ¼ c. butter with spoon and gradually stir in 1 tblsp. lemon juice (fresh, frozen or canned) and add ½ tsp. salt. If available, add 1 tblsp. chives or parsley, snipped fine with scissors, to the butter mixture.

Pan-broiled Lamb Use loin, sirloin, rib or shoulder chops or leg steaks ½" to ¾" thick. Trim piece of fat from meat and rub over surface of a heated, heavy skillet. Remove fat. Cook meat in greased skillet over moderate heat until well browned; turn and continue cooking. Turn occasionally while cooking. Test for doneness by cutting a slit near bone and observing color.

Broiled Lamb Patties Mix 1½ lbs. ground lamb with 1½ tsp. salt and ¼ c. or 6 tblsp. milk. Shape lightly into 6 patties. Score both sides with spatula. Place on broiler pan and broil 4" to 5" from heat, 10 to 12 minutes. Turn and broil 5 to 8 minutes longer or until patties are cooked. Serve plain or topped with dabs of Garlic Butter (see Index). A little marjoram added to the uncooked ground lamb adds flavor.

LAMB-SAUSAGE GRILL

Broil the meat for a special-occasion, hurry-up meal. A mixed grill is especially attractive and good. Excellent teammates are lamb chops, little pig sausages and canned pineapple rings. It's easy to fix such a combination of foods this way.

Mixed Grill To prevent meat from curling, slash fat edges of rib lamb chops. Lay on broiler rack with pork-sausage links. (There are 12 to 16 sausages in a pound.) Broil 5" to 6" from source of heat, 7 to 8 minutes. Turn chops and season; turn sausages. Place well-drained, canned pineapple slices on rack and dot with butter or margarine. Broil 7 to 8 minutes longer.

Note: Cook frozen lima beans while meats broil; toss a green salad. While taking up the meats and pineapple, warm hard rolls in the oven. Presto! your dinner menu will be: Mixed Grill, buttered lima beans, green salad, hard rolls and chocolate cake for dessert.

ARIZONA WAGON WHEEL

½ c. chopped onion
2 tblsp. butter or margarine
⅔ c. chili sauce
1 (1 lb.) can kidney beans
1 (1 lb.) pkg. frankfurters,
  cut in ¼" slices

⅛ tsp. black pepper
⅛ tsp. cayenne pepper
1 tsp. chili powder
2 c. shredded Cheddar cheese

Cook onion in butter until soft. Add chili sauce, kidney beans, frankfurters and seasonings. Simmer 10 minutes.

Add cheese and simmer, stirring frequently, until cheese is melted and blended. Makes 6 servings.

Note: To make dish to take to a pot-luck supper, pour hot bean mixture into greased 2 qt. casserole. Trim top with extra strips of cheese to represent spokes in wheel. Bake in hot oven (400°) to melt cheese.

CHILI FRANKS

½ c. chopped onion
2 tblsp. butter
1 (15½ oz.) can chili with
  beans
¼ c. water
¼ tsp. chili powder

Dash cayenne pepper
6 frankfurters
6 frankfurter buns, split and
  toasted
½ c. shredded Cheddar cheese

Sauté onion in butter until tender. Stir in chili, water, chili powder, pepper and frankfurters. Simmer for 10 minutes or until mixture is well heated.

Serve on buns. Top with cheese. Makes 6 servings.

SAUERKRAUT AND FRANKFURTERS

2 (1 lb.) cans sauerkraut
1 (1 lb.) pkg. frankfurters
   (about 10)

1 large apple, cored and sliced
½ tsp. caraway seeds (optional)

Place 1 can sauerkraut in bottom of 2 qt. casserole. Top with frankfurters, then with remaining sauerkraut. Spread apple slices on top. Sprinkle with caraway seeds.

Bake covered in moderate oven (350°) 1 hour. Makes 5 servings.

Note: Serve with instant mashed potatoes prepared as directed on package.

PENNY PANCAKES

1½ c. milk
2 eggs, beaten
2 tblsp. salad oil

2 c. buckwheat pancake mix
8 frankfurters, cut in ¼″ slices

Combine milk, eggs and oil; add pancake mix; stir lightly. Arrange frankfurters in clusters of six on hot griddle; pour 2 tblsp. batter over each cluster; brown. Makes 15 cakes.

BLACK-EYE PEAS WITH FRANKS

1 tblsp. finely chopped onion
2 tblsp. bacon fat
1 (1 lb.) can black-eye peas
   and pork
¼ c. ketchup

2 tblsp. molasses or brown
   sugar
1 tsp. dry mustard
Frankfurters

Cook onion in fat until soft. Combine in casserole with peas, ketchup, molasses and mustard. Lay frankfurters, two for every person, on top.

Cover and bake in moderate oven (350°) 30 minutes. Makes 3 servings.

Variation: Substitute canned pork and beans for black-eye peas.

FRANKFURTER-SUCCOTASH SKILLET

6 frankfurters
⅓ c. chopped onion
⅓ c. chopped green pepper
2 tblsp. butter or margarine
¾ c. chili sauce
1 (12 oz.) can whole kernel
corn

1 (10 oz.) pkg. frozen lima
beans
½ tsp. salt
Dash pepper

Slice frankfurters diagonally in ¼" slices and cook with onion and green pepper in butter in skillet until onion is soft.

Add remaining ingredients to mixture and simmer, covered, until lima beans are cooked, about 20 minutes. Stir occasionally to separate frozen limas. Makes 5 to 6 servings.

FRANK-TOPPED ZESTY SUCCOTASH

1 (10 oz.) pkg. frozen lima
beans
1 (10 oz.) pkg. frozen whole
kernel corn
1 c. dairy sour cream

2 tblsp. prepared mustard
¼ tsp. salt
6 frankfurters, halved
lengthwise

Cook lima beans and corn according to package directions. Drain well and combine. Spread in bottom of 7×11" baking dish.

Blend together sour cream, mustard and salt. Spread over vegetables. Top with halved franks, cut side down, and bake in moderate oven (350°) for 15 minutes or until franks are hot. Makes 6 servings.

10-Minute Main Dish Heat canned beans with franks in tomato sauce as label on can directs. Serve over toast or corn chips with a hot dog relish alongside.

BOY-SCOUT SPECIAL

Fast-fix Stuffed Frankfurters Split each frankfurter, but not quite through. Stuff with 1 tsp. canned spaghetti sauce and 1 tsp. pickle relish. Wrap with bacon slice and fasten with toothpick. Broil cut side down 2" to 3" from heat in preheated broiler, about 3 minutes. Turn and continue broiling until bacon is cooked, about 3 minutes. Serve in split long bun if desired.

SAUSAGE-APPLE-SAUERKRAUT SUPPER

1 lb. bulk pork sausage
2 tblsp. chopped onion
1 apple, cored and sliced
1 (1 lb.) can sauerkraut,
    drained

½ tsp. caraway seeds
4 servings instant seasoned
    mashed potatoes (2 cups)
⅓ c. shredded Cheddar cheese
Paprika

Brown sausage in skillet. Drain; turn into 1½ qt. casserole. Sauté onion in 2 tblsp. of drippings.

Place onion and apple on sausage. Cover with sauerkraut and caraway seeds. Spread potatoes on top; garnish with cheese and paprika.

Bake in moderate oven (350°) for 35 minutes or until top is golden brown. Makes 4 servings.

SAUSAGE AND APPLE SKILLET

1 lb. pork sausage links
4 medium red apples, sliced
⅓ c. brown sugar, firmly
    packed

¼ tsp. cinnamon
Dash cloves

Pan-fry sausage; remove and keep hot.

Pour off all but 2 tblsp. of drippings. Add apples to drippings in skillet. Combine sugar, cinnamon and cloves and sprinkle over apples. Cook slowly until apples are tender and glazed.

Serve with sausage. Makes 4 servings.

SAVORY SAUSAGE RICE

2 lbs. bulk sausage
1 c. finely chopped green
    pepper
¾ c. chopped onion
2½ c. coarsely chopped celery
2 (2⅛ oz.) pkgs. chicken
    noodle soup mix

4½ c. boiling water
1 c. uncooked rice
½ tsp. salt
¼ c. melted butter or
    margarine
1 c. blanched almonds, slivered
    (optional)

Brown sausage in large skillet; pour off excess fat. Add green pepper, onion and 1 c. celery; sauté.

Combine soup mix and water in large saucepan; stir in rice.

Skip work with BEEF VEGETABLE BAKE (recipe page 19). Meat and vegetables cook together in the same pan. Double recipe if you like—fill one loaf with frozen vegetables and freeze for later use.

HASH-STUFFED CRESCENTS (recipe page 35) and SALMON BISCUIT ROLL (recipe page 50) look mighty glamorous. Actually they are everyday foods dressed up with lots of imagination. Easy to fix, too!

Cover and simmer 20 minutes, or until tender. Add sausage mixture and salt; stir well.

Pour into greased baking dish (about 12×8×2″). Sprinkle remaining celery over top; drizzle with melted butter. Bake in moderate oven (375°) 20 minutes. Makes 10 servings.

If almonds are used, sauté all celery with green pepper and onion. Mix most of almonds with other ingredients; save a few to sprinkle on top. Omit melted butter.

POTATO-SAUSAGE SKILLET

½ (9 oz.) pkg. frozen hash-
  brown potatoes
½ lb. pork sausage
1 c. chopped onion

½ tsp. salt
¼ tsp. celery salt
¼ tsp. ground sage
⅛ tsp. pepper

Prepare potatoes as directed on package; drain well.

Cook sausage and onion together in skillet until sausage browns. Drain off fat if more than ¼ c. Add potatoes and seasonings.

Cook, stirring occasionally, until golden brown. Makes 6 servings.

SAUSAGE APPLE ROLL-UPS

1 lb. pork sausage links
1 (15 oz.) can unsweetened
  applesauce
¼ c. dark brown sugar, firmly
  packed
¼ tsp. cinnamon
¼ tsp. nutmeg

1 tblsp. butter
1 tsp. vanilla
1 c. pancake mix
1 c. milk
1 egg
1 tblsp. vegetable oil
½ c. maple syrup (optional)

Pan-fry sausages until thoroughly cooked and brown.

Combine applesauce, brown sugar, spices, butter and vanilla in 1½ qt. saucepan. Heat to boiling.

Combine pancake mix, milk, egg and oil; beat with rotary beater until smooth. Fry 5″ pancakes on hot griddle. As cakes come off griddle, spread with 1 rounded tblsp. of applesauce mixture. Place sausage in middle and bring sides of pancake up around sausage. Overlap at top and secure with toothpick. Drizzle with maple syrup, if desired; serve immediately. Makes 10 to 12 roll-ups.

BUTTERED APPLESAUCE

Heat together 2 c. applesauce and ¼ c. butter, stirring together. Makes about 2 cups.

BACON-POTATO SKILLET

½ (9 oz.) pkg. frozen hash- brown potatoes	⅛ tsp. pepper
6 slices bacon	4 eggs, slightly beaten
½ tsp. salt	¼ c. milk

Simmer potatoes as directed on package; drain well.

Pan-broil bacon until crisp. Drain on paper toweling and crumble. Remove all but ¼ c. bacon fat from skillet. Stir in potatoes. Add salt and pepper. Cook, turning occasionally, until golden brown.

Reduce heat to low. Combine eggs and milk; add, with bacon, to potatoes. Cook, stirring occasionally, until eggs are set. Makes 6 servings.

CONFETTI CORN BAKE

4 slices bacon	4 eggs, slightly beaten
1 tblsp. minced onion	1½ c. milk
2 tblsp. chopped green pepper	1 tblsp. chopped pimiento
1 tblsp. flour	1 tsp. salt
2 c. whole kernel corn	⅛ tsp. pepper

Fry bacon until crisp. Drain and crumble. Sauté onion and green pepper until tender in 3 tblsp. of the bacon drippings. Set aside. Sift flour into corn. Add bacon, sautéed vegetables and remaining ingredients. Pour into buttered 9″ pie plate. Bake in moderate oven (325°) for 30 minutes until set. Makes 5 to 6 servings.

TAMALE PIE

1 small bag corn chips	⅓ c. water
2 (15 oz.) cans beef tamales	1 c. chopped onion
2 (15 oz.) cans chili without beans	1 c. shredded Cheddar cheese

Crush corn chips. Sprinkle ½ over bottom of 9×11″ baking dish. Arrange unwrapped tamales over chips. Combine chili and water;

pour over tamales. Sprinkle onions then cheese over chili, top with remaining corn chips. Bake in moderate oven (350°) for 35 to 40 minutes. Makes 8 servings.

CHILI-MAC CASSEROLE

1 c. macaroni
2 (16 oz.) cans chili with
  beans

½ c. dill pickle slices

Cook macaroni as directed on package.
Heat chili to boiling point.
Drain cooked macaroni and combine with chili. Place in a 1½ qt. casserole. Top with pickle slices.
Bake in moderate oven (375°) 20 minutes. Makes 4 servings.

DEVILED CORNED BEEF HASH

1 (1 lb.) can corned beef hash
½ c. mayonnaise

1 tsp. prepared mustard
2 tblsp. chopped onion

Cut chilled corned beef hash in 4 slices and place in shallow baking pan. Top with mayonnaise, mustard and onion, mixed. Bake in hot oven (400°) until lightly browned, 15 to 20 minutes. Makes 4 servings.

HASH-STUFFED CRESCENTS

1 c. pancake mix
1 c. milk
1 egg
1 tblsp. shortening
¼ c. chopped onion
2 tblsp. butter

1 (15½ oz.) can corned beef
  hash
2 tblsp. pickle relish
2 tblsp. ketchup
1 c. sour cream
2 tblsp. prepared mustard

Combine pancake mix, milk, egg and shortening; beat batter until smooth. Bake 6 pancakes on a hot griddle; set aside.
Sauté onion in butter until tender. Add hash, pickle relish, and ketchup; heat. Spoon ⅙ of hash onto half of each pancake, folding other half over. Combine sour cream and mustard; spoon over top of each crescent. Makes 6 servings.

DOUBLE-QUICK COMBINATIONS

Chili-Spaghetti   Combine 1 (15½ oz.) can chili with beans with 1 (15½ oz.) can spaghetti in tomato sauce. Simmer gently until thoroughly heated. Serve over toast or with toast on the side; add a lettuce-cucumber salad and cantaloupe à la mode for dessert. Makes 6 servings.

Beef-Corn   Sauté 2 medium onions, chopped, in 2 tblsp. butter or margarine. Add 1 (12 oz.) can corned beef, shredded, and 1 (16 oz.) can cream-style corn. Simmer gently until thoroughly heated. Try this over canned chow mein noodles. Makes 6 servings.

Ham-Chicken   Spread 6 slices of toast with deviled ham—you'll need about 3 (2¼ oz.) cans. Heat 3 (10½ oz.) cans chicken à la king. Pour ½ c. mixture on each toast slice. Makes 6 servings.

CHILI AND CORN BREAD SUPPER

2 (15½ oz.) cans chili with
beans
2 c. cubed ham
1 (1 lb. 13 oz.) can tomatoes
1 (1 lb.) can mixed vegetables,
drained
2 tblsp. instant minced onion

¾ tsp. chili powder
1 (10 oz.) pkg. corn bread
mix
2 tblsp. grated cheese
1 egg, beaten
⅓ c. milk

Combine chili with beans, ham, tomatoes, mixed vegetables, instant minced onion and chili powder in a 4 qt. Dutch oven. Bring to a boil, stirring often.

Meanwhile, combine corn bread mix, cheese, egg and milk; stir until moistened. Spoon batter onto boiling stew; cover, reduce heat. Simmer for 20 minutes. Makes 6 to 8 servings.

CHEESE-MEAT LOAF

2 (12 oz.) cans luncheon meat
¼ tsp. ground cloves
4 tsp. prepared mustard
16 slices process American
cheese

1 (1 lb. 8 oz.) jar cherry-pie
filling

Cut each can of meat into 9 slices, cutting almost through to bottom of loaf. Spread between slices mixture of cloves and mustard; put 1 cheese slice into each slash in loaf.

Place meat in baking dish; pour cherries around it. Bake in hot oven (400°) 15 minutes, or until cheese melts. To serve, slice loaf at right angle to cuts. Makes 8 servings.

Variation: Instead of cherries, use thick applesauce or drained crushed pineapple, lightly sprinkled with cinnamon.

MEAT AND BEANS BAKE

2 (1 lb.) cans pork and
   beans
2 tblsp. minced onion
¼ c. brown sugar
2 tblsp. pickle relish

1 tsp. dry mustard
1 (12 oz.) can luncheon meat,
   sliced
8 slices American cheese,
   diagonally cut

Combine pork and beans, onion, brown sugar, pickle relish and mustard in a 1½ qt. casserole. Arrange meat and cheese on top. Bake in moderate oven (350°) for 30 minutes. Makes 6 servings.

JIFFY MEAT PIE

¼ c. chopped onion
¼ c. chopped green pepper
⅛ tsp. oregano
Dash garlic powder
1 tblsp. butter

1 (1½ lb.) can beef stew
½ c. peas or any vegetable
½ bay leaf
1 (8 oz.) pkg. refrigerator
   biscuits

Sprinkle onion and green pepper with oregano and garlic powder. Sauté in butter until tender. Add stew, peas and bay leaf; heat to boiling. Remove bay leaf. Pour into 1½ qt. casserole. Top with biscuits. Bake in hot oven (450°) until biscuits are brown, 15 to 20 minutes. Makes 6 servings.

Poultry

GOLDEN FRIED CHICKEN

2 (2½ to 3 lb.) frying chickens   2 c. cheese-cracker crumbs
    cut in serving pieces   2 tsp. salt
⅔ c. salad oil

Dip chicken pieces in oil, then in cracker crumbs, with salt added, to coat. Bake in a foil-lined, shallow baking pan or on baking sheet in moderate oven (375°) 45 to 60 minutes. Makes 6 to 8 servings.

CRISPY FRIED CHICKEN

1 (2½ to 3 lb.) frying chicken,   2 tsp. salt
    cut in serving pieces   ¼ tsp. pepper
3 tblsp. melted fat   1 c. corn flake crumbs

Rub chicken with 1 tblsp. fat, salt and pepper.
Roll chicken in corn flake crumbs until well coated.
Place in greased, shallow baking pan and sprinkle with remaining fat. Bake in moderate oven (375°) until browned and tender, 45 to 60 minutes. Makes 4 to 5 servings.

Variation: Instead of rubbing chicken with fat, dip it in ½ c. evaporated milk. Do not use regular milk.

SAUCY CHICKEN BAKE

2 to 3 medium zucchini   1 c. Basic Red Sauce (see
1 (2½ to 3 lb.) frying chicken,   Index)
    cut in pieces   2 to 3 tblsp. grated Parmesan
½ tsp. oregano   cheese

Slice unpeeled squash in ½″ slices. Arrange in bottom of 3 qt. baking dish. Place chicken, skin side up, over zucchini.
Add oregano to Basic Red Sauce; pour evenly over the chicken and zucchini.
Bake uncovered in hot oven (400°) 30 minutes. Baste chicken

and zucchini with drippings; bake another 30 minutes, or until chicken is tender. Sprinkle with cheese and return to oven for a few minutes. Makes 4 to 6 servings.

BARBECUED CHICKEN

¼ c. vinegar
¼ c. water
1 small onion, grated
2 tblsp. ketchup
1 tblsp. Worcestershire sauce
1 tsp. sugar

1 tsp. salt
¼ tsp. paprika
¼ tsp. dry mustard
2 broiler-fryer chickens, quartered

Combine vinegar, water, onion, ketchup, Worcestershire sauce, sugar, salt, paprika and dry mustard.

Place chicken in a 13×9×2″ oblong baking dish. Pour sauce over chicken. Bake in moderate oven (375°) for 1½ hours or until tender. Makes 8 servings.

BAKED CHICKEN WITH DRESSING

¼ c. butter or margarine
⅓ c. hot water
2 c. herb-seasoned stuffing mix
1 (10¾ oz.) can chicken gravy

1 (6 oz.) can boned chicken, cubed, or ⅔ c. cooked chicken
1 (10 oz.) pkg. frozen peas

Melt 3 tblsp. butter in water; toss lightly with 1 c. stuffing mix; place half in 1 qt. casserole.

Mix gravy, chicken, cooked peas, unsalted, and 1 c. dry stuffing mix; pour over mixture in casserole; top with rest of stuffing; dot with 1 tblsp. butter.

Bake in moderate oven (350°) 20 minutes. Makes 6 servings.

CHICKEN AND STUFFING PIE

Crust

1 (8 oz.) pkg. herb-seasoned stuffing mix (4 c.)
¾ c. chicken broth

½ c. melted butter
1 egg, beaten

Combine all ingredients; mix well. Press mixture into a greased 10″ pie plate.

Filling

1 (4 oz.) can mushrooms	1 c. peas, fresh, frozen or
2 tsp. flour	canned
½ c. chopped onion	2 tblsp. diced pimiento
1 tblsp. butter	1 tblsp. parsley flakes
1 (10½ oz.) can chicken giblet	1 tsp. Worcestershire sauce
gravy	½ tsp. thyme
2 to 3 c. cubed cooked	4 slices American process
chicken	cheese

Drain mushrooms. Combine mushroom liquid with flour; set aside. Sauté mushrooms and onion in melted butter. Stir in mushroom liquid, gravy, chicken, peas, pimiento, parsley flakes, Worcestershire sauce and thyme. Heat thoroughly.

Turn into stuffing crust. Bake in moderate oven (375°) for 20 minutes. Cut each cheese slice into 4 strips. Place in lattice design on pie. Bake 5 more minutes until crust is golden and cheese is melted. Makes 1 (10″) pie.

CHICKEN CASSEROLE

1 (10½ oz.) can condensed	1 (3 oz.) can chow mein
cream of mushroom soup	noodles
1 (10½ oz.) can condensed	¾ c. corn flake crumbs
chicken with rice soup	
⅔ c. cubed, cooked chicken	
or 1 (5 oz.) can boned	
chicken	

Mix soups together in greased 1½ qt. casserole. Stir in chicken and noodles. Top with corn flake crumbs.

Bake in moderate oven (350°) 30 minutes. Makes 4 to 5 servings.

CASSEROLE À LA KING

1 (15¼ oz.) can macaroni with	2 tblsp. butter or margarine,
cheese sauce	melted
1 (10½ oz.) can chicken à la	¼ c. shredded Cheddar cheese
king	Paprika
3 tblsp. bread crumbs	

Heat macaroni and chicken à la king on top of range in separate saucepans.

Place half of heated macaroni in bottom of greased 1 qt. casserole. Top with chicken mixture, then remaining macaroni. Combine bread crumbs and butter; sprinkle on top. Scatter on cheese and dust with paprika.

Broil until top is bubbly and brown, about 5 minutes. Makes 4 servings.

CHICKEN-ASPARAGUS CASSEROLE

1 (10½ oz.) can condensed cream of mushroom soup
⅓ c. milk
Dash nutmeg
1 c. diced cooked or canned chicken

1 (14½ oz.) can asparagus spears, drained
½ c. crushed corn chips

Combine soup and milk. Mix in nutmeg and chicken. Pour into a 1½ qt. casserole. Top with asparagus, attractively arranged. Sprinkle with corn chips. Heat in moderate oven (375°) 15 to 20 minutes. Makes 4 servings.

Variations: Substitute diced cooked ham for the chicken. Use buttered bread crumbs for the corn chips.

CHICKEN QUEEN

1 (10½ oz.) can condensed cream of mushroom soup
3 tsp. instant minced onion
1 tblsp. mayonnaise
1 (5 to 6 oz.) can boned chicken, (about ⅔ c. diced cooked chicken)

1 c. crushed potato chips
1 c. drained canned peas
1 (4 oz.) can or jar pimientos

Combine soup, onion and mayonnaise in greased 1½ qt. casserole. Add liquid from canned chicken, chicken, cut in pieces, ¾ c. potato chips, peas and pimiento, cut in strips. Mix gently. Sprinkle remaining potato chips on top.

Bake in moderate oven (350°) about 30 minutes. Makes 4 servings.

CHICKEN-RICE CASSEROLE

1 (10 oz.) pkg. frozen peas
and carrots
1 (10½ oz.) can condensed
cream of mushroom soup
1⅓ c. water
½ c. milk

½ tsp. salt
1⅓ c. precooked rice
1½ c. diced cooked chicken
or 2 (5 oz.) cans chicken
½ c. grated Cheddar cheese

Combine peas and carrots, soup, water, milk and salt in saucepan. Bring to a boil and simmer 3 minutes.

Pour half of soup mixture into greased 2 qt. casserole. Top with rice, chicken and remaining soup mixture. Sprinkle with cheese. Bake in moderate oven (350°) 20 minutes. Makes 6 servings.

CHOW MEIN HOT DISH

1 (10½ oz.) can condensed
cream of chicken soup
1 (10½ oz.) can condensed
cream of mushroom soup
1 c. milk
1 c. cubed cooked turkey or
chicken

1 (1 lb.) can chow mein
vegetables, drained
1 (8 oz.) can chow mein
noodles

Blend soups and milk in a greased 2 qt. casserole. Stir in turkey, vegetables and two-thirds of the noodles. Top with remaining noodles. Bake in moderate oven (350°) 50 minutes. Makes 8 servings.

CHICKEN ITALIANO

¼ c. flour
1½ tsp. salt
¼ tsp. pepper
1 (3 lb.) stewing chicken, cut
into pieces
2 tblsp. oil
½ c. chopped onion
1 small clove garlic, chopped

1¼ c. tomato juice
½ c. water
¼ c. chopped green pepper
¼ tsp. oregano
¼ tsp. basil
¼ tsp. rosemary
½ bay leaf
¼ c. sliced stuffed olives

Combine flour, salt and pepper. Roll chicken pieces in seasoned flour. Heat pressure cooker. Add oil and heat until oil sizzles. Add chicken pieces a few at a time and brown well on all sides in hot oil. Remove chicken pieces. Sauté onion and garlic in remaining oil until tender. Add tomato juice, water, green pepper, oregano, basil, rosemary, half bay leaf and bring to a boil. Add chicken pieces. Close cover securely. Place over high heat. Bring to 15 lbs. pressure, according to manufacturer's directions for your pressure cooker. When pressure is reached (control will begin to jiggle or rock), reduce heat immediately and continue to cook 25 minutes at 15 lbs. pressure. Remove from heat. Allow pressure to reduce naturally 5 minutes, then place cooker under running faucet or in pan of cold water.

Skim off any excess fat. Sprinkle with olives. Makes 4 to 5 servings.

TURKEY SHORTCAKES

½ lb. process American cheese	1½ tsp. instant minced onion
2 tblsp. chicken broth or milk	Salt
2 c. cubed cooked turkey, or	Pepper
3 (5 oz.) cans boned turkey	

Place cheese and broth in double boiler. Cook over boiling water until cheese is melted, stirring occasionally to blend. Add remaining ingredients, seasoning to taste.

Serve over toast, hot biscuits or corn bread. Makes 4 servings.

Variations: For Chicken Shortcakes, use cooked or canned chicken instead of turkey. For Superlative Burgers, serve the cheese sauce, with the onion added, over cooked hamburger patties on toasted bun halves.

Fish

FAST-FIX FISH You can depend on fish for a change of pace that's also kind to your budget. Fish is an excellent source of protein, low in cholesterol, and available in frozen food cases everywhere. Our recipes will help you serve fish in appetizing ways.

Read on, too, for some good ideas for serving canned seafood. Every last-minute cook who keeps a few cans of tuna and salmon in her cupboard also keeps her cool in the face of any meal emergency.

BAKED FISH FILLETS

1 (1 lb.) pkg. frozen fish fillets	1 tblsp. prepared mustard
1 egg white	½ tsp. salt
¼ c. mayonnaise	⅛ tsp. pepper

Thaw fish slightly. Cut in 4 pieces. Place skin side down in greased shallow baking dish.

Beat egg until stiff. Fold in mayonnaise, mustard, salt and pepper. Spread on fish. Bake in hot oven (425°) 20 minutes or until fish flakes with fork and topping is brown. Makes 4 servings.

FISH PIQUANT

2 lbs. frozen fish fillets (haddock, flounder or perch)	2 tblsp. butter or margarine
	1 small onion, chopped
	1 lemon
½ c. French dressing	Tartar Sauce (see Index)

Thaw fish as directed on package.
Dip pieces in French dressing.
Heat butter in skillet. Add fish; sprinkle onion over top.
Cook over moderate heat 7 to 8 minutes on each side, turning once.
Serve with lemon wedges and Tartar Sauce. Makes 6 servings.

BARBECUED SALMON STEAKS

6 (1″) salmon steaks	2 tsp. Worcestershire sauce
⅓ c. butter or margarine	2 tblsp. finely chopped onion
½ tsp. salt	Tartar Sauce (see Index)

Place salmon in greased shallow baking pan. Combine butter, salt and Worcestershire sauce. Brush mixture over salmon. Sprinkle on onion.

Bake in moderate oven (350°) about 30 minutes. Serve with Tartar Sauce. Makes 6 servings.

BROILED FISH

3 lbs. fish fillets (⅜ to ½″ thick)	½ tsp. salt
	½ tsp. dried tarragon
⅔ c. lemon juice	Rich Tomato Sauce (recipe follows)
2 tblsp. Worcestershire sauce	

Place fillets in large shallow dish. Combine remaining ingredients to form marinade; pour over fish. Cover dish, place in refrigerator for 2 to 3 hours.

Place fillets in broiler pan. Spoon marinade over. Broil 5" from heat 12 to 15 minutes. Baste with marinade. Serve with Rich Tomato Sauce. Makes 6 servings.

Rich Tomato Sauce

⅓ c. butter
1 clove garlic, crushed
1 green pepper, chopped
1 (1 lb.) can tomatoes

3 tblsp. reserved fish marinade
½ tsp. salt
2 tblsp. cornstarch
2 tblsp. water

Melt butter in skillet. Add garlic and cook 1 minute. Add green pepper; cook until tender. Remove garlic.

Stir in tomatoes, fish marinade and salt. Heat to bubbling. Dissolve cornstarch in water and gradually stir into hot mixture. Stir and cook until thick. Makes 2½ c.

FISH POACHED IN SHRIMP SAUCE

1 (10 oz.) can frozen cream
  of shrimp soup, thawed
1 c. water
1 tsp. instant parsley flakes

½ tsp. onion salt
¼ tsp. oregano
1 (1 lb.) pkg. frozen fish
  fillets, thawed to separate

Blend soup and water in skillet. Add parsley flakes, onion salt and oregano; bring to a boil. Add fish; cover, simmer 10 minutes or until fish flakes easily with fork. Makes 4 servings.

POTATO-CLAM SCALLOP

3 tblsp. butter or margarine
2 tblsp. flour
3 c. milk
2½ tsp. salt
¼ tsp. pepper

8 medium potatoes, sliced thin
2 tblsp. chopped onion
1 (7 oz.) can minced clams,
  drained

Melt butter; stir in flour and cook until smooth and bubbly. Remove from heat; add milk (you can substitute clam juice for equal amount of milk), 1½ tsp. salt and pepper. Boil 1 minute.

Arrange half the potatoes in bottom of 2 qt. casserole. Sprinkle with ½ tsp. salt and half of onion, clams and sauce. Repeat for top layer. Bake, uncovered, in moderate oven (350°) 50 to 55 minutes. Makes 8 servings.

SHRIMP BISQUE

1 (10½ oz.) can condensed
  cream of celery soup
1½ c. milk

1 (5 oz.) can shrimp
¼ c. chopped green pepper
3 drops Tabasco sauce

Dilute soup with milk in saucepan.
Chop shrimp, reserving some whole for garnish.
Add shrimp, green pepper, and Tabasco sauce to soup.
Heat and pour into soup bowls. Makes 6 servings.

SHRIMP CREOLE

1 lb. frozen shrimp, shelled
  and deveined
½ c. chopped green pepper
½ c. chopped celery

1 tblsp. salad oil
1 c. Basic Red Sauce (see
  Index)

Cook shrimp according to package directions.
Cook pepper and celery in hot oil until just soft. Add Basic Red Sauce and shrimp. Serve with rice. Makes 4 servings.

SCALLOPED OYSTERS

2½ c. coarse cracker crumbs
1 pt. oysters
¼ c. oyster liquor
¾ c. light cream

1 tsp. Worcestershire sauce
½ tsp. salt
⅛ tsp. pepper
⅓ c. butter or margarine

Arrange ⅓ cracker crumbs in well-buttered shallow 1 qt. baking dish. Cover with ½ of oysters; repeat layers of crumbs and oysters. Blend liquids and seasonings; pour over oysters. Top with remaining crumbs. Dot with butter.
Bake in moderate oven (350°) about 45 minutes. Makes 5 servings.

OVEN-FRIED OYSTERS

24 large oysters
1½ c. flour
1¼ tsp. salt
¼ tsp. pepper
2 eggs, slightly beaten

3 tblsp. cold water
Dry bread crumbs or cracker
  crumbs
Salad oil

Drain oysters; dry between paper towels.

Combine flour, salt and pepper. Coat oysters with seasoned flour.

Combine eggs and water; beat well. Dip floured oysters into egg mixture. Roll in bread crumbs. Sprinkle on both sides with salad oil.

Bake in a single layer in an oiled shallow pan in hot oven (400°) about 15 minutes. Good served with lemon wedges or Tartar Sauce (see Index).

FARMHOUSE OYSTER STEW

2 tblsp. flour	2 tblsp. cold water
1½ tsp. salt	1 pt. oysters
Few drops Worcestershire sauce	1 qt. milk

Combine flour, salt, Worcestershire sauce and water. Blend to a smooth paste. Stir in oysters and their liquor.

Simmer over very low heat until edges of oysters ruffle. Remove from heat, pour in the hot milk, cover and let stand 10 to 15 minutes to mellow.

Reheat stew and serve in warm bowls. Makes 3 to 4 servings.

TUNA-NOODLE SUPPER

1 (8 oz.) pkg. medium noodles	⅓ c. sliced stuffed olives
1 (10½ oz.) can condensed cream of mushroom soup	2 tsp. minced onion
1 c. milk	1 (8 oz.) pkg. process American cheese, sliced
2 (7 oz.) cans tuna, drained and broken in chunks	⅛ tsp. pepper

Prepare noodles according to package directions.

Combine noodles, soup, milk, tuna, olives, onion, cheese and pepper. Simmer until mixture is well heated and cheese is melted. Makes 6 servings.

TUNA-CORN BREAD CASSEROLE

1 (10 oz.) pkg. frozen mixed vegetables	Pepper
1 tblsp. instant minced onion	1 (10½ oz.) can condensed cream of celery soup
1 (6½ to 7 oz.) can tuna, drained and flaked	¾ c. milk
¼ tsp. salt	1 (8 oz.) pkg. corn muffin mix

Cook vegetables in boiling salted water until barely tender. Drain. Add onion, tuna, salt, pepper, soup and milk. Heat to boiling.

Meanwhile, prepare corn bread batter as directed on package. Pour hot tuna mixture into greased 2 qt. casserole. Top with batter.

Bake in hot oven (400°) until top is golden brown, 25 to 30 minutes. Makes 6 servings.

HOT TUNA SALAD

2 (7 oz.) cans tuna, drained and flaked
2 c. chopped celery
¼ c. chopped sweet pickles
2 tsp. grated onion
2 tblsp. lemon juice
½ tsp. salt
1 c. mayonnaise
½ c. shredded sharp cheese
1 c. crushed potato chips

Combine ingredients except cheese and potato chips. Pile lightly in individual bakers.

Top with layer of cheese and then potato chips. Bake in very hot oven (450°) 10 minutes. Makes 6 servings.

TUNA BISQUE

1 (10½ oz.) can condensed cream of tomato soup
1 (10½ oz.) can condensed pea soup
2 (6 to 7 oz.) cans tuna, drained and flaked
2 c. milk
½ c. light cream
1½ tsp. lemon juice
Thin lemon slices

Mix soups until smooth. Add tuna, milk and cream. Heat. Add lemon juice. Simmer a few minutes before serving. Float lemon slices on top. Makes 6 to 8 servings.

SALMON LOAF

1 (10½ oz.) can condensed cream of celery soup
⅓ c. mayonnaise or salad dressing
1 egg, beaten
½ c. chopped onion
¼ c. chopped green pepper
1 tblsp. lemon juice
1 (1 lb.) can salmon, drained, boned and flaked
1 c. cracker crumbs

Mix together all ingredients. Place in greased loaf pan (9×5×3″).

Bake in moderate oven (350°) 1 hour. Unmold and slice. Makes 6 to 8 servings.

LIGHTNING SALMON PIE

1 (1 lb.) can salmon, drained
½ pkg. instant mashed potatoes
2 tblsp. milk

½ c. grated process American cheese
1 tblsp. butter or margarine

Break salmon into pieces with fork; pile in center of greased 9" pie pan.

Prepare potatoes as directed on package. Place ring of hot potatoes around salmon.

Sprinkle milk over salmon, and cheese over potatoes. Dot with butter.

Bake in very hot oven (450°) until potatoes are lightly browned, 15 to 20 minutes. Makes 4 servings.

SALMON SCALLOP

1 (1 lb.) can salmon
3 eggs
1 c. milk
1¼ c. coarse cracker crumbs
½ tsp. salt
Dash pepper

1 tblsp. instant onion
¼ c. butter or margarine
½ c. cracker crumbs
2 tblsp. butter or margarine, melted

Empty salmon (including bones and liquid) into greased 1½ qt. casserole. Break up with fork. Add eggs and stir with fork until thoroughly mixed. Stir in milk, 1¼ c. cracker crumbs, salt, pepper and onion. Dot with butter, stirring it in.

Toss ½ c. cracker crumbs with 2 tblsp. melted butter. Sprinkle on top.

Bake in moderate oven (350°) 50 minutes. Makes 6 servings.

SOUR CREAM-SALMON

2 (1 lb.) cans salmon, drained
2 (10½ oz.) cans condensed clam chowder
1 tsp. instant minced onion

2 tblsp. dry bread crumbs
1½ c. dairy sour cream
2 tblsp. chopped chives

Combine salmon, chowder, onion and crumbs in greased baking

dish (8×8×2″); spread cream over top; sprinkle with chives (or green onion tops, chopped, or instant green onions).

Bake in moderate oven (375°) 20 to 25 minutes. Makes 6 to 8 servings.

SALMON BISCUIT ROLL

½ c. chopped celery	1 (10½ oz.) can condensed
½ c. chopped green pepper	cream of chicken soup
¼ c. chopped onion	2 c. biscuit mix
2 tblsp. butter	⅔ c. milk
½ c. chopped black olives	1 egg
(optional)	1 tblsp. water
1 (1 lb.) can red salmon	Piquant Sauce (recipe follows)

Sauté celery, pepper and onion in butter until tender; add olives. Drain salmon; reserve liquid. Add salmon with ¼ c. of the chicken soup to vegetables; set aside.

Combine biscuit mix and milk; turn onto floured surface. Knead 12 times. Roll dough into 9×12″ rectangle; set aside trimmings. Cover dough with salmon mixture; roll up as for jelly roll. Place on baking sheet, seam side down. Combine egg and water and brush on roll to glaze. If you wish, decorate roll with reserved dough trimmings. Brush with egg mixture.

Bake in a hot oven (400°) for 25 minutes, until golden brown. Serve hot with Piquant Sauce. Makes 8 servings.

Piquant Sauce Add milk to reserved salmon liquid to make ½ c. Combine with remaining chicken soup and 1 tblsp. lemon juice in small saucepan; heat to boiling. Spoon over individual servings.

SKILLET SALMON CHOWDER

6 slices bacon	1 (1 lb.) can whole kernel
½ c. chopped onion	corn
1 (10½ oz.) can chicken broth	⅛ tsp. pepper
1 (5½ oz.) pkg. au gratin	1 (1 lb.) can salmon, drained
potato mix	and flaked
2 c. water	⅓ c. evaporated milk
1½ c. milk	

Sauté bacon until crisp; drain and crumble. Reserve 2 tblsp. bacon fat. Sauté onion in fat until tender. Stir in chicken broth, au gratin potato mix (add both potatoes and sauce mix), water, milk, corn, pepper and bacon. Bring to a boil; reduce heat. Simmer for 15 minutes, stirring often.

Stir in salmon and evaporated milk. Simmer for 5 minutes. Makes 6 to 8 servings.

Eggs

FIRST-CHOICE EGG DISHES If you're *really* in a hurry, there's nothing faster than scrambled eggs for supper. When you have a few more minutes, you can do something different with eggs. These recipes are favorites of busy cooks *and* their families.

EGGS FOO YOUNG

4 eggs, beaten
1 (1 lb.) can bean sprouts, drained
½ c. chopped cooked or canned chicken
1 small onion, chopped

½ tsp. salt
⅛ tsp. pepper
1 tblsp. soy sauce (optional)
2 tblsp. salad oil
Chinese Sauce (recipe follows)

Combine all ingredients except oil. Drop by spoonfuls into hot oil in skillet; spread bean sprouts gently with tip of spoon to cover egg mixture.

Cook until little cakes set and brown on edges. Turn and brown on the other side. Add more oil to skillet if necessary as you cook additional patties. Place on hot platter and serve at once with Chinese Sauce. Makes 10 patties.

Chinese Sauce

1½ c. chicken broth
1 tsp. molasses
1 tsp. soy sauce

2 tblsp. cornstarch
2 tblsp. water

Combine chicken broth, molasses and soy sauce. Dissolve cornstarch in water; add to chicken broth and cook, stirring constantly, over low heat until mixture comes to a boil.

OMELET SQUARES

6 eggs beaten
⅔ c. milk
1 c. instant mashed potatoes
½ tsp. instant minced onion
½ tsp. salt
⅛ tsp. pepper

1 tsp. mustard
½ c. crumbled, cooked bacon
¼ c. pickle relish
1 tblsp. butter or margarine
Tomato Sauce (recipe follows)

Combine eggs and milk; beat in rest of ingredients except butter. Melt butter in 10″ electric skillet; add egg mixture; cook over low heat (280°) 30 minutes or until set (occasionally make cuts in omelet to let uncooked egg run down). Cut in squares; serve hot with Tomato Sauce. Makes 6 servings.

Tomato Sauce

1 (10½ oz.) can condensed
    tomato soup
1 tsp. brown sugar

1 tsp. parsley flakes
½ tsp. Worcestershire sauce
¼ tsp. oregano

Combine soup, brown sugar, parsley flakes, Worcestershire sauce and oregano in a saucepan. Heat well, but do not boil.

OMELET PANCAKES

¾ c. sifted flour
1 tsp. salt
¼ tsp. pepper

¾ c. milk
6 large eggs, beaten

Combine flour, salt and pepper in mixing bowl. Stir in milk slowly and beat to form a smooth batter.

Stir in beaten eggs, blend well.

Pour ½ cup of batter on very hot, greased 10″ griddle; spread batter to edges.

Cook about 20 seconds until browned. Turn, brown on other side.

Remove to warm plate. Spread with cooked bulk sausage, cranberry sauce, jam or cinnamon and sugar. Roll up if you wish.

Keep warm in oven while cooking other pancakes. Makes 6 pancakes.

PUFFY OMELET

¼ c. butter or margarine	4 eggs, separated
3½ tblsp. flour	2 tblsp. shortening
1 tsp. salt	Chopped parsley
1 c. milk	

Melt butter in small saucepan over low heat. Blend in flour and salt; cook 1 minute, stirring constantly.

Remove from heat; gradually stir in milk; return to heat. Cook, stirring constantly, until white sauce is thick and smooth. Cool.

Beat egg whites until stiff enough to hold firm peaks. Then beat the yolks.

Blend egg yolks into white sauce. Then fold in beaten egg whites.

Heat shortening over low heat in a 10″ skillet. Pour in the omelet mixture. Cover with a close fitting lid.

Cook over low heat 15 to 20 minutes, or until a light brown crust is formed on bottom and top is firm.

Loosen the omelet from the sides of skillet and cut through the center down to crust in bottom. Tilt pan; fold one half over the other. Slide onto platter.

Sprinkle with chopped parsley. Makes 4 servings.

Variation: Just before folding omelet, sprinkle lower half with ⅓ c. shredded cheese.

DENVER-STYLE SCRAMBLED EGGS

¼ c. chopped green pepper	¼ tsp. salt
2 tblsp. chopped onion	⅛ tsp. pepper
3 tblsp. butter	4 English muffins, split and
1 c. chopped ham	toasted
8 eggs	Butter
2 tblsp. milk	

Sauté pepper and onion in melted butter in a skillet until tender. Add ham and toss to heat thoroughly.

Beat together eggs, milk, salt and pepper. Add eggs to sautéed vegetables. Cook over low heat, gently lifting egg mixture so uncooked egg seeps to bottom.

Spoon eggs onto buttered English muffins. Makes 4 servings.

CHEESE SCRAMBLED EGGS

6 eggs
6 tblsp. light cream
½ tsp. onion salt

⅛ tsp. pepper
3 tblsp. butter
½ c. shredded Cheddar cheese

Combine eggs, cream, onion salt and pepper.

Melt butter in skillet. Add eggs and cook over low heat, gently lifting egg mixture so uncooked egg will flow to bottom. Add cheese when eggs are partly cooked. Cook eggs until set, but remove from heat while they are moist. Makes 4 servings.

MUSHROOM-EGG SCRAMBLE

8 eggs
1 (10½ oz.) can condensed
   cream of mushroom soup
¼ c. milk

⅛ tsp. pepper
2 tblsp. butter
½ c. shredded yellow cheese
Parsley

Beat eggs slightly. Add soup and beat gently with rotary beater. Blend in milk and pepper.

Melt butter in skillet. Pour in egg mixture. Cook slowly until eggs are set, stirring occasionally. Sprinkle with cheese and chopped parsley just before serving. Makes 6 servings.

EGGS IN POTATO POCKETS

8 c. instant mashed potatoes
1 tsp. instant minced onion
2 tblsp. chopped pimiento
½ tsp. pepper
8 eggs

½ tsp. salt
2 c. grated process American
   cheese
⅓ c. crumbled cooked bacon

Prepare potatoes as directed on package. Mix in onion, pimiento and pepper; spread in greased shallow 2½ qt. baking dish.

Break eggs into ½″ depressions in potatoes. Sprinkle with salt, cheese and bacon. Bake in moderate oven (325°) 35 minutes or until eggs are consistency you desire. Makes 8 servings.

POTATO-EGG SUPPER

4 strips bacon
4 c. diced cooked potatoes
6 hard-cooked eggs, sliced
1 (10½ oz.) can condensed
cream of chicken soup
1 c. milk
⅛ tsp. oregano

½ tsp. onion salt
¼ tsp. garlic salt
⅛ tsp. pepper
1 tblsp. instant minced onion
1 c. shredded sharp Cheddar
cheese

Fry bacon until crisp; crumble. Brush 2 qt. casserole with drippings. Layer potatoes, bacon and eggs in casserole. Blend soup, milk, seasonings and onion; pour over potato mixture. Sprinkle cheese over top. Bake in moderate oven (375°) for 25 minutes. Makes 6 servings.

EGGS IN SPINACH CUPS

2 (10 oz.) pkgs. frozen
chopped spinach, cooked and
drained
1 (10½ oz.) can condensed
cream of mushroom soup

¼ tsp. onion salt
8 eggs
Paprika

Mix spinach with soup and onion salt. Butter 8 (6 oz.) baking cups; line with spinach; break one egg into each cup. Bake in moderate oven (325°) 15 minutes. Sprinkle with paprika. Makes 8 servings.

Eggs Baked in Tomatoes   Place thin slices of tomatoes, peeled, in bottom of greased, large muffin-pan cups. Top each with an egg. Season with salt and pepper and sprinkle with shredded process American cheese. Bake in moderate oven (325°) until eggs are set, about 25 minutes. Serve on rounds of buttered toast.

TUNA-EGG SCRAMBLE

6 eggs
⅓ c. light cream or milk
½ tsp. salt

1 (6½ oz.) can tuna, drained
and flaked
2 tblsp. butter or margarine

Blend together eggs, cream and salt. Stir in tuna. Pour into hot skillet with butter. Cook over low heat, stirring occasionally until eggs are thickened, but still moist. Makes 6 servings.

EGGS BENEDICT

6 thin, small ham slices	3 hamburger buns, split
6 eggs	Hollandaise Sauce (see Index)

Score fat edges of ham slices. Place on broiler rack, 3″ from heat. Broil 3 minutes; turn.

Poach eggs; keep warm.

Place bun halves on broiler. Broil until light golden.

Place ham on buns. Top with poached eggs. Pour Hollandaise Sauce over all. Makes 6 servings.

CREAMED EGGS

½ c. butter or margarine	⅛ tsp. pepper
6 tblsp. flour	¼ tsp. Tabasco sauce
1 qt. milk	2 tsp. finely grated onion
1½ tsp. salt	12 hard-cooked eggs, coarsely
½ tsp. paprika	cut

Melt butter over low heat. Add flour, stir until bubbly (do not let brown) and add milk. Cook, stirring constantly, until mixture thickens. Add remaining ingredients. Heat thoroughly.

Serve over split hot biscuits, toast, rice, baked potatoes, broccoli or asparagus. Makes 6 to 8 servings.

CURRIED EGGS WITH MUSHROOMS

1 (10½ oz.) can condensed cream of mushroom soup	1 (4 oz.) can sliced mushrooms, drained
½ c. milk	1 tblsp. chopped parsley
½ tsp. curry powder	8 slices toast, buttered
4 hard-cooked eggs, sliced	

Combine soup, milk and curry powder. Stir in eggs, mushrooms and parsley.

Heat, stirring occasionally. Serve over toast. Makes 4 servings.

HOT DEVILED EGGS

¼ c. butter or margarine	2 c. milk
¼ c. flour	12 deviled-egg halves
½ tsp. salt	½ c. dry bread crumbs
¼ tsp. pepper	½ c. grated sharp cheese

Make medium white sauce with butter, flour, salt, pepper and milk. Pour over eggs, arranged in rows in greased 8×8×2″ baking dish. Top with crumbs, then cheese. Bake in moderate oven (350°) until cheese melts. Makes 6 servings.

Cheese

BAKED SWISS FONDUE

8 slices bread
6 (1 oz.) slices process Swiss
  cheese
3 eggs, beaten
2 c. milk

½ tsp. salt
⅛ tsp. white pepper
½ tsp. instant minced green
  onion

Trim crusts from bread; cut in halves diagonally. Arrange 8 halves in pinwheel pattern in greased round pan (or in 1½ qt. casserole). Cover bread with cheese slices cut in halves for easy placement. Top with remaining bread like first layer.

Combine beaten eggs, milk, salt and pepper with rotary beater. Pour over bread and cheese. Sprinkle with onion.

Bake in moderate oven (325°) until puffy and golden brown, about 1 hour. Serve at once. Makes 6 servings.

CHEESE-BREAD CASSEROLE

5 slices bread
Butter
3 eggs, separated
1 c. milk
2 tblsp. chopped chives
½ tsp. salt

⅛ tsp. pepper
1 tsp. prepared mustard
½ lb. grated sharp cheese
Curried Dried Beef (recipe
  follows)

Trim crusts from bread; spread generously with butter, then cut into cubes. Place in greased 1½ qt. casserole.

Beat egg yolks until foamy; add milk, chives, salt, pepper, mustard and cheese. Beat egg whites until stiff; fold into yolk mixture. Pour over bread. Bake in moderate oven (375°) for 25 to 30 minutes or until puffed and browned. Serve hot, topped with Curried Dried Beef. Makes 6 to 8 servings.

Curried Dried Beef

¼ c. butter	¼ tsp. curry powder
¼ c. flour	2½ c. light cream
1 tblsp. instant minced onion	1 (4 oz.) pkg. dried beef

Melt butter in saucepan. Stir in flour, instant minced onion, and curry powder. Cook for 1 minute, stirring constantly. Gradually stir in light cream; cook until thickened, stirring constantly.

Rinse dried beef in cold water. Shred and add to sauce. Serve hot. Makes 3 cups.

HASTY-TASTY RAREBIT

2 (10½ oz.) cans condensed cream of celery soup	8 slices toast
2 (6 oz.) links smoke-flavor cheese	Stuffed green olives
	Parsley

Blend together soup and cheese over hot water. Serve immediately on toast. Garnish with pimiento-stuffed green olives and parsley. Makes 8 servings.

QUICK MACARONI AND CHEESE

8 oz. elbow macaroni	1 tblsp. instant minced onion
¼ c. butter	1 tblsp. chopped parsley
1 (8 oz.) pkg. process cheese, shredded	⅛ tsp. pepper
1 c. milk	Paprika

Cook macaroni as directed on package. Drain, then return to saucepan. Add remaining ingredients except paprika. Cook over low heat, stirring frequently, until cheese melts, about 5 minutes. Sprinkle with paprika. Makes 8 servings.

STUFFED GREEN PEPPERS

Speed up this favorite main dish with a quick stuffing—a package of Spanish rice and a can of tomato sauce or a can of macaroni and cheese. You can get the peppers ready for stuffing in 10 minutes. But fix Spanish rice first and then cut 4 medium peppers in halves. Remove seeds and cook in boiling, salted water until barely tender, about 8 minutes. Drain.

SPANISH-RICE STUFFING

½ lb. ground beef
2 c. water
1 beef bouillon cube
1 (6 oz.) pkg. Spanish-rice mix

2 tblsp. butter or margarine
1 (8 oz.) can tomato sauce
½ c. grated Cheddar cheese

Brown beef in skillet over low heat. Add water and bouillon cube and bring to a boil.

Remove from heat and stir in Spanish-rice mix and butter. Cover and let stand 20 minutes. Prepare peppers.

Fill peppers with rice mixture and place in baking pan (13×9 ×2"). Spoon tomato sauce over rice in peppers; sprinkle with cheese. Broil until cheese melts, about 5 minutes. Makes 4 to 6 servings.

MACARONI AND CHEESE STUFFING

2 (15¼ oz.) cans macaroni
and cheese
1 hard-cooked egg, chopped
1 (2 oz.) can sliced
mushrooms, drained
3 tblsp. chopped pimiento

½ tsp. onion salt
½ tsp. celery salt
4 green peppers, halved,
seeded and parboiled
½ c. shredded Cheddar cheese
Paprika

Combine first 6 ingredients in 2 qt. saucepan; heat to boiling. Fill parboiled pepper halves with mixture. Top with cheese; sprinkle lightly with paprika. Broil to melt cheese, about 4 minutes. (Or bake in moderate oven [350°] for 15 minutes.) Makes 4 servings.

Section 2
Vegetables, Salads, Salad Dressings, Sauces, Relishes

Does your imagination bog down when it comes to fixing vegetables? Many women have this difficulty. And many serve the same salad over and over again. This is often the hardest part of the meal to make interesting to the family.

We have culled and collected the best ideas from country women, many of whom garden and have large yields. They have had to avoid monotony! And we have developed many quick and easy tricks in our Test Kitchens. For example, cauliflower can be bland and uninteresting but when it is served under a blanket of cheese sauce—not an ordinary cheese sauce but a delicate Swiss Cheese Sauce—it's a winner every time.

Canned vegetables, those handy right-off-the-shelf specials, are invaluable for last minute cooks. Seasonings and quick mixes can turn them into gourmet creations. Our recipe for Creole Beans, for instance, is peppy with onion soup mix. We team corn with canned onion rings for a new taste treat. You'll find new twists with baked beans—a bubbling casserole with deviled ham, cloves and pineapple.

Then to complement a meal there's a selection of salads that can truly be "tossed" together—each one enhanced with an imaginative touch. For instance, the Cabbage Salad Bowl—a tangy combo of cabbage, orange juice, raisins and carrots.

Every cook is always looking for new dressings to dress up a salad—we included some that you can make up last minute.

COUNTRY VEGETABLE ALPHABET Many country cooks find that color-bright vegetables boost their cooking fame. They substitute imagination for time and come up with tempting dishes. The recipes that follow show how they do it.

ASPARAGUS WITH BACON

24 asparagus stalks	1 tblsp. lemon juice
1 c. dairy sour cream	4 slices toast
¼ c. mayonnaise	2 slices crisp bacon, crumbled

Cook tender part of stalks, scales removed if sandy, in just enough salted water to cover, until tender, about 15 minutes.

Meanwhile combine sour cream, mayonnaise and lemon juice.

Drain asparagus and arrange on toast. Top with cream mixture. Run under broiler until top bubbles. Scatter bacon on top; serve. Makes 4 servings.

Variation: Substitute Speedy Cheese Sauce (see Index) for the cream-mayonnaise mixture.

CREAMED ASPARAGUS ON TOAST

1 (10½ oz.) can condensed cream of asparagus soup	1 (14½ oz.) can cut asparagus
¼ c. milk	4 slices toast

Combine soup and milk in saucepan. Add asparagus and heat. Serve on toast. Makes 4 servings.

Note: If you have hard-cooked eggs in refrigerator, garnish servings with egg slices. For a heartier dish, lay cheese slices on toast before spooning on hot asparagus.

Asparagus with Herbs Cook 2 (10 oz.) pkgs. frozen asparagus as directed on package. Drain. Meanwhile cream ¼ c. butter; add a dash each of rosemary and thyme. Blend in juice of ½ lemon. Serve on the hot asparagus. Makes 4 to 6 servings.

Beets in Cream Heat 24 small canned or cooked beets, drained. Season with salt and add 1 c. dairy sour cream to hot beets. Serve at once. Makes 6 servings.

GREEN BEANS—18 WAYS

To Cook Green Beans   Place 2 lbs. beans in kettle containing ½″ to 1″ boiling salted water (¾ tsp. salt to 2 c. water) with 1 tsp. sugar added. Cook, covered, until barely tender, 10 to 30 minutes. Usually much of the water evaporates in cooking, but if it doesn't, cook it down to 2 or 3 tablespoonfuls after the beans have been removed from the kettle. Add to beans. Makes 6 to 7 cups, or 6 servings.

Let imagination be your guide in seasoning. Here are 17 ways to dress up the cooked beans; 1 for raw beans.

Plain Buttered   Add ¼ to ½ c. melted butter.

Deviled   Add 2 tsp. prepared mustard mixed with ¼ to ½ c. butter.

With Mushrooms   Sauté 1 (3 oz.) can chopped mushrooms (or ½ c. fresh mushrooms) in ½ c. melted butter.

With Bacon and Onions   Sauté 4 cut-up bacon slices with 3 tblsp. chopped onion until bacon is crisp and onion is soft.

With Bacon and Pepper   Add ¼ to ½ c. bacon drippings and 1 small red-pepper pod; top with ½ c. crumbled crisp bacon. Or cook beans as directed, adding 6 slices bacon cut up, and 1 small red-pepper pod.

With Almonds   Lightly sauté ½ c. blanched, slivered almonds (or pecans or Brazil nuts) in ¼ to ½ c. butter.

With Bread Crumbs   Sauté ½ c. bread crumbs in ½ c. butter until delicately browned.

With Savory   Add ½ tsp. dried summer savory or a few leaves of the fresh savory (known in Europe as the "bean herb") to ¼ to ½ c. butter.

With Water Chestnuts   Add ½ c. thinly sliced water chestnuts (canned) to ¼ to ½ c. butter.

With Cheese   Sprinkle hot, buttered beans liberally with grated cheese.

With Cheese Sauce   Pour your favorite cheese sauce over beans.

With Eggs Put 2 hard-cooked egg yolks through sieve. Add ¼ c. soft butter, 1½ tblsp. lemon juice and salt to taste. Beat with electric mixer or rotary beater until fluffy. Serve on hot beans.

With Mushroom Sauce Heat cream of mushroom soup, thinned with milk as you like it. Pour over beans.

With Quick Hollandaise Blend 2 tblsp. hot water into ½ c. mayonnaise in measuring cup. Set cup in hot water to heat sauce, stirring occasionally. Spoon sauce on hot beans.

In Broiler Place cooked beans in broiler pan. Broil ham slices on rack above. Drippings season beans.

Bundles Cook small whole beans and season as you like. Arrange in bundles with band of pimiento over each. Or circle beans with lemon rings. (Save lemons after juice is extracted and cut in slices.) Garnish platter of meat or chicken with bundles.

Salad Add 1 tsp. prepared horse-radish to ½ c. French dressing and 3 tblsp. chopped onion. Add to hot beans; cool, cover and chill several hours. Serve on 6 lettuce-lined salad plates; garnish with hard-cooked egg slices and white or red onion rings.

Oriental Add raw beans to ¼ c. butter or margarine melted in a heavy skillet. Add ¼ c. water, salt and pepper. Cover and cook on high heat until they steam. Then reduce heat and cook slowly 20 to 25 minutes. Add more water during the cooking if necessary to prevent burning. When crisp-tender, add ½ c. light cream.

ELEGANT GREEN BEANS

1 (10½ oz.) can condensed
  cream of mushroom soup
1 tblsp. instant minced onion
⅛ tsp. oregano
⅛ tsp. garlic salt

¼ c. sour cream
2 (1 lb.) cans green beans,
  drained
½ c. shredded Cheddar cheese

Combine soup, onion, oregano, garlic salt and sour cream. Toss with beans. Place in greased 1½ qt. casserole. Top with cheese. Bake in moderate oven (350°) for 30 minutes. Makes 6 to 8 servings.

TANGY GREEN BEANS

1 tblsp. butter or margarine   1 tblsp. crumbled blue cheese
1 tsp. vinegar   1 (1 lb.) can green beans

Melt butter and add vinegar and cheese. Heat, stirring, to melt cheese.

Heat beans; drain. Pour cheese mixture over beans and toss lightly. Makes 4 servings.

CREOLE BEANS

8 slices bacon   1 tblsp. onion soup mix
2 (1 lb.) cans green beans,   1 (1 lb.) can stewed tomatoes
  drained   1 tsp. sugar

Sauté bacon until crisp; drain on paper toweling. Pour off all but 3 tblsp. drippings.

Empty beans carefully into skillet; add onion soup mix; heat thoroughly.

Snip bacon into small pieces; add half to beans; also add stewed tomatoes and sugar. Top with remaining bacon. Makes 8 servings.

Peppy Green Beans Heat canned green beans in their own liquid; drain. Serve topped with whipped cream, unsweetened, with prepared horse-radish folded in. Taste for salt.

PIMIENTO GREEN BEANS

2 (10 oz.) pkgs. frozen green   1 pimiento, chopped
  beans   ¼ tsp. salt
½ c. French or Italian salad
  dressing

Cook beans as directed on package. Drain; add dressing, pimiento and salt. Toss to mix and serve piping hot. Makes 6 servings.

Southwestern Beans Cook a little diced bacon and chopped onion in a heavy skillet until bacon is crisp and onions are soft. Toss into hot canned, or cooked fresh, or frozen green beans, drained. Serve at once.

SAUCY CHICKEN BAKE (recipe page 38) gets its red-gold color and wonderful seasoning from Basic Red Sauce. Keep a jar of this sauce in your refrigerator or freezer for other tasty recipes in this book.

SKILLET SALMON CHOWDER (recipe page 50) and CHILI AND
CORN BREAD SUPPER (recipe page 36) are two dandy one-pot main
dishes that you can prepare with canned goods and packaged mixes.

SMART COUNTRY COOKS SAY: "If you have green beans in your garden, cook small ones when you are in a hurry. Cook them whole in salted water—no breaking, chopping or cutting into short lengths. Serve them buttered. For special occasions, delicately brown ¼ c. slivered almonds (you can buy them slivered) in the melted butter and pour over the hot beans. Or serve the hot, crisp-tender baby green beans with cheese sauce."

BEANS WITH DEVILED HAM

2 (1 lb.) cans New England-
   style pork and beans

2 (4½ oz.) cans deviled ham
⅛ tsp. ground cloves

Place beans in saucepan over moderate heat. Blend ham and cloves thoroughly through beans. Heat about 10 minutes, stirring occasionally. Makes 6 to 8 servings.

DOUBLE-QUICK BEAN BAKE

1 (1 lb. 5 oz.) can pork and
   beans
1 tblsp. instant minced onion
¼ c. ketchup

2 drops Tabasco sauce
2 tblsp. brown sugar
½ tsp. salt
½ tsp. dry mustard

Combine all ingredients in saucepan. Bring to a boil and simmer 10 minutes. Makes 4 servings.

BAKED BEANS WITH PINEAPPLE

2 (1 lb.) cans pork and beans
1 (8¾ oz.) can pineapple
   tidbits, drained
½ c. ketchup

½ c. brown sugar, firmly
   packed
1 tsp. dry mustard
2 bacon slices

Combine beans, pineapple, ketchup, brown sugar and mustard in saucepan. Simmer 30 minutes, stirring occasionally, to cook down liquid.

Pour into greased 1½ qt. casserole. Top with bacon. Bake in moderate oven (350°) 30 minutes. Makes 6 servings.

BAKED KIDNEY BEANS

2 (1 lb.) cans red kidney beans
1 large onion, finely chopped
½ c. ketchup
3 tblsp. brown sugar
2 slices bacon

Combine beans, onion, ketchup and sugar in greased 2 qt. casserole. Top with bacon.

Bake in hot oven (400°) 1¼ hours. Makes 6 servings.

Note: Substitute 3 tblsp. instant minced onion for chopped onion and bake beans 1 hour.

WONDERFUL LIMA BEANS

1 (10 oz.) pkg. frozen lima beans
2 tblsp. butter or margarine
1 tblsp. instant parsley flakes
1 tblsp. instant minced green onion, or 1 medium onion, chopped
½ tsp. sugar
1 tsp. lemon juice
⅛ tsp. pepper

Cook beans as directed on package; drain. Add remaining ingredients and cook over low heat until butter melts. Makes 4 servings.

LIMA BEANS WITH CELERY

2 chicken bouillon cubes
1 (1 lb.) can green lima beans
1 c. sliced celery
2 tblsp. butter or margarine

Place bouillon cubes, liquid drained from lima beans and celery in saucepan. Cook, covered, until celery is almost tender. Stir once to help dissolve bouillon cubes.

Add limas and butter. Mix and heat. Makes 5 servings.

CALIFORNIA BROCCOLI

2 lbs. fresh broccoli
½ c. mayonnaise
2 tblsp. tarragon vinegar
2 hard-cooked eggs, chopped

Wash broccoli and trim off ends from stems. Cut stems lengthwise almost to the flowerets. (Stems will cook almost as quickly as flowerets.) Drop into a small amount of boiling salted water. Cover and cook until just tender, 12 to 15 minutes. Drain. Meanwhile heat mayonnaise in double boiler with vinegar and eggs. Serve broccoli topped with mayonnaise mixture. Makes 6 servings.

Note: Another way to cook broccoli quickly is to chop it before dropping it into the boiling salted water.

Broccoli Two Ways Cook the flower heads for one meal. Serve with Brown Butter-Crumb Sauce (see Index). For a second meal, slice the stems very thin diagonally. Cook in salted water no longer than 5 minutes. Drain and serve with melted butter or sour cream.

Buttered Cabbage Cook 1 lb. shredded cabbage in ½ c. water, 3 tblsp. butter or margarine added, until water is absorbed, 5 to 7 minutes. Season with salt, pepper and 1 tsp. caraway seeds, lightly crushed.

CREAMY CABBAGE

1 medium head cabbage	½ tsp. salt
½ c. butter or margarine	¼ tsp. caraway seeds
½ c. light cream or evaporated milk	

Shred cabbage. Melt butter in skillet; add cabbage and cook, covered, 5 minutes.

Pour in cream; add salt and caraway seeds. Heat 3 or 4 minutes longer. Makes 6 servings.

Swedish Cabbage Cook 1 lb. cabbage shredded, in salted water to cover 5 minutes. Drain and add 3 tblsp. butter, 1 tsp. lemon juice and 2 tsp. dill weed. Makes 6 servings.

CARROTS AND ONIONS ON TOAST

6 to 10 carrots (1½ to 2 lbs.)	1 (10½ oz.) can condensed cream of celery soup
1 (8 oz.) can whole cooked onions	12 slices buttered toast
⅓ c. milk	

Scrape carrots and cut in thin slices. Cook in 1″ boiling salted water (½ tsp. salt to 1 c. water) 15 minutes.

Add onions; heat. Drain. Add milk and soup. Stir carefully; bring to boiling point. Season.

Spoon carrots and onions on buttered toast. Makes 6 servings.

HASTY CREAMED CARROTS

6 to 10 carrots (1½ to 2 lbs.)	½ c. dairy sour or sweet cream
2 c. water	½ c. chopped parsley or chives
1 tsp. salt	

Peel carrots; cut them into thin lengthwise slices, using vegetable peeler or slicer.

Bring water and salt to boil; add carrots; cover and cook 5 to 7 minutes, just until they are tender-crisp. Drain.

Slowly stir in cream and parsley. (Parsley snips quickly with kitchen scissors.) Makes 6 servings.

Variation: Season cooked, shaved carrots with butter and a pinch of dill weed (not seeds). Add a few drops of lemon juice to accent the flavor.

SKILLET CARROTS AND ONIONS

2 to 3 tblsp. butter or margarine	2 c. sliced onions
4 c. sliced raw carrots (⅛″ slices)	1 tsp. salt
	¼ tsp. pepper

Melt butter in heavy skillet; add carrots and onions. Season with salt and pepper. Brown slowly on one side, then turn and brown other side. Do not cover. Makes 6 servings.

HOLIDAY CAULIFLOWER

1 large head cauliflower	2 c. milk
1 (4 oz.) can sliced mushrooms	1 tsp. salt
¼ c. diced green pepper	1 c. shredded Swiss cheese
¼ c. butter	2 tblsp. chopped pimiento
⅓ c. flour	

Break cauliflower into medium-size flowerets; cook in boiling water until crisp-tender, about 10 minutes. Drain well; set aside.

In a 2 qt. saucepan, sauté mushrooms and green pepper in butter until tender. Blend in flour. Gradually stir in milk. Cook, stirring constantly, over medium heat until mixture is thick. Stir in salt, cheese and pimiento.

Place half of the cauliflower in a buttered 2 qt. casserole. Cover with half of the sauce; add remaining cauliflower. Top with sauce. Bake in moderate oven (325°) for 15 minutes. Makes 8 servings.

Cauliflower with Sour Cream Quick cooking makes for superior flavor. Boil cauliflower flowerets in salted water about 10 minutes. Drain and add dairy sour cream with chopped chives.

Pronto Saucy Cauliflower Cook cauliflower flowerets in boiling salted water until barely tender, 8 to 10 minutes. Drain. Pour in enough heavy cream to cover bottom of saucepan. Break sliced process American cheese over the top. Cover and let stand a few minutes or until cheese is melted.

Stuffed Celery Fill celery stalks with peanut butter for the children. They'll like it fixed this way. Or add 2 tblsp. drained crushed pineapple to 1 (3 oz.) pkg. cream cheese and press in celery stalks. You can speed up the preparation by using a pineapple-cheese spread.

IOWA CORN ON THE COB An Iowa woman says, "Most good cooks in our neighborhood rush the corn from the garden, husk it; use a dry vegetable brush to brush away the stubborn silk, and drop the ears into boiling water to cover. They cook it 5 to 8 minutes—never more than 10. But I get more praise from folks around the table when I cover the corn with cold water; bring it to a boil—then drain the steaming ears and serve them at once. No smart country cook around here adds salt to the water when cooking sweet corn. It toughens the kernels."

CORN DELICIOUS

2 (12 oz.) cans whole kernel corn	¼ c. light cream
1 (3½ oz.) can French-fried onions	

Heat corn; stir in onions and cream. Heat 2 minutes longer and serve immediately. (Onions become soggy if they wait.) Makes 6 to 8 servings.

CREAMY CHEESE-CORN BAKE

1 egg, beaten
1 (1 lb.) can cream-style corn
½ c. cubed process American cheese

Combine egg, corn and cheese. Pour in greased 1 qt. casserole. Bake in moderate oven (350°) until cheese is melted, about 30 minutes. Makes 5 servings.

ROASTED CORN

In Foil Spread husked ear of corn with butter and wrap securely with foil. Roast over embers, 15 to 25 minutes, or in hot oven (400°) 15 to 30 minutes (time varies with size of ears). Turn ears several times while cooking.

CHICKEN CORN SOUP

3 strips bacon
2 tblsp. chopped onion
1 chicken bouillon cube
¼ c. boiling water
1 (10½ oz.) can condensed
   cream of chicken soup
1 (1 lb.) can cream-style corn

2 c. milk
¼ tsp. salt
¼ tsp. thyme
½ tsp. celery salt
⅛ tsp. sage
Chopped parsley

Fry bacon until crisp in heavy 2 qt. saucepan. Drain and crumble. Set aside.

Sauté onion in drippings until tender; drain off drippings. Dissolve bouillon cube in water; add with remaining ingredients, except parsley, to onion. Bring to boiling point over low heat. Sprinkle with parsley. Makes 6 servings.

OKRA AND TOMATOES

3 c. okra, cut in rounds
¼ c. butter or margarine
3 c. tomatoes, peeled and cut
   in wedges or chopped

¾ c. onion slices
2 tsp. salt
¼ tsp. pepper

Sauté okra in butter until tender.

Add remaining ingredients and simmer gently, covered, 5 minutes. (Don't overcook.) Makes 6 servings.

Variation: Use green tomatoes instead of ripe ones.

ONION TIPS FROM A SMART COUNTRY COOK

Speedy Onion Juice Cut a slice from a peeled onion. Scrape cut onion surface with a knife. Cut a second slice and repeat. When you have enough onion juice, place slices in a plastic bag, close tightly and refrigerate to use in stew, over the pot roast or in any dish you wish to season with onion. Good cooks know the flavor magic of adding a few drops of onion juice to fruit salads, cottage cheese, tomato juice and many other foods.

Green Onions on Toast Trim and cook small green onions in a little salted water until tender, about 12 minutes. Drain and serve on buttered toast. Spoon over cheese sauce.

NEW PEAS IN CREAM

4 c. shelled peas	Water
2 tsp. sugar	2 tblsp. butter
2 tsp. salt	½ tsp. pepper
Pea pods	1 c. light cream
1 small green onion with top, chopped	

Cook peas with sugar, salt, 5 or 6 pea pods, onion and enough water to cover for 10 to 15 minutes, or until just tender (water should almost evaporate). Add butter and hold over heat to melt. Add pepper and cream. Heat but do not cook. Makes 6 servings.

NEW PEAS, 12 WAYS

With Mint Cook 2 or 3 fresh mint leaves with the peas.

With Mint Jelly Omit sugar and add 3 to 4 tblsp. mint jelly to peas with butter. Hold over heat to melt. Add pepper and cream and heat to warm.

With Pimiento   Add ¼ c. chopped pimiento to peas just before adding cream.

With Sour Cream and Chives   Add 3 tblsp. chives, chopped, to peas before buttering. Then add 1 c. dairy sour cream instead of light cream and heat to warm; do not cook.

With Potatoes   Cook 12 small new whole potatoes until just tender. Mix with peas before adding cream.

With Mushrooms   Sauté 1 c. canned sliced mushrooms in 1 tblsp. butter. Mix with peas before adding cream.

With Onions   Cook 1 c. small green onions, sliced (use tops, too), until just tender. Add to peas before buttering.

With Carrots   Cook 1½ c. thinly sliced carrots until just tender. Add to peas before buttering.

With Celery   Cook ¼ c. chopped celery in small amount of water until tender. Add to peas before buttering.

With Bacon   Sprinkle ½ c. finely crumbled bacon over top of peas just before serving.

With Ham   Cut ham slices (boiled or baked) in thin strips 1″ in length. Mix with peas just before serving.

With Lettuce Leaves   Line saucepan with several leaves of leaf lettuce, wet from washing. In center place peas, salt, pepper, sugar, tops of small green onions and 3 or 4 tblsp. water. Cover and cook until tender. Discard lettuce; season peas with cream.

POTATOES CHANTILLY

1 pkg. instant mashed potatoes (4 servings) 1 c. heavy cream	½ c. grated sharp cheese Salt and pepper to taste

Prepare potatoes as directed on package; place in greased shallow baking dish.

Whip cream; fold in cheese. Season with salt, pepper. Spread over potatoes.

Bake in moderate oven (350°) until golden, about 20 minutes. Serve immediately. Makes 4 to 6 servings.

HERB POTATO CHIPS

1 (7 oz.) pkg. potato chips   Oregano
¼ c. grated Parmesan cheese

Spread potato chips in shallow baking pan. Sprinkle with cheese
and dust lightly with oregano. Bake in moderate oven (350°)
5 minutes. Makes about 12 servings.

Note: Instead of oregano, you may use a touch of mixed salad
herbs, thyme, dill or curry powder.

OVEN-ROASTED POTATOES

½ c. butter   Dash pepper
6 or 8 medium potatoes,   1 tsp. paprika
  peeled   2 tsp. chopped parsley
½ tsp. salt

Place butter in a shallow pan (13×9×2"). Put in moderate
oven (350°) until butter is melted.

Roll potatoes in butter. Sprinkle with salt and pepper. Cover pan
tightly with foil. Return to oven and bake 1¼ hours.

Put potatoes in serving dish and pour over butter from baking
pan. Sprinkle with paprika and parsley if desired. Makes 6 servings.

Note: If dinner is delayed, remove foil. Continue baking up to
30 minutes longer; the potatoes brown attractively.

BROILED POTATO SLICES

3 medium potatoes   ½ tsp. salt
⅓ c. salad oil   Paprika

Scrub potatoes, but do not peel. Cut into ¼" crosswise slices.
Dip slices in oil and place one-layer deep on broiler rack. Season with
salt and dust with paprika.

Broil until potatoes are golden brown, about 7 minutes. Turn and
continue broiling until brown. Serve hot. Makes 4 servings.

CHEESE FRENCH FRIES

2 (9 oz.) pkgs. frozen French-   ¼ tsp. paprika
  fried potatoes   ⅓ c. grated Parmesan cheese
1 tsp. onion salt

Place potatoes in shallow baking pan. Sprinkle with onion salt and paprika. Bake as directed on package.

Sprinkle with cheese, shake pan to coat evenly. Makes 6 servings.

OVEN-FRIED POTATO SLICES

⅔ c. salad oil	Salt
5 medium potatoes, scrubbed	Pepper

Pour ⅓ c. oil into each of two large shallow pans. Slice potatoes crosswise ¼″ thick. Turn slices to coat both sides in salad oil. Arrange potato slices in pans, one layer deep.

Bake in very hot oven (450°) until potatoes are lightly browned, 20 to 25 minutes. Sprinkle with salt and pepper and serve hot. Makes 6 servings.

DELICIOUS MASHED POTATOES

4 servings instant mashed potatoes	¼ tsp. onion salt
½ c. dairy sour cream	Dash black pepper

Prepare potatoes as directed on package, omitting butter. Stir in sour cream, salt and pepper; heat until piping hot. Makes 4 servings.

POLISH POTATOES

1 (1½ lb.) pkg. frozen whole potatoes	2 tblsp. chopped pimiento
1 c. dairy sour cream	1 tblsp. chopped chives
	Salt and pepper

Cook potatoes according to package directions; drain.

Stir together sour cream, pimiento and chives. Pour over potatoes and toss. Salt and pepper to taste. Makes 6 servings.

HASH-BROWN ONION POTATOES

8 c. cubed raw potatoes	1 c. water
¼ c. butter or margarine	
1 (1½ oz.) pkg. onion soup mix	

Lightly brown potatoes in butter in a large skillet. Add onion soup mix and water. Cover and simmer until potatoes are tender, about 10 minutes. Uncover and cook a few minutes until liquid is absorbed. Stir occasionally. Makes 8 servings.

SWISS POTATOES

1 (1 lb.) can whole white potatoes	1 small onion, chopped
2 tblsp. bacon drippings or shortening	½ tsp. salt
	⅛ tsp. pepper

Drain potatoes and chop fine. Cook with onion in hot fat until browned and crisp, stirring occasionally with a broad spatula. Season with salt and pepper. Makes 4 servings.

SPEEDY STUFFED POTATOES

Shape baked potato "shells" of heavy aluminum foil, or buy oval foil containers. Fill foil shells with instant mashed potatoes prepared as directed on package. Heap up attractively; then make a depression in each "potato" with spoon. Just before serving, heat in hot oven; fill centers with sour cream and chopped chives (or green onions added). Serve at once.

SAUERKRAUT WITH APPLES

1 c. chopped onion	1½ c. apple slices
¼ c. butter or margarine	2 tblsp. brown sugar
1 (1 lb. 11 oz.) can sauerkraut	¼ tsp. dry mustard

Sauté onion in butter until soft and clear, but not brown. Mix with sauerkraut.

Place alternate layers of sauerkraut and apples in greased 1½ qt. casserole; sprinkle with brown sugar and mustard.

Cover, bake in moderate oven (375°) 30 minutes. Good with sliced ham, pork chops and meat loaf. Makes 6 to 8 servings.

SAUERKRAUT AND TOMATOES

1 (1 lb. 11 oz.) can sauerkraut	2 tsp. sugar
¾ tsp. salt	1 (1 lb.) can stewed tomatoes
½ tsp. caraway seeds	1 bay leaf

Combine ingredients in saucepan; heat thoroughly, about 15 to 20 minutes. Makes 6 servings.

SQUASH-PINEAPPLE CASSEROLE

2 (12 oz.) pkgs. frozen squash,
  thawed, or 4 c. cooked,
  mashed squash
1 (8½ oz.) can crushed
  pineapple, undrained

2 tblsp. sugar
½ tsp. salt
2 tblsp. butter or margarine

Combine squash, pineapple, sugar and salt in a greased 1½ qt. casserole. Dot with butter. Bake in moderate oven (350°) 35 to 40 minutes. Makes 8 servings.

SUMMER SQUASH WITH SOUR CREAM

2 lbs. squash, cut in 1" strips
1 tsp. salt
⅓ c. chopped onion
2 tblsp. butter or margarine

1 c. dairy sour cream
4 tsp. flour
Paprika

Sprinkle squash with salt; let stand 1 hour to improve flavor; drain.

Cook squash and onion in butter over low heat. When squash is tender, add sour cream mixed with flour. Bring to a boil; remove from heat. Sprinkle with paprika. Makes 6 servings.

SUCCOTASH CHOWDER

2 (10 oz.) pkgs. frozen lima
  beans
2 (10½ oz.) cans condensed
  cream of celery soup
2 (12 oz.) cans Mexicorn

2 tsp. sugar
2 tsp. salt
½ tsp. celery salt
½ tsp. garlic salt
1 qt. milk

Cook beans as directed on package; add remaining ingredients. Heat thoroughly; do not boil. Makes 8 servings.

NEW ORLEANS SUCCOTASH

2 (10 oz.) pkgs. frozen
  succotash
2 slices bacon

1 (1 lb.) can stewed tomatoes
1 tsp. cornstarch
2 tblsp. butter

Cook succotash as directed on package.

Meanwhile, pan-fry bacon until crisp. Drain and crumble bacon. Reserve bacon drippings.

Drain succotash; stir in tomatoes and cornstarch. Cook until slightly thickened, about 2 minutes. Add butter and bacon with drippings. Makes 5 to 6 servings.

ORANGE SWEET POTATOES

3 (1 lb. 2 oz.) cans whole
   sweet potatoes
1 (6 oz.) can frozen orange
   juice concentrate
2 orange juice cans water

½ c. sugar
1 tsp. salt
2 tblsp. cornstarch
¼ c. butter or margarine

Empty sweet potatoes into shallow pan. Combine orange juice, water, sugar and salt in saucepan. Bring to boil.

Mix cornstarch with a little cold water to make thin paste. Pour slowly into orange mixture, stirring constantly. Cook 2 or 3 minutes until thickened. Add butter. Pour over potatoes in pan.

Bake in moderate oven (350°) 30 minutes. Or make sauce in electric skillet; add potatoes and simmer over low heat. Makes 8 to 10 servings.

CINNAMON-CANDIED SWEET POTATOES

3 tblsp. butter or margarine
¼ c. brown sugar
½ tsp. cinnamon

1 (1 lb. 7 oz.) can sweet
   potatoes in syrup

Melt butter in skillet. Add brown sugar, cinnamon and ¼ c. syrup drained from sweet potatoes. Simmer a few minutes and add drained sweet potatoes. Cook over medium heat, stirring frequently, to coat potatoes with glaze. Makes 4 servings.

A SMART COUNTRY COOK SUGGESTS: "When tomatoes are in season and plentiful, Hot Buttered Tomatoes are a favorite of my family and friends. To make them: Peel 2 lbs. (about 6 medium) ripe tomatoes and squeeze out the seeds and pulp around them. Cut the tomato flesh in pieces and add to a heavy skillet containing ¼ c. butter, melted. Season with salt, pepper, a touch of sugar and a dash of basil. Cover and cook 3 to 5 minutes to heat tomatoes." Makes 4 to 6 servings.

Variation: Omit basil and add ¼ to ½ tsp. chili powder for Mexican Skillet Tomatoes.

BAKED TOMATO HALVES

8 medium tomatoes   2 tblsp. butter or margarine
1 c. herb-seasoned stuffing
  mix

Wash tomatoes; remove stem and flower ends. Cut in crosswise halves. Place in shallow baking pan.

Top each tomato half with 1 tblsp. bread-stuffing mix. Dot with butter. Bake in moderate oven (375°) until tender and top browns, about 20 minutes. Makes 8 servings.

BAKED TOMATO CASSEROLE

1 (1 lb.) can tomatoes   ½ c. butter or margarine
1 tsp. salt   8 oz. medium-sharp cheese,
¼ tsp. pepper   cut into 4 slices
⅓ c. sugar   3 slices dry bread or toast

Put half of tomatoes in greased, deep 1 qt. baking dish. Sprinkle with half of salt, pepper and sugar and dot with half of the butter. Top with half the cheese and half the bread, broken in pieces. Finish with remaining ingredients in same order.

Bake in moderate oven (350°) 30 minutes. Makes 3 or 4 servings.

VEGETABLES IN FOIL

6 medium-size carrots   Salt
6 small whole onions   6 tblsp. Basic Red Sauce
3 celery stalks   (see Index)
1 medium green pepper

Peel carrots and onions; clean celery. Remove seeds from green pepper. Cut carrots in quarters lengthwise, celery in diagonal strips and green pepper in lengthwise strips. Leave onions whole.

Place vegetabes on 6 pieces of aluminum foil, dividing them evenly. Sprinkle salt over them and add 1 tblsp. Basic Red Sauce to each of the six groups. Close foil around vegetables, using drugstore wrap and folding ends. Do not wrap tightly.

Bake in hot oven (400°) 50 to 60 minutes or until vegetables are tender. Serve steaming hot in foil, opening tops of packages and folding edges back. Makes 6 servings.

VEGETABLE MEDLEY SUPPER

4 c. zucchini squash in 1"
cubes
1 c. coarsely chopped onion
1½ c. green pepper in 1"
cubes
1 c. sliced carrots
1 c. stewed tomatoes
1 c. diced potatoes

1 c. frozen peas, thawed
1 c. frozen whole kernel corn,
thawed
¼ c. oil
2 tsp. salt
⅛ tsp. pepper
½ tsp. oregano
1 beef bouillon cube

Put all ingredients in pressure cooker. (No extra water is needed.)
Close cover securely. Place over high heat. Bring to 15 lbs. pressure,
according to manufacturer's directions for your pressure cooker.
When pressure is reached (control will begin to jiggle or rock),
reduce heat immediately and continue to cook at 15 lbs. pressure
for just 2 minutes. Remove from heat. Reduce pressure instantly by
placing cooker under running faucet or in pan of cold water.

If you wish, thicken juices with a paste of 1 tblsp. cornstarch and
1 tblsp. water. Makes 6 servings.

SHORT-CUT ZUCCHINI

1 lb. small zucchini
¼ c. butter or margarine
¼ tsp. garlic salt
⅛ tsp. pepper

2 tblsp. water
2 tblsp. grated Parmesan
cheese

Slice zucchini (do not peel). Melt butter in skillet; add zucchini
and seasonings and water.

Cover tightly and simmer over low heat about 10 minutes.
Sprinkle with cheese. Simmer an additional 5 minutes. Makes 3
servings.

RICE PLAYS THE VEGETABLE ROLE Rice is not a vegetable,
but it often serves as one. It's an accompaniment to meats and
poultry; it rates high with many excellent cooks.

BAKED TOMATO RICE

3 tblsp. butter or margarine
1 c. regular rice
1 small onion, finely chopped
 or grated

1 c. tomato juice
1 (10½ oz.) can condensed
 beef broth
2 tblsp. instant minced parsley

Melt butter in heavy skillet; add rice and cook, stirring, 3 minutes, or until rice is golden. Stir in remaining ingredients, cover tightly and bake in moderate oven (350°) 30 minutes.

Remove lid and toss rice lightly with a fork; cover and continue to bake until rice is tender and dry. Add salt if needed. Makes 6 servings.

QUICK TOMATO RICE

1 small onion, chopped
2 tblsp. butter or bacon
 drippings
1⅓ c. precooked rice
1 (15 oz.) can meatless
 spaghetti sauce

¼ c. water
¼ tsp. basil or chili powder

⅛ tsp. pepper

Cook the onion in butter in heavy skillet. Stir in the remaining ingredients. Heat to boiling; cover and simmer over very low heat until rice is tender and liquid is absorbed, 8 to 10 minutes. Makes 4 servings.

RED AND GREEN RICE

1⅓ c. precooked rice
1 tblsp. butter or margarine

¼ c. chopped parsley
¼ c. chopped canned pimiento

Prepare rice as directed on package. Toss with butter, parsley and pimiento. Serve at once. Makes 4 servings.

Salads

CRUNCHY APPLE SALAD

1 c. diced apples, unpeeled
1 c. diced bananas
1 tblsp. lemon juice
½ c. drained pineapple tidbits

½ c. raisins
½ c. coarsely chopped pecans
⅓ c. mayonnaise

Place apples, bananas, and lemon juice in a bowl and toss. Add pineapple, raisins and pecans.

Toss lightly. Add mayonnaise. Toss just until mayonnaise is mixed thoroughly. Spoon into individual lettuce cups or into a salad dish. Serves 6.

CHERRY-PINEAPPLE SALAD

1 (3 oz.) pkg. cream cheese
1 tblsp. mayonnaise
1 (9 oz.) can sliced pineapple, drained

1 (8 to 9 oz.) can light sweet cherries, drained and pitted
Salad greens
Paprika

Have cream cheese at room temperature; blend in mayonnaise.

Arrange chilled pineapple and cherries on crisp greens. Top each with spoonful of cheese mixture and sprinkle with paprika. Makes 4 servings.

PINEAPPLE-CUCUMBER SALAD

1 (8½ oz.) can sliced pineapple
1 (3 oz.) pkg. cream cheese
½ c. finely chopped cucumber

⅛ tsp. salt
Lettuce cups
French dressing

Drain pineapple, reserving syrup.

Combine cheese with 1 tblsp. syrup. Stir in cucumber and salt.

Place each of the 4 pineapple slices in a lettuce cup. Top with cream-cheese mixture. Serve with French dressing. Makes 4 servings.

CABBAGE SALAD BOWL

½ c. light raisins
¼ c. orange juice
1 medium head cabbage, shredded
1 carrot, shredded

2 tblsp. sugar
½ tsp. salt
¼ c. mayonnaise
2 tblsp. tarragon vinegar

Soak raisins in orange juice while preparing other ingredients. Combine cabbage, carrot, sugar and salt in salad bowl. Blend mayonnaise and vinegar. Add to cabbage along with raisins and orange juice.

Toss lightly. Makes 8 servings.

CREOLE SALAD

3 tomatoes, peeled and sliced
Lettuce
4 crosswise slices green pepper
1 hard-cooked egg, sliced

1 tsp. salt
4 chopped green onions
Salad dressing

Place 3 tomato slices on each of 4 lettuce-lined salad plates. Top each with green-pepper ring and a slice of hard-cooked egg. Sprinkle with salt and green onions.

Serve with your favorite salad dressing. Makes 4 servings.

BACON-SPINACH SALAD

4 slices bacon
1 tblsp. dry mustard
¼ c. salad oil
¼ c. vinegar

½ tsp. onion salt
1 lb. spinach, washed and stems removed

Pan-broil bacon until crisp. Remove and save for later use. Measure bacon drippings. Place 3 to 4 tblsp. in skillet. Stir in mustard, oil, vinegar and onion salt; heat to boiling. Add spinach leaves and toss to coat with dressing. Serve at once in salad bowl or vegetable dish, crumbling bacon over top. Makes 8 servings.

KIDNEY BEAN-APPLE SALAD

1 (1 lb.) can kidney beans, drained
¼ c. chopped onion
¼ c. chopped celery
1 unpeeled red apple, cored and diced
⅓ c. diced Cheddar cheese
½ tsp. salt
⅓ c. mayonnaise or salad dressing
Lettuce

Combine all ingredients. Serve on lettuce. Makes 4 servings.

TOMATO-HERB SALAD

½ tsp. minced fresh basil
½ tsp. minced fresh marjoram
¼ c. French dressing
2 large tomatoes, peeled and sliced
Lettuce

Combine herbs and dressing. Place tomatoes on 6 lettuce-lined salad plates. Pour over dressing. Makes 6 servings.

Variation: Use fresh thyme, rosemary or savory for basil or marjoram.

TOMATO-SALAD PLATTER

8 medium tomatoes, peeled and sliced or cut in quarters
1 (⅝ oz.) pkg. Italian salad-dressing mix

Arrange chilled tomatoes on platter or chop plate. Just before serving, sprinkle on salad-dressing mix. The juicy tomatoes make their own dressing. Makes 8 servings.

SAUSAGE-POTATO SALAD

1 (12 oz.) pkg. smoked sausages
1 c. dairy sour cream
2 tblsp. prepared mustard
1 tsp. salt
1 tsp. sugar
1 tsp. instant minced green onion
4 c. hot cooked potato cubes

Simmer little sausages in hot water as directed on package. Combine cream, seasonings and green onion. Heat, but do not let boil. Pour over hot potatoes and toss.

Serve potato salad topped with hot sausages. Makes 4 to 5 servings.

Salad Dressings

CREAM DRESSING

½ c. light or heavy cream   1 tblsp. vinegar
2 tblsp. sugar

Mix ingredients; pour enough over lettuce to coat leaves. Makes
¾ cup.

Variation: Add 2 tsp. horse-radish.

SHORT-CUT SALAD DRESSING

½ c. mayonnaise   1 hard cooked egg, finely
2 tblsp. Basic Red Sauce   chopped
   (see Index)   Salt to taste

Combine all ingredients. Chill until ready to use. Makes about
¾ cup.

PINK-CLOUD DRESSING

1 c. dairy sour cream
2 tblsp. red raspberry jam

Combine ingredients and spoon over fruit salads. Makes about
1 cup.

Sauces

SAUCES FOR VEGETABLES AND MEATS You can lift
plain cooked vegetables and plain broiled meat right into the
gourmet class with sauces. Many sauces are time-consuming and
tricky—but you won't find them here! Our recipes are as easy and
quick as they are tasty. And we include a basic recipe you can
make by the quart, to use in a number of ways, with meat,
vegetables and in salad dressing.

Brown Butter-Crumb Sauce   Delicately brown ¼ c. fine, dry bread crumbs in ¼ c. butter. Add another ¼ c. butter and melt over low heat. Use to top cooked green beans or cauliflower. Try both white or rye bread crumbs.

SPEEDY CHEESE SAUCE

1 c. undiluted evaporated milk	¼ tsp. dry mustard
1½ c. cut-up process American cheese	½ tsp. Worcestershire sauce
	Few drops Tabasco sauce

Heat milk over low heat. Add cheese and continue cooking, stirring constantly, until cheese melts. Add seasonings. Serve hot. Makes about 1½ cups.

NOBBY CHEESE SAUCE

4 tblsp. butter or margarine	¼ tsp. pepper
4 tblsp. flour	1 tsp. Worcestershire sauce
2 c. milk	1 c. (¼″) sharp Cheddar
1 tsp. salt	cheese cubes

Melt butter in heavy skillet over low heat; add flour and blend, but do not brown. Remove from heat; add milk and stir to blend. Add salt, pepper and Worcestershire sauce.

Return to low heat and cook, stirring, until mixture is smooth and thickens. Just before serving, stir in the cheese. Makes about 2 cups.

Variation: To make Deviled Cheese Sauce, add 1 tsp. dry mustard and 1 tsp. grated onion.

Creamy Curry Sauce for Hamburgers or Meat Loaf   Blend 1 c. dairy sour cream with ½ to 1 tsp. curry powder. Season with salt to taste. Serve at room temperature with hot meat.

Note: This sauce also may be served with hot vegetables.

Easy Hollandaise Sauce   Cream thoroughly ½ c. butter or margarine; gradually beat in 3 egg yolks, 1½ tblsp. lemon juice, ½ tsp. salt, dash paprika and few grains cayenne pepper; blend well. Slowly stir in ¼ c. boiling water. Place in top of double boiler. Cook over 1½″ boiling water (so water doesn't touch top part of double boiler) 5 minutes, stirring constantly. Remove from heat; beat 1 minute.

Mock Hollandaise Sauce   Blend ½ c. mayonnaise or salad dressing, ½ c. heavy cream and 2 tblsp. lemon juice.

MUSTARD BUTTER SAUCE

¼ c. butter   1 tsp. lemon juice
1 tsp. prepared mustard

Heat butter until light brown; stir in mustard and lemon juice. Pour over broiled fish just before serving. Makes about ¼ cup.

ORIENTAL SAUCE

1 tblsp. dry mustard   1 tblsp. vinegar
½ tsp. curry powder   1 tblsp. soy sauce
½ c. ketchup

Combine ingredients and bring to a boil. Serve hot with pork. Makes about ½ cup.

BASIC RED SAUCE

1 c. finely chopped onion   ¼ c. sugar
⅓ c. salad oil   ¼ c. Worcestershire sauce
1½ c. ketchup   2½ tsp. salt
½ c. water   ½ tsp. pepper
½ c. lemon juice   4 drops Tabasco sauce

Cook onion in hot oil until soft and golden. Add remaining ingredients; simmer 15 minutes. Cool and store in refrigerator or freezer. Makes about 1 quart.

Variations: For a more tart sauce, use an additional 2 tblsp. lemon juice. For a hotter sauce, add more Tabasco sauce to suit taste.

Note: The following recipes are made with Basic Red Sauce: Better Burgers, Saucy Chicken Bake, Nippy Cheese Dip, Vegetables in Foil, Short-cut Salad Dressing and Shrimp Creole (see Index).

Relishes

REALLY GOOD RELISHES Count on relishes to add a bright touch to quick meals. Their job is to make other foods taste better. They accompany meats, poultry and fish to point up their flavor. Most relishes are make-aheads, but here are two jiffy ideas to add color and zest to your meat platters.

SPICY APPLE RELISH

4 medium apples	1 tblsp. honey
2 tblsp. butter or margarine	1 c. chili sauce

Cut unpeeled apples in wedges, removing cores.

Melt butter in skillet, add honey and chili sauce, mix thoroughly and heat. Add apples, coating them with the chili-sauce mixture, and cook until slightly soft, about 10 to 12 minutes, turning occasionally to baste fruit. Serve hot or cold as meat relish and garnish. Makes 6 servings.

GLAZED APRICOTS

1 (1 lb.) can apricot halves	1 stick cinnamon
2 tblsp. butter	1/8 tsp. nutmeg
1 tblsp. brown sugar	1/4 tsp. vanilla

Drain apricots, reserving 1/2 c. syrup. Combine syrup, butter, sugar, cinnamon, nutmeg and vanilla in 1 qt. saucepan; boil 5 minutes. Gently add apricots; reduce heat and simmer 5 minutes. Serve hot with poultry or meat. Makes 6 servings.

Section 3
Sandwiches and
Breads

Sandwiches and quickie hot breads have long been favorite stand-bys to perk up breakfast, lunch or dinner. They can be the mainstay of the meal or an added attraction to give a menu that little extra lift.

We feature, in this section, a stunning variety of sandwiches and breads to suit everyone in the family. A hearty breakfast in a bun will surprise and please the men. You'll find a collection of skillet sandwiches, a host of hamburgers, from tomato cheeseburgers to nippy burgers tucked in a long bun.

We have "push-button" biscuits that are ready-to-bake in a jiffy. We've combined refrigerator biscuits and biscuit mix with imagination for glamorous go-alongs with any meal. Our light, golden, onion/buttermilk biscuits are delicious by themselves—and can make a jiffy meal split and topped with creamed chicken or tuna fish.

You'll like our basic coffee-cake mix, actually starting with biscuit mix dressed up to make apricot swirl or spicy apple, streusel or strawberry/nut creations.

Do try the Hot Crusty Loaf fashioned from a package of refrigerator rolls. And our snappy-to-fix French bread that starts with 2 cans of refrigerator biscuits.

You'll discover recipes for everyday muffins and fancy varieties for company—but always easy and quick.

SPEEDY SUBSTANTIAL SANDWICHES They're hot and satisfying.

BETTER BURGERS

1 lb. ground beef
1 tblsp. fat
½ tsp. salt

1 c. Basic Red Sauce (see Index)

Brown beef in hot fat. Add salt and sauce; cover and simmer 10 minutes. Serve on hamburger buns, split and toasted. Makes 4 to 6 servings.

TOMATO CHEESEBURGERS

1½ lbs. lean ground beef
1 small onion, chopped
2 tblsp. salad oil
1½ tsp. salt
¼ tsp. pepper

1 (1 lb.) can tomatoes
½ lb. sharp Cheddar cheese, chopped
Hamburger buns

Brown beef and onion in hot salad oil. Pour excess fat from skillet. Season beef with salt and pepper; add tomatoes. Cook 15 to 20 minutes, or until mixture has absorbed most of the juice. Add cheese; cook about 5 minutes.

Serve on heated soft buns. Makes about 8 servings.

WEST COAST CHEESEBURGERS

1 tblsp. instant minced onion
¼ c. bread crumbs
1 egg
⅓ c. milk
1 tsp. salt
1 tsp. prepared mustard

1 lb. lean ground beef
6 sticks process American cheese (¼ × ¼ × 5″)
6 frankfurter buns
Butter or margarine

Combine onion, crumbs, egg, milk, salt and mustard. Add beef and mix thoroughly. Divide into six portions. Shape into logs around the cheese sticks, covering cheese.

Place meat-cheese logs in shallow pan. Bake in hot oven (400°) about 20 minutes or until well browned.

Split buns and toast; spread with butter. Place a cheeseburger in each bun and serve at once. Makes 6 servings.

OLIVE CHEESEBURGERS

1½ c. soft bread crumbs	1½ lbs. lean ground beef
3 tblsp. olive brine	Prepared mustard
3 tblsp. water	12 large pimiento-stuffed olives
1 tsp. Accent	8 slices Swiss cheese (½ lb.)
⅛ tsp. pepper	8 hamburger buns

Combine first five ingredients; mix well. Add beef; form into 8 patties.

Broil meat on one side about 7 minutes, with patties about 3" below heat source. Turn, spread with mustard and top with olive slices. Top each patty with a cheese slice. Broil 5 minutes longer or until cheese melts and browns.

Serve in split buns. Makes 8 servings.

CORNBURGERS

1 lb. ground beef	⅛ tsp. pepper
¼ c. finely chopped onion	½ c. ketchup
¼ c. finely chopped green pepper	½ c. milk
1 tblsp. flour	1 (1 lb. 1 oz.) can whole kernel corn
1 tsp. salt	8 sandwich buns

Cook beef, onion and green pepper in skillet until meat browns. Sprinkle on flour, salt and pepper and stir to blend. Add remaining ingredients, except buns.

Cook over low heat 5 to 10 minutes to blend flavors. Serve between split sandwich buns. Makes 8 servings.

Note: For a flavor change add ½ tsp. chili powder and a dash of oregano.

SPOON BURGERS

1 lb. ground beef	⅓ c. ketchup
1 tblsp. instant minced onion	⅛ tsp. pepper
1 (10½ oz.) can condensed chicken gumbo soup	1 tsp. chili powder
	8 hamburger buns

Brown ground beef in skillet; drain off excess fat. Stir in onion, soup, ketchup and seasonings. Simmer 5 minutes. Serve between split hamburger buns. Makes 8 servings.

SURPRISE HAMBURGERS

1 lb. ground beef   Pepper
4 tsp. onion soup mix
4 (3″ square) slices mozzarella
  cheese

Divide ground beef into 8 equal portions. Flatten each into thin 4″ patties. Top 4 patties with 1 tsp. soup mix, 1 slice cheese and then with remaining beef patties, pressing edges together to seal. Sprinkle with pepper; broil or pan-fry. Serve plain or with your favorite tomato sauce. Makes 4 servings.

TOASTED CHEESE TREAT

6 tomato slices   12 strips cooked bacon
6 slices Cheddar cheese   6 hamburger buns, toasted

Layer tomato slice, cheese and bacon on buns. Broil until cheese melts and is golden brown. Makes 6 servings.

GOLDEN SAUSAGE BOAT

12 pork sausage links   Pinch salt
6 eggs   6 frankfurter buns
⅓ c. milk   Syrup

Place links in an unheated skillet. Do not prick skins. Add 3 tblsp. water. Cook, covered, 5 minutes over low heat. Uncover; drain off liquid. Finish cooking links over low heat, turning until well browned on all sides.

Meanwhile, beat together eggs, milk and salt. Dip buns in mixture. Grill on both sides until browned.

Place sausages in buns. Serve with syrup. Makes 6 servings.

SUNSHINE SPECIAL

8 eggs   1 (3 oz.) pkg. cream cheese,
½ tsp. onion salt   cut into cubes
⅛ tsp. pepper   6 frankfurter buns, toasted
1 tblsp. parsley flakes   12 strips cooked bacon
3 tblsp. butter

Beat together first 4 ingredients. Cook over low heat in melted butter, gently lifting egg mixture so uncooked egg seeps to bottom. Stir in cheese when eggs are partially cooked.

Spoon eggs into buns. Add bacon strips. Makes 6 servings.

BAKED HEARTY CHEESE SANDWICHES

½ c. butter
12 slices bread
1 (8 oz.) tube sandwich spread

6 slices process American cheese
2 tblsp. ketchup

Melt butter in skillet. Dip one side of bread slices very quickly in butter. Place 6 slices, buttered side down, on baking sheet. Spread with sandwich spread. Top each slice with cheese and 1 teaspoon ketchup, then with remaining bread, buttered side up. Bake in very hot oven (500°) until golden brown, about 5 minutes. Makes 6 servings.

CONEY ISLAND HOT DOGS

1 (15 oz.) can chili con carne
1 (6 oz.) can tomato paste
1 tsp. prepared mustard

10 frankfurters
10 frankfurter buns

Combine chili con carne, tomato paste and mustard in saucepan; heat.

Heat frankfurters in hot water, but do not boil.

Toast split buns. Place frankfurter in each bun and spoon sauce over. Makes 10 servings.

Tomato-Bacon Sandwiches Split buns in half, toast and butter. Lay a slice of peeled tomato on each bun half. Pour your favorite cheese sauce, heated, over tomatoes and top each sandwich with 2 slices (crisscross fashion) of crisp bacon.

Bologna Sandwiches Buy unsliced bologna, cover with water and bring to boiling. Serve hot, sliced, in toasted, buttered buns. Pass ketchup and prepared mustard. Excellent with Hot Potato Salad (see Index).

Ham-Egg Sandwiches Spread toast with deviled ham. Top with hard-cooked egg slices. Heat canned cream of mushroom soup, adding milk for the consistency you desire. Spoon over toast and serve at once.

BARBECUED STEAK SANDWICHES

4 minute steaks
1 tblsp. hot fat
1 (10¾ oz.) can beef gravy

4 slices buttered toast
¼ c. barbecue pickle relish
¼ c. finely chopped onion

Brown steaks in hot fat. Pour gravy over steaks and heat. Place each steak on a slice of toast. Spoon gravy over steaks. Top with relish and onion. Makes 4 servings.

DEVILED DENVER SANDWICH FILLING

2 eggs
1 tblsp. instant or fresh minced
  onion
1 tblsp. minced green pepper

1 tblsp. milk
1 (2¼ oz.) can deviled ham
1 tblsp. butter or bacon
  drippings

Put ingredients, except butter, in jar. Cover and shake to blend. Pour into skillet containing butter, melted, and brown on both sides. Makes filling for 2 sandwiches.

Note: Serve on split buns or between buttered bread slices.

Deviled Ham and Egg Sandwiches Spread toast slices with deviled ham. Cover with slices of hard-cooked eggs. Spoon on a hot sauce like Speedy Cheese Sauce (see Index) or a can of condensed cream of mushroom soup with ⅓ c. milk and a pinch of herbs added.

Butter-browned Peanut Sandwiches Make sandwiches with peanut butter and raisin bread. Spread outside of sandwiches (both sides) with soft butter or margarine. Brown in heavy skillet.

SKILLET TUNA SANDWICHES

1 (6½ oz.) can tuna, drained
  and flaked
¼ c. chopped celery
3 tblsp. mayonnaise
2 tsp. lemon juice
1 tsp. finely chopped onion

8 slices bread
1 to 2 tblsp. shortening or
  salad oil
2 eggs
½ tsp. salt
½ c. milk

Combine tuna, celery, mayonnaise, lemon juice and onion. Mix with fork. Spread on 4 slices bread; top each with another slice of bread. Cut each sandwich in half to make triangles.

Heat shortening over medium heat in large skillet.

Beat eggs; add salt and milk; mix. With slotted pancake turner, dip one side of each sandwich in egg mixture. Turn, and dip second side; place in hot skillet. Brown quickly. Turn and brown other side (quick browning makes the best sandwiches). Serve immediately. Makes 8 sandwiches.

TUNA-CHEESE BUNS

1 (9¼ oz.) can tuna,
    drained and flaked
5 hard-cooked eggs, chopped
3 tblsp. sweet pickle relish
2 tblsp. chopped onion

1 tsp. seasoned salt
½ c. mayonnaise
1 (8 oz.) pkg. sliced process
    American cheese
8 long buns, split and buttered

Combine tuna, eggs, pickle relish, onion, salt and mayonnaise. Spread between split buns. Cut each cheese slice in half. Put 2 halves, end to end, in bun on top of tuna filling.

Place buns on large sheet of foil and wrap. Arrange on baking sheet.

Bake in moderate oven (350°) 20 minutes. Makes 8 servings.

Note: You can make and wrap sandwiches in advance and store in refrigerator to heat just before serving. Bake chilled sandwiches 25 minutes.

TUNA-CHEESE SANDWICHES

2 tsp. lemon juice
1 (3¼ oz.) can tuna, drained
    and flaked
1 (12 oz.) carton onion-chive
    cottage cheese

14 slices buttered bread
Lettuce

Sprinkle lemon juice on tuna (finely flaked) and toss lightly. Gently stir in cottage cheese.

Spread tuna-cheese mixture over 7 bread slices. Top with lettuce leaves and remaining bread slices. Makes 7 sandwiches.

Variation: Use plain cottage cheese instead of onion-chive cottage cheese and add 1 tblsp. finely chopped onion.

FRENCHED CHICKEN SANDWICH

1 egg, beaten	8 slices cooked chicken
2 tblsp. milk	1 (10½ oz.) can condensed
4 slices day-old bread	cream of chicken soup

Blend together egg and milk.

Cut bread slices diagonally. Dip in milk-egg mixture. Brown lightly on both sides in small amount of hot fat in heavy skillet. Arrange in baking pan.

Cover with chicken. Pour on soup. Bake in moderate oven (375°) 20 minutes. Makes 4 servings.

GRILLED TURKEY SANDWICH

8 slices bread	8 slices process American
1 (4½ oz.) can deviled ham	cheese (8 oz. pkg.)
8 to 12 slices cooked turkey	

Toast bread lightly on one side under broiler. Turn over and spread untoasted side with deviled ham. Cover with turkey; top with cheese slice.

Broil until cheese is delicately browned and bubbly. Serve hot. Makes 8 sandwiches.

TURKEY AND GRAVY SANDWICH

6 slices buttered toast	2 (10¾ oz.) cans chicken gravy
6 thick slices cooked turkey	

Lay turkey slices on toast. Heat gravy and spoon over turkey. Serve at once with buttered asparagus or Mexicorn. Makes 6 open-faced sandwiches.

KNIFE AND FORK SANDWICHES A fast-fix, hearty sandwich that's almost a meal in itself comes in handy. Serve it with hot coffee or tea to a hungry man who arrives too late for supper. Have it for lunch at noon or any time of the day. It satisfies.

These substantial, invitingly thick sandwiches are favorite fare in Denmark. You can borrow the Danish way of stacking tempting foods on buttered bread slices, using favorite American foods. You need no recipes. Just look in your refrigerator and freezer for tasty tidbits and left-overs.

The next three open-faced sandwiches, made in our Countryside Test Kitchens, are typical examples, but you need not follow the recipes to the letter to get good results. They are not the finger kind and neither are they dainty. Serve them with knives and forks. You will find they are eye-catching and that they appease lively appetites. Each sandwich is pretty as a picture.

Company Sandwich   Spread rye bread with butter. On right side of each slice, lay two cheese slices; on left side of same slice, pile your favorite potato salad. Top cheese with crisp bacon slices; add cheerful topknot of red-ripe tomato slices to potato salad.

Hawaiian Favorite   Cover buttered white bread with two or three layers of sliced corned beef. Mix crushed pineapple with cottage cheese; spread on top. Garnish with thin carrot curls.

Southern Special   Spread buttered whole wheat bread with thin layer of peanut butter. Cover with slices of ham, then chicken or turkey. Mix hard-cooked eggs, cubed, with mayonnaise, salt, pepper, pimiento and parsley. Spread over meat. Top with thin, unpeeled cucumber slices, sliced pickles or olives.

Breads

REFRIGERATOR BISCUIT SPECIALS

BISCUIT STICKIES

⅓ c. butter or margarine
½ c. dark corn syrup
¼ c. chopped nuts

1 (8 oz.) pkg. refrigerator biscuits

Divide butter evenly in bottoms of 10 muffin-pan cups. Set in oven just long enough to melt butter.

Remove from oven; pour corn syrup and nuts in each cup.

Cut biscuits into thirds; roll each in syrup mixture. Put three pieces in each cup. Bake in preheated hot oven (400°) about 15 minutes. Makes 10 biscuits.

VEGETABLE MEDLEY SUPPER—The best-tasting dish of vitamins you'll ever eat! Perfect seasoning, heavenly aroma. Make in a pressure pan (2 minutes' cooking time) or skillet (simmer 25 minutes). Recipe page 79.

LACE-CRUSTED APPLES are a stunning dessert to serve and are incredibly easy to make. This really is a hot fruit compote with a sweet broiled-on topping. Tap crisp crust to break, spoon into serving dishes. Recipe page 125.

ONION BUTTERMILK BISCUITS

2 tblsp. butter, melted
2 tblsp. minced onion
⅛ tsp. onion salt

1 (8 oz.) pkg. refrigerator
buttermilk biscuits

Combine butter, onion and salt. Flatten biscuits on ungreased baking sheet with bottom of floured custard cup. Leave rim that cup makes. Fill biscuit centers with about 1 tsp. butter-onion mixture. Bake in hot oven (425°) 8 minutes or until biscuits are light golden brown. Makes 10 biscuits.

CORN-KERNEL BISCUITS

3 c. biscuit mix
2 tsp. sugar
½ tsp. salt
2 tblsp. chopped onion
2 tblsp. chopped parsley

1 c. whole kernel corn
1 egg, beaten
½ c. milk
2 tblsp. salad oil
Milk for tops

Combine biscuit mix, sugar, salt, onion, parsley and corn.

Mix egg with milk and oil; add all at once to flour mixture. Stir with fork into a soft dough; beat about 30 seconds (dough should be stiff and a bit sticky).

Dust board with flour; roll dough around in flour. Knead about 10 times to smooth dough. Roll out ½″ thick.

Cut with 3″ floured biscuit cutter. Brush tops with milk. Bake on ungreased baking sheet in very hot oven (450°) 12 to 15 minutes. Makes 1 dozen.

POTATO-CORNMEAL BISCUITS

3 c. biscuit mix
½ c. cornmeal
1 tsp. baking powder
½ tsp. salt
1 tblsp. sugar

1 c. warm mashed potatoes
1 egg, beaten
1 tblsp. salad oil
½ c. milk
Milk for tops

Combine biscuit mix, cornmeal, baking powder, salt and sugar in mixing bowl.

Blend potatoes, egg, oil and milk until smooth. Add to dry ingredients; blend until completely mixed.

Knead half a minute on floured board to smooth dough. Roll out ½″ thick.

Cut with 3″ floured biscuit cutter. Place on ungreased baking sheet; brush with milk. Bake in very hot oven (450°) 12 to 15 minutes, or until done. Makes 15 biscuits.

Note: Place biscuits close together on baking sheet if you like soft sides, 1″ apart if you like crusty biscuits.

Use instant mashed potatoes when in a hurry.

HASTY-TASTY BISCUIT TRICKS

Sage Biscuits Add ¼ tsp. sage to the dry ingredients for biscuits (2 c. flour or biscuit mix) and bake as usual. Wonderful with chicken or pork.

Onion Biscuits When you have leftover canned French-fried onions, chop them fine and add ½ c. of them to biscuits (2 c. flour or biscuit mix). Excellent with beef or lamb.

Waffled Biscuits Place canned refrigerator biscuits on hot waffle iron. Bake until light golden brown. The grid flattens the biscuits. They are crunchy-crisp outside, light within.

Strawberry Biscuits Place 1 tblsp. strawberry preserves in bottom of each greased muffin-cup pan. Top with refrigerator biscuits and bake as directed on package. Turn out of pan at once.

CHEESE ROLLS

⅔ c. Cheddar-cheese spread
2 tblsp. butter

1 (8 oz.) pkg. refrigerator butterflake rolls

Soften cheese spread and butter at room temperature; combine and mix thoroughly.

Spread cheese mixture on rolls, pulling sections to separate a little so some of cheese will melt between them.

Bake in moderate oven (375°) 15 minutes. Makes 12 rolls.

Variations: Add ½ to ¾ tsp. caraway seeds to the cheese-butter mixture. Or fix ready-to-bake brown-and-serve rolls this way.

FRUITED FANTAN ROLLS

3 tblsp. Cranberry Relish (see Index), thawed and drained
3 tblsp. butter or margarine

1 (8 oz.) pkg. refrigerator butterflake rolls

Combine Cranberry Relish with butter. Spread mixture between one slit in each roll.

Set rolls in large muffin-pan cups; bake in moderate oven (350°) 15 minutes. Makes 12 rolls.

Dill Biscuits Break package of refrigerator biscuits apart. Dip in butter and then sprinkle with poppy seeds and dried dill. Place on greased baking sheet; bake in hot oven (400°) about 10 minutes.

BASIC COFFEE CAKE

2 c. biscuit mix
2 tblsp. sugar

1 egg
⅔ c. milk

Blend biscuit mix, sugar, egg and milk; beat vigorously 3 minutes or 75 strokes. Use one of the following three recipes. You'll want to work out other variations.

APRICOT SWIRL COFFEE CAKE

1 c. apricot jam
1½ tblsp. orange juice

½ tsp. grated orange rind
1 Basic Coffee Cake recipe

Combine apricot jam, orange juice and rind.
Spread two-thirds of Basic Coffee Cake batter in a 9" round pan.
Alternate spoonful of apricot-jam mixture and remaining batter on top. Run a knife through batter in spiral fashion to give a marbled appearance.
Bake in hot oven (400°) until golden brown, about 25 minutes. Serve warm. Makes 8 servings.

Variation: Substitute pineapple jam for apricot jam.

SPICY APPLE COFFEE CAKE

1 Basic Coffee Cake recipe
2 medium apples, peeled, cored
    and sliced (1⅓ c. chopped)
½ c. sugar

1½ tsp. cinnamon
2 tblsp. biscuit mix
2 tblsp. soft butter or margarine

Spread batter in greased 9" round pan. Sprinkle apples over top. Top with sugar, cinnamon, biscuit mix and butter, mixed together.
Bake in hot oven (400°) 25 to 30 minutes. Serve warm. Makes 8 servings.

STREUSEL COFFEE CAKE

1 Basic Coffee Cake recipe
½ c. brown sugar
½ c. chopped nuts
2 tblsp. biscuit mix

2 tblsp. butter or margarine, melted
1 tsp. cinnamon

Spread Basic Coffee Cake batter in greased 9″ round layer-cake pan. Top with remaining ingredients, mixed.

Bake in hot oven (400°) 25 to 30 minutes. Serve warm. Makes 8 servings.

STRAWBERRY SWIRL COFFEE CAKE

3½ c. biscuit mix
¼ c. sugar
1 egg, beaten
1 tsp. vanilla
Milk

2 tblsp. melted butter
⅔ c. strawberry preserves
½ c. chopped nuts
½ c. confectioners sugar
1 tblsp. milk

Blend biscuit mix and sugar. Add enough milk to egg and vanilla to make 1 c.; add to sugar mixture. Stir with fork into soft dough; beat vigorously 20 strokes until stiff and slightly sticky. Knead on well-floured board ½ minute. Roll into 7×18″ rectangle. Leaving 1″ uncovered on long sides for sealing, spread with butter and ½ cup of preserves. Sprinkle with nuts; moisten edge. Roll lengthwise like jelly roll; let rest on sealed side one minute, then turn seam to side. Cut roll in half lengthwise. Cut 5″ from one strip; form loosely into circle on center of greased baking sheet, keeping cut surfaces up. Coil remainder of strip loosely in circle around it. Make outer circle with second strip; seal end. Spoon remaining jam between strips. Bake in moderate oven (375°) for 25 to 30 minutes, until lightly browned.

Combine confectioners sugar and milk; brush over hot coffee cake. Serve warm. Makes 8 to 10 servings.

ORANGE SUGAR BREAD

2 (8 oz.) pkgs. refrigerator
  biscuits
¼ c. butter, melted
2 tblsp. orange juice

½ c. sugar
½ c. brown sugar
1 tsp. grated orange rind
¼ tsp. nutmeg

Separate biscuits. Combine butter and orange juice. Mix remaining ingredients in separate bowl. Dip biscuits in butter then sugar mixtures. Stand upright in well-greased 1½ qt. ring mold. Bake in very hot oven (450°) for 12 to 15 minutes. Turn out on plate. Makes 1 coffee ring.

HOT ONION BREAD

2 medium onions, peeled	1 egg
3 tblsp. butter or margarine	1 c. dairy sour cream
2 c. biscuit mix	½ tsp. salt
½ c. milk	1 tsp. poppy seeds

Slice onions thinly and separate into rings. Cook gently in butter until soft, 10 to 15 minutes. (Do not brown.)

Meanwhile combine biscuit mix and milk as directed on package. Spread into a greased pan (8×8×2"). Top with onions.

Beat egg with sour cream and salt; spoon over onions. Sprinkle with poppy seeds.

Bake in moderate oven (375°) 30 minutes or until topping is set. Serve hot; makes 8 servings.

QUICK CRUMB COFFEE CAKE

2 (8 oz.) pkgs. refrigerator biscuits	¼ c. finely chopped nuts
½ c. sugar	2 tblsp. butter or margarine. melted
2 tblsp. brown sugar	Glaze (recipe follows)
1 tsp. cinnamon	

Flatten biscuits. Place 10 biscuits in a greased 9" layer pan; press biscuit edges together so they cover the bottom of the pan.

Combine remaining ingredients. Spread over biscuits. Place remaining flattened biscuits on top to cover filling.

Bake in very hot oven (450°) until browned, about 15 minutes. Remove from pan.

Cool 5 minutes. Spread top with glaze. Makes 6 servings.

Glaze Combine ¾ c. sifted confectioners sugar, ½ tsp. vanilla and 3 to 4 tsp. water.

CRANBERRY COFFEE CAKE

3 tblsp. butter or margarine,
  melted
⅓ c. honey
¾ c. Cranberry Relish (see
  Index) partially thawed

2 (8 oz.) pkgs. refrigerator
  biscuits

Melt butter in tube pan (8" or 9"). Add honey and relish; mix well.

Arrange biscuits on end around outer edge of pan. Bake in hot oven (425°) 10 minutes; reduce heat to 400° and bake about 20 to 25 minutes, until browned on top and inner edges. Let cake set 5 minutes before turning upside-down on serving plate. Serve hot. Makes 8 to 10 servings.

MADE WITH BROWN-AND-SERVE ROLLS   Many busy women keep brown-and-serve rolls on hand. They add their own touches and heat them at mealtime or when serving coffee. You can get some of their specialties ready and hot out of the oven in less than 20 minutes.

MAPLE-NUT STICKIES

1 tblsp. butter or margarine
½ c. maple blended syrup

½ c. chopped nuts
12 brown-and-serve rolls

Place ¼ tsp. butter, 2 tsp. syrup and a sprinkling of chopped nuts in each muffin-pan cup.

Place a roll, top side down, over mixture in muffin-pan cup.

Bake in hot oven (400°) about 10 minutes. Serve warm. Makes 12 rolls.

CRUNCHY ORANGE ROLLS

12 brown-and-serve rolls
1 tblsp. butter or margarine,
  melted

2 tblsp. grated orange rind
1 c. sugar
Orange juice

Brush rolls with butter. Combine orange rind, sugar and enough orange juice to moisten. Turn rolls in mixture until well coated.

Place rolls on baking sheet and bake in hot oven (400°) about 10 minutes, or until browned. Makes 12 rolls.

BUTTERFLAKE BREAD

1 (8 oz.) pkg. refrigerator butterflake rolls
1 tsp. sesame seeds

On ungreased baking sheet place 2 rolls side by side, slightly overlapping. Place the next 2 rolls so that they overlap the first 2 rolls a little and also overlap each other. Repeat until all 12 rolls are used. Sprinkle with sesame seeds.

Bake in moderate oven (350°) 15 minutes. Makes 1 loaf.

QUICK FRENCH BREAD It's disappointing not to find French bread in your store when you want it. Nine chances out of ten, you don't have time to bake the conventional crusty loaf. And your heart may be set on serving garlic bread as a part of a spaghetti or other dinner. We have a solution. Make a quick French bread.

NEW-WAY FRENCH BREAD

2 (8 oz.) pkgs. refrigerator   1 egg white, slightly beaten
   biscuits   1 tsp. poppy seeds

Place biscuits on ungreased baking sheet, press together lightly, shaping ends to form a long loaf. Brush with egg white, sprinkle with poppy seeds.

Bake in moderate oven (350°) until rich, golden brown, 30 to 40 minutes. Makes 1 (14") loaf.

Garlic Bread Slice New-Way French Bread and spread with Garlic Butter. Heat in oven a few minutes. Serve hot.

To make Garlic Butter: Crush 2 or 3 garlic cloves, peeled, and add to ½ c. butter. Let stand at room temperature while baking the bread, stirring occasionally. Remove garlic.

Butter-Pecan Doughnuts Slice plain doughnuts from the bakery in half, crosswise. Spread cut sides with soft butter or margarine and sprinkle with brown sugar and chopped pecans. Spread in shallow pan and bake in hot oven (400°) about 5 minutes. Serve with coffee or for dessert alongside canned pears or other fruit.

HOT DINNER BREAD

1 (1 lb.) loaf white bread
¼ c. butter

1 c. shredded Cheddar cheese
Paprika

Spread bread slices on one side with softened butter; sprinkle with cheese and paprika. Put back in shape of loaf. Tie with string. Wrap loaf in foil and heat in moderate oven (375°) for 25 minutes or until cheese is melted. Unwrap, cut and remove string and serve piping hot. Makes 10 to 12 servings.

HOT BREAKFAST BREAD

1 (1 lb.) loaf white bread
¼ c. butter
⅔ c. sugar
1 tsp. cinnamon

½ c. sifted confectioners sugar
1½ to 2 tblsp. light cream
2 tblsp. finely chopped nuts

Spread bread slices on one side with softened butter; sprinkle with combined sugar and cinnamon. Put back in shape of loaf. If desired, cut in lengthwise halves and tie with string. Wrap loaf securely in foil and heat in moderate oven (375°) for 20 to 25 minutes. Unwrap, cut and remove string. Make glaze from confectioners sugar and cream; pour glaze over top and sprinkle with nuts. Serve piping hot. Makes 10 to 12 servings.

Tea-party Chocolate Toast Instead of cinnamon toast, make the teatime treat this way: mix together ½ c. cocoa, 6 tblsp. soft butter, 1 tsp. cinnamon and 6 tblsp. sugar. Spread on hot toast and serve at once with tea or coffee.

Sesame Toast Sticks Spread slices of whole-wheat bread, crusts removed, with equal amounts of butter or margarine and honey, mixed. Sprinkle with sesame seeds. Cut bread slices in finger lengths and place on baking sheet. Toast in very hot oven (450°) until crisp and browned, about 6 minutes. Serve with fruit salad or with tea or coffee.

WAFFLED FRENCH TOAST

2 eggs	2 tblsp. salad oil
1 c. milk	10 slices bread
¼ tsp. salt	

Beat eggs slightly; blend in milk, salt and oil. Pour into shallow pan.

Dip bread in egg-milk mixture, coating both sides.

Bake in hot waffle iron until steam no longer appears and bread is brown. Serve at once with honey, syrup or jam. Makes 5 servings.

MUFFINS—PLAIN AND FANCY Muffins lift simple, plain meals above the commonplace. They are a snap to make. And the cook's imagination is the limit to the variety in this hot bread. If you ever are lucky enough to have left-over muffins, cut them in crosswise halves, butter and toast them. They're delicious. Here are country-favorite muffins you'll want to try.

CRANBERRY-CORN MUFFINS

1 (7 oz.) can jellied cranberry
   sauce
1 (8 oz.) pkg. corn muffin mix

Cut cranberry sauce into ¼" cubes.

Prepare muffin mix as directed on package. Fold in cranberry sauce. Fill paper-lined muffin-pan cups half full and bake as directed on package. Makes 12 muffins.

SPICED RAISIN MUFFINS

2 c. biscuit mix	1 c. finely cut raisins
¼ c. sugar	1 egg, slightly beaten
½ tsp. ground cinnamon	¾ c. milk

Combine biscuit mix, sugar, cinnamon and raisins (if you cut them with scissors in mixing bowl, raisins distribute better).

Blend together egg and milk; add to dry ingredients. Stir until batter is just moistened. Bake in hot oven (425°) about 15 minutes. Makes 12 muffins.

SPICY MUFFINS

1 (14 oz.) pkg. muffin mix, any desired kind	1 tsp. cinnamon
½ c. butter or margarine, melted	½ c. sugar

Prepare and bake muffins as directed on mix package.

Dip hot muffins into melted butter. Shake in paper sack with cinnamon and sugar. Makes 12 to 16 muffins.

MUFFIN STRATEGY One of the most successful tricks busy cooks use to avoid meal monotony is to change the shape of familiar foods. Muffins are a classic example. Here are 2 ways to give them a new look and to cut down on time—no paper liners or pouring of batter into lots of muffin-pan cups. The baking is quicker, too. Use your favorite muffin mix, like orange, blueberry or corn.

Muffin Fingers Prepare batter with 1 (14 oz.) pkg. muffin mix, using 2 envelopes, as directed on package. Pour into greased 13×9 ×2″ pan. Bake in hot oven (400°) 15 minutes. Cut in half lengthwise, then in 8 crosswise strips. Makes 16 muffins.

Muffin Squares Prepare batter from ½ (14 oz.) pkg. (1 envelope) as directed on muffin-mix package. Pour into greased 9×9×2″ pan. Bake in hot oven (400°) 15 minutes or until top is lightly browned. Cut in squares to serve. Makes 9 (3″) squares.

Note: You can bake Muffin Squares from 1 (14 oz.) pkg. muffin mix, using 2 envelopes, in a greased 9×9×2″ pan. Increase baking time to 20 to 25 minutes. The muffins will be thicker and their tops will brown more.

SPANISH CORN BREAD

1 (12 oz.) pkg. corn muffin mix	1 small onion, finely chopped
1 (12 oz.) can Mexicorn	1 egg, beaten
½ tsp. dry mustard	⅔ c. milk

Combine muffin mix, Mexicorn, mustard and onion. Add egg and milk; blend according to package directions.

Spread in greased 8″ square baking pan; bake in hot oven (400°) about 20 minutes or until corn bread tests done. Serve warm. Makes 9 to 10 servings.

OVEN-BAKED PANCAKES If you have trouble keeping up with the appetites of the people who are eating pancakes, let the oven take over the work. Here's how to make pancakes that require no turning.

Baked Pancakes Prepare 2 c. pancake mix as directed on package. Pour into well-greased jelly-roll pan (15×10×1″). Bake in hot oven (425°) until top is lightly browned, 15 to 20 minutes. Cut in rectangles and serve at once with butter and syrup or jam. Makes 4 servings.

Country Kitchen Pancakes Make batter as directed on pancake-mix package. Add ½ c. each canned whole kernel corn, drained, and cooked ham, cut in small pieces. Bake and serve hot with butter and syrup.

MEAT-IN-A-PANCAKE

1½ c. milk	1½ c. pancake mix
1 egg, beaten	2 (12 oz.) cans luncheon meat,
1 tblsp. salad oil	sliced ¼″ thick
½ c. yellow cornmeal	

Blend milk, egg and oil; add cornmeal and pancake mix; stir until smooth. Dip meat in batter; brown on preheated griddle. Makes 24 cakes.

PANCAKES ORIENTAL

1 (12 oz.) can luncheon meat, cubed	3 tblsp. chopped parsley
3 tblsp. shortening	12 (4″) pancakes (from mix)
1 c. chopped celery	Gravy (recipe follows)
1 (1 lb.) can bean sprouts, drained	

Brown meat in shortening; add celery, bean sprouts and parsley; heat through.

Serve mixture between 2 warm pancakes; pass gravy. Makes 6 servings.

Gravy   Combine 2 c. chicken broth, 2 tblsp. cornstarch and 1 tblsp. soy sauce. Cook, stirring constantly, until thick and clear. Serve hot. Makes about 2 cups.

BACON-PEANUT BUTTER WAFFLES

4 c. pancake mix	1 c. crumbled, crisp-cooked
1 c. peanut butter	bacon

Mix waffle batter according to package directions. Blend in peanut butter. Fold in bacon. Bake as directed. Makes 6 (9") square waffles or 4 (12") square waffles.

PANCAKE WAFFLES

3 c. pancake mix	½ c. melted shortening
3 c. milk	3 tblsp. crumbled, cooked bacon
3 eggs, beaten	Apricot Fluff (recipe follows)

Combine pancake mix, milk and eggs; beat with rotary beater until fairly smooth; blend in shortening and bacon.

Bake in preheated waffle baker. Serve with Apricot Fluff. Makes about 6 (11×6") waffles.

Apricot Fluff   Beat ½ c. butter until fluffy; beat in ½ c. apricot preserves. Makes 1 cup.

Section 4
Desserts

No meal is complete without the grand finale—dessert. And you can prepare a dessert that takes only a few minutes of your time but tastes divine.

Take advantage of the hundreds of dessert mixes that flood the supermarket shelves: instant pie crusts, instant puddings, cake mixes, almost instant frostings, ready-prepared topping mixes and you'll discover many, many more.

Apricot Pie à la Mode—sounds fancy doesn't it? Looks it too—but it's made from canned apricot halves and a pie shell that you have made ahead and frozen (or an unbaked shell from the supermarket frozen foods section). Cherry-Banana Pie is another almost instant glamorous ending for a meal—made with canned cherry-pie filling and bananas, topped with a layer of whipped cream and nuts.

Whip together a batch of Ginger-Apple Fluff—a quick folding of crushed gingersnaps, whipped cream, canned applesauce. Instant glamour in less than 10 minutes!

For a party you will want to try the Ice-Cream Cookie Pie. After baking a refrigerator cookie to golden brown, fill it with scoops of assorted ice creams and drizzle with strawberry topping. Raspberry Crunch will make a hit at any meal—only 5 ingredients and 5 minutes' preparation for a superb sweet.

Pies

APRICOT PIE À LA MODE

1 (1 lb. 13 oz.) can apricot
   halves, drained
1 unbaked 9″ pie shell
1 tblsp. lemon juice
½ c. flour

¾ c. sugar
¼ tsp. cinnamon
¼ tsp. nutmeg
¼ c. butter or margarine
1 pt. vanilla ice cream

Spread apricots in pastry-lined pan. Sprinkle with lemon juice. Combine flour, sugar and spices. Mix with butter until crumbly. Sprinkle over apricots.

Bake in hot oven (400°) 40 minutes. Serve warm or cold, topped with scoops of ice cream. Makes 1 (9″) pie.

Variation: Your own apple or favorite berry pie also may be served this way.

CHERRY-BANANA PIE

2 medium bananas
1 baked 9″ pie shell
1 (1 lb. 6 oz.) can cherry pie
   filling

1 c. heavy cream
2 tblsp. sugar
⅓ c. chopped nuts

Slice bananas into bottom of pie shell. Top with cherry-pie filling. Whip cream, add sugar and spread over cherry filling. Sprinkle nuts over. Makes 1 (9″) pie.

Variation: Substitute flaked or shredded coconut for nuts.

BROWNIE PIE

1 stick pie-crust mix
1 (1 lb.) pkg. brownie mix
¼ c. chocolate syrup

¼ c. chopped nuts
Whipped cream

Prepare pie mix as directed on package. Line a 9″ pie pan with pastry.

Prepare brownie mix as directed on package for fudgy brownies. Spread mixture evenly in unbaked pie shell. Pour chocolate syrup evenly over the top. Sprinkle with nuts.

Bake in moderate oven (350°) 40 to 45 minutes. Serve warm topped with whipped cream. Makes 1 (9″) pie.

DAMSON PLUM WHIPPED CREAM PIE

1 pkg. pie-crust mix for 8″ pie
¾ c. damson plum preserves
1 (2 oz.) pkg. dessert-topping mix
½ tsp. vanilla
⅛ tsp. almond extract
1 tblsp. confectioners sugar
Nutmeg

Mix, bake and cool 8″ pie shell as directed on package. Spread preserves over bottom of pie shell.

Prepare topping as directed on package, adding flavorings and sugar before whipping. Spread over preserves. Sprinkle very lightly with nutmeg. Chill before serving. Makes 1 (8″) pie.

Variation: To make Damson Custard Pie, prepare a package of instant vanilla-pudding mix as directed on package. Pour over preserves. When set, add topping.

CRANBERRY-MINCEMEAT PIE

3 c. ready-to-use mincemeat
1 c. Cranberry Relish (see Index)
1 unbaked (9″) pie shell

Combine mincemeat and relish; pour into pie shell.
Bake in hot oven (400°) 35 minutes. Makes 1 (9″) pie.

EASY PECAN PIE

20 round buttery crackers, crushed
1 c. chopped pecans
1 c. sugar
3 egg whites
1 tsp. vanilla
½ c. heavy cream, whipped
½ c. flaked or shredded coconut

Combine crackers, pecans and ½ c. sugar.

Beat egg whites until stiff; beat in remaining sugar and vanilla. Fold into cracker mixture.

Spread in greased 9″ pie pan and bake in slow oven (325°) 30 minutes. Cool.

Top with whipped cream and sprinkle with coconut. Makes 1 (9″) pie.

CRUMB PIE CRUSTS   Some short-order cooks find crumb crusts help them to make pies in a jiffy. These crusts for open-faced pies are simple to make and introduce great variety in desserts because so many different kinds of crumbs can be used.

The universal favorites are graham crackers, vanilla and chocolate wafers, gingersnaps, corn flakes, zweibach and rusks. Almost any dry cereal or bread crumbs may be used. Corn flake, vanilla-wafer and graham cracker crumbs are excellent for a lemon-meringue pie. Spiced crusts are especially tasty for pumpkin-, chocolate- and mocha-pie fillings. Here is a basic recipe with variations.

CRUMB CRUSTS

| 1⅔ c. very finely crushed crumbs | ½ c. butter or margarine, melted
2 to 4 tblsp. sugar, or to taste |

Mix crumbs, butter and sugar. Spread in a greased 9″ pie pan and press firmly against the bottom and sides of the pan, molding with an 8″ or 9″ pie pan.

Bake 8 minutes in moderate oven (375°). Cool and fill.

Variations

Chocolate-Crumb Crust   Add 2 (1 oz.) squares unsweetened chocolate, melted, to corn flake, vanilla-wafer or graham cracker crumb mixture.

Coconut-Crumb Crust   Reduce crumbs to 1⅓ c. and add ⅓ c. flaked coconut.

Orange-Crumb Crust   To basic crumb-crust mixture, add 2 tblsp. grated orange rind.

Nut-Crumb Crust Reduce crumbs to 1¼ c. and add ½ c. finely chopped nuts.

Spiced-Crumb Crust Mix 1 tsp. cinnamon or ½ tsp. ginger with crumbs.

COCONUT PIE CRUST

1⅓ c. flaked coconut	2 tblsp. sugar
2 tblsp. butter, melted	¼ c. graham cracker crumbs

Combine coconut and butter; mix well. Add sugar and graham cracker crumbs; mix and press firmly into bottom and on sides of an 8″ pie pan. Bake in moderate oven (375°) 10 to 12 minutes, or until golden brown. Makes 1 (8″) pie shell.

Variation: Substitute chocolate wafer (cookie) crumbs for graham cracker crumbs.

OIL PASTRY

½ c. salad oil	2 c. sifted flour
5 tblsp. iced water	1 tsp. salt

Beat oil and water until mixture is thick and creamy. Sift flour and salt into bowl and pour over the oil-water mixture to completely cover flour. Mix with a fork to form a ball. Makes enough pastry for 1 (8″ or 9″) two-crust pie.

Cakes and Frostings

Country cakes never were better tasting or more glamorous than they are today. Cooks have little time to fuss over decorations, but their quick tricks yield big dividends. Angel food cakes continue to hold their own. And it's a rare woman who does not have a few simple dress-ups for these tall, light cakes.

SURPRISE ANGEL FOOD CAKE

1 (15 oz.) pkg. angel food cake mix
3 tblsp. instant cocoa mix

Prepare batter as directed on package. Pour one-fourth of batter in a 10″ tube pan. Spread evenly to eliminate air pockets. Sprinkle half of cocoa mix over batter. Add another fourth of the batter; spread evenly with spatula. Sprinkle on remainder of cocoa mix. Top with remaining batter. Run a knife in batter in spiral fashion.

Bake as directed on package. Makes 1 (10″) cake.

Note: For a festive dessert, frost the cake in white and sprinkle tiny chocolate decorating candies on frosting.

Angel Food à la Mode   Brush angel food cake slices with melted butter and sprinkle lightly with brown sugar and flaked or shredded coconut. Run under broiler to melt sugar and brown coconut delicately. Top with vanilla ice cream and serve immediately.

BUSY COOK'S SHORTCAKES   One busy country woman prefers to bake angel food cake batter in individual servings. She cools the little cakes, freezes them and then stores them in the freezer in plastic bags. This enables her to take out as many servings as she needs without cutting a big cake.

Angel Shortcakes   Prepare batter from angel food cake mix as directed on package. Drop from ½-cup measure about 2″ apart on ungreased baking sheet. Bake in moderate oven (375°) until a light golden brown, 10 to 15 minutes. Remove from baking sheet immediately. Repeat until all the batter is used. Makes 18 to 20 shortcakes. Serve little cakes topped with ice cream and your favorite dessert sauce or partly thawed frozen strawberries, raspberries or sliced peaches.

WHIZ CHOCOLATE CAKE

¼ c. shortening	1 tsp. vanilla
2 (1 oz.) squares unsweetened chocolate	¼ c. buttermilk
	1 c. sifted flour
½ c. water	½ tsp. baking powder
1 c. sugar	½ tsp. baking soda
½ tsp. salt	1 egg

Heat shortening, chocolate and water together in a 1 qt. saucepan until they are melted. Remove from heat. Cool.

Stir in sugar, salt, vanilla and buttermilk. Beat in flour, baking powder and soda, which have been sifted together. Add egg and beat well.

Pour batter into greased 9×9×2″ pan.

Bake in moderate oven (350°) 30 minutes. Remove from oven. Turn out of pan. Frost with Saucepan Chocolate Frosting (see Index) or as desired. Makes 1 (9″) square cake.

CRESTED DESSERT CAKE

1 (8″ or 9″) layer white or
  sponge cake
½ c. chunk-style peanut butter

1 c. apricot jam
½ c. flaked or shredded coconut

Turn cake bottom side up on baking sheet. Spread with peanut butter, then with jam. (Or mix peanut butter with jam before spreading—it goes on easier.) Sprinkle with coconut.

Place cake in cold oven, then turn on heat and set temperature control at 350°. Turn off heat in 5 minutes. Leave cake in oven while first part of dinner is eaten. Cut in wedges. Makes 1 (8″ or 9″) layer.

Variation: Use raisins, rinsed in warm water and wiped dry with paper towel, instead of coconut. Raisins puff up in oven. For a company touch, top cake with scoops of vanilla ice cream.

SWEET CREAM CAKE

2½ c. sifted flour
1¾ c. sugar
3 tsp. baking powder
½ tsp. salt

1⅓ c. heavy cream
⅓ c. milk
1 tsp. vanilla
3 eggs

Sift dry ingredients into mixing bowl. Add cream, milk and vanilla. Mix to dampen dry ingredients. Beat 1 minute at medium speed of electric mixer, or 150 vigorous strokes by hand.

Add eggs and mix 1 minute longer.

Pour into 2 paper-lined 8″ round cake pans. Tap sharply on table top to remove air bubbles. Bake in moderate oven (350°) about 40 minutes. Makes 1 (8″) layer cake.

NUT-TOPPED GINGERBREAD

1 (14½ oz.) pkg. gingerbread   2 tblsp. melted butter or
   mix   margarine
½ c. brown sugar, firmly packed   ⅔ c. chopped walnuts
2 tblsp. flour
1½ tsp. cinnamon

Prepare gingerbread batter as directed on package. Pour into greased 9″ square pan.

Combine brown sugar, flour and cinnamon. Blend in butter and nuts. Sprinkle mixture over batter.

Bake in moderate oven (350°) 25 to 30 minutes. Cut in squares; serve hot. Makes 1 (9″) square cake.

Variation: Omit nut topping; sprinkle 1 c. flaked or shredded coconut on top.

TROPICAL GINGERBREAD

1 (14½ oz.) pkg. gingerbread   ¼ c. sifted confectioners sugar
   mix   ½ tsp. vanilla
1¼ c. grated coconut   1 c. heavy cream, whipped
   (packaged)   2 large bananas

Prepare gingerbread batter as directed on package. Fold in coconut. Pour into greased 9″ square pan. Bake in moderate oven (350°) 25 to 30 minutes. Cut in squares.

Fold sugar and vanilla into whipped cream. Spoon on top of hot gingerbread. Decorate whipped cream with bananas, sliced. Serve at once. Makes 1 (9″) square cake.

Variations: Omit bananas. Fold 3 tblsp. instead of ¼ c. confectioners sugar into whipped cream. Fold in 1 (9 oz.) can crushed pineapple, well drained (about ¾ c.), and ¼ c. chopped and drained maraschino cherries. Serve on warm gingerbread. Or top with ice cream or whipped cream.

LEMON-COCONUT CAKE PIE

1 (7 or 8 oz.) baker's loaf cake   2 eggs, separated
½ c. flaked or shredded coconut
1 (3¼ or 4 oz.) pkg. lemon
   flavor pudding and pie filling

Cut cake into 12 or 14 slices. Line sides and bottom of a 9″ pie pan with them to make pie shell.

Sprinkle half of coconut over cake slices.

Prepare pudding according to package directions, using egg yolks. Pour immediately into pie shell.

Make meringue from the egg whites, using 6 tblsp. sugar or as directed on pudding package. Spread over filling; sprinkle with remaining coconut. Bake in moderate oven (350°) 12 minutes or until lightly browned. Cool and cut. Makes 1 (9″) pie.

MERRY CHRISTMAS CAKE

1 (8″) square white cake layer
2 tblsp. soft butter or margarine
⅓ c. brown sugar, firmly packed
2 tblsp. heavy cream
⅓ c. chopped candied mixed fruits
⅔ c. broken nuts
⅓ c. flaked or shredded coconut
Candied cherries

Set cake on baking sheet. Cream together butter, sugar and cream. Add candied mixed fruits, nuts and coconut. Spread on cake. Dot with candied cherries.

Broil in preheated broiler until top bubbles and has a glazed appearance, 3 to 5 minutes. Serve warm. Makes 1 (8″) layer.

Note: Make 2 (8″) square cake layers from cake mix. Store in freezer. When company comes, add topping and broil.

ORANGE-RAISIN CAKE

1 (1 lb. 3 oz.) pkg. yellow cake mix
Rind of 1 orange, grated
1 c. raisins
1 c. orange juice
Juice of 1 lemon
¾ c. brown sugar

Prepare cake batter as directed on package. Fold in orange rind and raisins. Bake in a greased 13×9×2″ pan in moderate oven (350°) 30 minutes.

Remove cake from pan and, while warm, prick top with fork. Pour over it the orange and lemon juices mixed with the brown sugar. Serve topped with whipped cream, ice cream or plain. Makes 1 (13×9×2″) cake.

Note: Omit raisins and orange rind when in a hurry.

DRESS-UPS FOR CAKE DESSERTS   You'll find that glamorous cake desserts frequently consist of layers or loaves cut in horizontal halves and put together with luscious fillings. Sometimes it's difficult to cut tender cakes without breaking them. Women who have freezers have a perfect solution to the problem. Freeze the cake before cutting it into crosswise halves.

NUT-CRESTED CAKE

3 tblsp. butter or margarine	½ c. coarsely chopped nuts
2 tblsp. brown sugar	1 (10 oz.) pkg. spice cake mix

Combine butter and brown sugar. Pat on sides and bottom of 9″ layer pan. Sprinkle nuts over butter mixture.

Prepare cake mix as directed on package. Pour into pan and bake in moderate oven (350°) 30 to 35 minutes. Serve warm or cold, plain or topped with vanilla ice cream. Makes 1 (9″) layer.

Variation: Substitute peanuts for nuts and banana cake mix for spice cake mix. (This is a small package of cake mix.)

MOCHA DREAM CAKE

1 c. miniature marshmallows	2 (8″ or 9″) baked devil's food
4 tsp. instant coffee	cake layers
2 c. heavy cream	

Add marshmallows and instant coffee to cream and stir to blend. Allow to stand at least 3 hours, or overnight, in refrigerator.

Cut each cake layer horizontally into 2 equal layers, making 4 layers.

Whip cream mixture until all marshmallows are dissolved and mixture stands in soft peaks. Spread between cake layers and on sides and top of them. Store in refrigerator until ready to serve. Makes 1 (8″ or 9″) layer cake.

Note: A good way to cut unfrozen cake in even layers horizontally is to mark around it with a knife, cutting into the cake about ½″. Anchor a length of thread in the slit and gently pull it through the cake.

MINCEMEAT CAKE

2 tblsp. butter or margarine
1 c. brown sugar, firmly packed
2 c. prepared mincemeat

1 (1 lb. 1 oz.) pkg. orange
  cake mix
1 c. heavy cream, whipped

Put butter, sugar and mincemeat in 10½″ ring mold. Heat in moderate oven (375°) while making cake.

Prepare cake batter as directed on package and pour over hot mincemeat mixture in pan. Bake in moderate oven (375°) about 25 minutes or until cake is delicately brown and springs back to light touch.

Let stand a few minutes; turn out upside-down on chop plate. Or cool in pan, and just before serving, warm in slow oven (300°) 10 to 15 minutes. Place small dish of whipped cream in center. Makes 1 (10½″) ring.

Busy Women's Cupcakes Make cupcakes as directed on package of yellow cake mix. Cool. Spread tops with orange marmalade and miniature marshmallows, 8 to 10 on each cake. Broil until marshmallows melt slightly and are golden brown. Extra delicious with hot tea.

ALMOND GLAZE

⅓ c. chopped or slivered
  unblanched almonds
2 tblsp. butter

1 c. apricot or peach jam
2 to 3 tblsp. water

Lightly brown almonds in butter over low heat. Add jam and water. Heat until jam melts. Drizzle over sponge or angel food cake.

BANANA FROSTING

½ c. mashed banana
1 tsp. lemon juice

¼ c. butter
3½ to 4½ c. confectioners sugar

Combine banana and lemon juice. Cream together butter and 1 c. confectioners sugar. Beat in banana and enough confectioners sugar to make mixture of spreading consistency. Makes enough for tops and sides of two 8″ cake layers.

Note: If you have ripe bananas that will not keep long, mash them and freeze to use in this frosting.

BROILED CARAMEL GLAZE

¼ c. butter   2 tblsp. heavy cream
½ c. brown sugar, firmly packed

Melt butter; stir in brown sugar and cream.

Place cake layers on baking sheet, one at a time. Spread each layer evenly with butter mixture, spreading out to edges.

Place cake in broiler 6" to 8" from heat, and broil until bubbly and golden brown, 2 to 3 minutes. Broil each layer separately.

When second layer is removed from broiler, place on cake plate immediately and place first layer on it. Layers will hold together, and glaze will have run down the side to give cake a finished, appetizing look. Makes enough glaze for 2 (8" or 9") layers.

Variations

Caramel-Nut Glaze   Remove glazed top layer from broiler; sprinkle immediately with chopped nuts.

Pineapple Glaze   Spread top layer with glaze, dip well-drained pineapple tidbits in some of the glaze mixture and arrange in sunburst effect on top of cake at least 1" from edge all around. Broil like plain Caramel Glaze.

Sour Cream-Caramel Glaze   Use dairy sour cream for heavy cream.

Whipped Cream-Cocoa Frosting   Pour 1 c. heavy cream into bowl; stir in ⅓ c. cocoa mix. Chill thoroughly. Whip until light and fluffy. Spoon on slices of angel food or unfrosted white cake. Makes enough for 12 cake slices.

Note: You also can frost an angel food cake with Whipped Cream-Cocoa Frosting if you wish.

FRUIT WHIP

2 egg whites   ½ c. sugar
½ c. preserves, jam or   Dash salt
    marmalade

Place all the ingredients in double boiler. Beat 1 minute with electric or rotary beater. Cook over boiling water, beating constantly, until mixture forms stiff peaks, 5 to 7 minutes. Remove from heat and beat until of spreading consistency. Makes enough frosting for tops and sides of 2 (8″ or 9″) cake layers.

ORANGE BUTTER CREAM

½ c. butter
3 c. sifted confectioners sugar

⅓ c. frozen orange juice
    concentrate, thawed

Cream butter. Add sugar alternately with orange juice, creaming well after every addition until mixture is light and fluffy. Makes frosting for tops and sides of 2 (8″ or 9″) round layers.

SAUCEPAN CHOCOLATE FROSTING

1 (1 oz.) square unsweetened
    chocolate
2 tblsp. butter or margarine

3 tblsp. light cream
½ tsp. vanilla
1 c. sifted confectioners sugar

Place chocolate, butter and cream in saucepan; heat until chocolate and butter are melted. Add vanilla and confectioners sugar and beat until mixture is of spreading consistency. Makes enough frosting for 2 (8″ or 9″) cake layers or for Saucepan Brownies (see Index).

Cheese-Cherry Cake Topping Spread cream cheese, softened at room temperature, on squares of unfrosted chocolate cake. Spoon on canned cherry-pie filling. A simple, easy, pretty and extra-good dessert.

Cookies

TEMPTING BAR COOKIES If you are the kind of cook who likes to stir up brownies from scratch, you will never find a quicker recipe than the one that follows. Nor will you ever taste a more delicious brownie.

SAUCEPAN BROWNIES

½ c. butter or margarine	1 tsp. baking powder
2 (1 oz.) squares unsweetened chocolate	1 tsp. vanilla
	½ c. chopped walnuts
1 c. sugar	2 eggs
½ c. sifted flour	

Melt butter and chocolate together in saucepan. Remove from heat and stir in sugar, flour, baking powder, vanilla and nuts. Add eggs and beat thoroughly.

Spread in a greased pan (9×9×2″). Bake in moderate oven (350°) 30 minutes. Dust with confectioners sugar if desired.

Cut in 18 bars to serve as cookies or in 9 squares to serve as dessert topped with vanilla ice cream. Chocolate fans may wish to pour a chocolate dessert sauce over the ice cream.

BROWNIES—MANY A KIND The smart cook finds a package of brownie mix a challenge. So many different flavorings may be added for a tasty, personal touch. Here are a few favorites of farm women. In all of them the batter is prepared as directed on the mix package, but with these additions to the batter:

Cherry Brownies Add ¼ c. chopped and well-drained maraschino cherries.

Date Brownies Add 1 c. chopped dates instead of nuts. Roll baked brownies, cut in squares, in confectioners sugar.

Mocha Brownies Add 1½ tblsp. powdered instant coffee, stirring it into dry mix.

Double Fudge Brownies Add ½ c. semi-sweet chocolate pieces. Cool brownies before cutting.

Peanut Brownies Omit nuts and add 3 tblsp. chunk-style peanut butter.

Frosted Brownies Frost brownies when cool, and before cutting in squares, with white or chocolate frosting made from packaged mix.

BROWNIES WITH NUTS

Cashew Brownies   Make fudgy brownies as directed on package of brownie mix, only omit nuts from batter. Before baking, sprinkle batter with ¼ c. (¼ lb.) chopped salted cashew nuts.

Variation: Instead of cashew nuts, used chopped nuts from package of assorted salted nuts.

CHOCOLATE PEANUT BARS

½ c. soft butter or margarine
½ c. peanut butter
1 c. brown sugar, firmly packed
⅓ c. light corn syrup

6 c. toasted rice cereal
1 (6 oz.) pkg. semi-sweet
  chocolate pieces

Cream butter and peanut butter together. Add brown sugar and cream well. Stir in syrup.

Add cereal and chocolate pieces. Mix until cereal is coated with butter mixture.

Pack mixture into a greased 13×9×2" pan.

Bake in hot oven (400°) 12 to 15 minutes. Makes 4 dozen (1½") bars.

PRALINE COOKIES

24 graham crackers
1 c. light brown sugar, firmly
  packed

½ c. butter or margarine
1 c. chopped pecans

Grease a (15½×10½×1") jelly roll pan. Line bottom of pan with whole graham crackers.

Place brown sugar and butter in a small saucepan. Bring to a rolling boil over medium heat and cook for 1½ minutes. Remove from heat. When mixture has stopped bubbling, stir in nuts. Spoon it on and spread over graham crackers.

Bake in moderate oven (350°) for 10 minutes. Cool and cut into 48 (1×2") bars.

SCOTCH SHORTBREAD

1 c. butter or margarine
½ c. sugar

2 c. sifted flour

Cream butter thoroughly. Add sugar gradually. Beat in the flour a little at a time.

Divide dough in half and place each half on a greased baking sheet. Pat in 8" circles; flute edges. Prick surface with fork and mark each circle into 8 wedges.

Bake in moderate oven (325°) for 25 to 30 minutes, or until pale brown. Remove from oven and cool on baking sheet 5 minutes. Cut each circle in 8 wedges. Makes 16 servings.

JUST-RIGHT DROP COOKIES

CRUNCHY CHOCOLATE-CHIP COOKIES

1 (13 oz.) pkg. chocolate chip cookie mix
⅓ c. corn flake crumbs

Prepare cookie dough as directed on package. Drop teaspoonfuls into corn flake crumbs. Roll into balls.

Bake on greased baking sheet in moderate oven (375°) 13 to 15 minutes. Makes 2½ dozen.

PEANUT BUTTER DROPS

1 c. sugar
1 c. light corn syrup
½ c. peanut butter
4 c. ready-to-eat high protein
    cereal

1 c. thin pretzel sticks, broken
    into 1" lengths

Mix sugar and syrup in large saucepan. Bring to boil over medium heat; cook for about 30 seconds. Remove from heat and add peanut butter. Stir until smooth. Stir in cereal and pretzel sticks.

Drop by spoonfuls onto waxed paper. Makes 4½ dozen cookies.

CHOCOLATE CRACKLES

1 (1 lb. 2½ oz.) pkg. devil's
    food cake mix
2 eggs, slightly beaten

1 tblsp. water
½ c. vegetable shortening
Confectioners sugar

Combine cake mix, eggs, water and shortening. Mix with a spoon until well blended.

Shape dough into balls the size of small walnuts. Roll balls in confectioners sugar.

Place on greased baking sheets. Bake in moderate oven (375°) for 8 to 10 minutes. Makes 48 cookies.

Other Desserts

LACE-CRUSTED APPLES

5 tart cooking apples	½ tsp. cinnamon
3 tblsp. raisins	1½ c. brown sugar, firmly packed
1 tblsp. lemon juice	½ c. finely chopped walnuts
Water	½ c. melted butter
1½ tsp. grated lemon peel	Vanilla ice cream
1 tblsp. lemon juice	

Peel and core apples. Cut into ½" thick lengthwise slices. Place in saucepan with raisins, lemon juice and water to cover halfway. Cover, bring to a boil, simmer until tender, about 5 minutes. Drain well. Turn into a 10" oven glassware pie plate.

Sprinkle with lemon peel, lemon juice and cinnamon. Combine brown sugar, walnuts and melted butter. Sprinkle over fruits.

Broil about 6" from heat until sugar is melted and golden brown. Cool slightly. Tap crust to break, and top with ice cream. Makes 6 servings.

PEACH-PINEAPPLE-PECAN BROIL

1 (1 lb. 4 oz.) can pineapple chunks, well drained	1 c. brown sugar, firmly packed
	¾ c. finely chopped pecans
1 (1 lb. 13 oz.) can sliced peaches, well drained	½ tsp. ground ginger (optional)
	6 tblsp. melted butter
1 tblsp. lemon juice	Vanilla ice cream

Gently toss together pineapple chunks, peaches and lemon juice. Turn into a 9" oven glassware pie plate.

Combine brown sugar, pecans, ginger and melted butter. Sprinkle over fruits.

Broil about 6 inches from heat until sugar is melted and golden brown. Cool slightly. Tap crust to break, and top with ice cream. Makes 6 servings.

BROILED AMBROSIA

2 large bananas, sliced about
⅜" thick
3 oranges (or 2 oranges plus
1 c. chopped dates), cut into
bite-size pieces

1 tblsp. fresh lemon juice
1 c. brown sugar, firmly packed
1 c. flaked or shredded coconut
6 tblsp. butter, melted
Vanilla ice cream

Gently toss bananas, oranges, and dates with lemon juice; turn into a 10" oven glassware pie plate or comparable shallow broiling-serving dish. Mix together sugar, coconut, and butter; sprinkle over fruits. Broil about 6" from heat until sugar is melted and coconut toasted. Cool slightly. Tap crust to break, and top with ice cream. Makes 6 servings.

JIFFY AMBROSIA

1 (1 lb. 13 oz.) can fruit
cocktail, drained
1 (3½ oz.) can flaked or
shredded coconut
1 large banana, sliced

1 (6 oz.) can frozen orange juice
concentrate, thawed
8 maraschino cherries
(optional)

Combine fruit cocktail, half of the coconut, banana and orange juice. Garnish mixture with remaining coconut and top each serving with a cherry. Makes 8 servings.

APPLE-ORANGE DESSERT

1 (16 to 17 oz.) can applesauce
1 c. miniature marshmallows

1 c. orange sections, fresh or
canned

Combine ingredients, spoon into dessert glasses and chill a few minutes or an hour. Makes 5 servings.

Note: Crisp cookies make an excellent teammate.

GINGER-APPLE FLUFF

1 c. gingersnap crumbs
½ c. heavy cream, whipped

1 (1 lb.) can applesauce
Maraschino cherries

Reserve 2 tblsp. crumbs. Fold remaining crumbs and cream into applesauce. Spoon into sherbet or other dessert glasses. Sprinkle tops with the remaining crumbs. Top each serving with a cherry. Chill. Makes 6 servings.

VIRGINIA APPLE PUDDING

½ c. butter or margarine
1 c. sugar
1 c. sifted flour
2 tsp. baking powder
¼ tsp. salt

¼ tsp. cinnamon
1 c. milk
2 c. cooked or canned apple
slices

Melt butter in 2 qt. casserole.

Combine next 6 ingredients to make batter; pour on butter. Drain apples; pile in center of batter.

Bake in moderate oven (375°) until batter covers fruit and crust browns, 30 to 40 minutes. Makes 4 to 6 servings.

QUICK BANANA PUDDING

1 (3¼ oz.) pkg. vanilla pudding
mix

27 vanilla wafers
2 large bananas, sliced

Prepare pudding mix as directed on package. Cool.

Line the bottom of a 9×5×3″ loaf pan with 12 cookies. Top with 1 banana, sliced. Spread half the pudding on top. Top with remaining cookies, then with 1 banana, sliced, and remaining pudding. Chill. Makes 4 to 6 servings.

LEMON-PEAR VELVET

1 (3¼ or 4 oz.) pkg. lemon
pudding mix
1 c. heavy cream, whipped

1 (1 lb. 14 oz.) can pear halves
Tiny chocolate decorating
candies

Prepare pudding mix as directed on package; chill. Stir until smooth and fold in whipped cream.

Spoon pudding into dessert glasses and top with drained, chilled pear halves. Sprinkle with candies. Makes 6 to 8 servings.

Variation: Instead of pear halves, use canned apricot or peach halves.

MINTED GRAPEFRUIT

2 (1 lb.) cans grapefruit
⅓ c. small peppermint-flavored
candy mints (pillow type)

Combine ingredients. Chill. Makes 6 servings.

Variation: Add 1 orange, peeled and sectioned, for a touch of color and interesting flavor.

FROSTED PINEAPPLE

1 (1 lb. 4 oz.) can pineapple
tidbits, drained
1 c. flaked or shredded coconut

1 pt. lemon sherbet
1 c. blueberries (optional)

Place chilled pineapple in 6 dessert dishes. Sprinkle on ¾ c. coconut. Top with sherbet and scatter on remaining coconut. Garnish with blueberries. Makes 6 servings.

HONEYED BAKED PEARS

8 pear halves, peeled and cored
¼ c. lemon juice
½ c. honey

1 tblsp. butter
½ tsp. cinnamon

Arrange pears in a shallow, greased 1½ qt. casserole. Combine lemon juice and honey. Dot with butter and sprinkle with cinnamon.
Bake, covered, in moderate oven (350°) until pears are tender, 25 to 30 minutes. Serve warm or chilled. Makes 4 servings.

Variation: Substitute peeled and pitted peaches for pears.

BROILED PEACHES

2 (1 lb.) cans peach halves,
drained
1 (6 oz.) can frozen orange
juice concentrate

2 tblsp. red raspberry preserves
1 c. shredded coconut

Arrange peach halves in baking dish; fill each with 1 tblsp. thawed concentrate and ½ tsp. preserves; sprinkle with coconut.
Bake in hot oven (425°) 10 minutes, until coconut browns. Serve warm. Makes 6 servings.

STRAWBERRY SHORTCAKE ROYALE — The classic luscious, old-fashioned shortcake with a heavenly sauce that combines sour cream, softened ice cream and whipped cream. Beautiful to look at, to eat. Recipe page 138.

Melting marshmallows float atop SPICED STEAMER, a hot milk drink sweetened with SPICED SYRUP (recipe page 148). Keep a supply of this syrup in your refrigerator for speedy use.

PINEAPPLE SUPREME

1 (13½ oz.) can frozen   2 tsp. sugar
   pineapple, thawed and drained   Nutmeg
½ c. dairy sour cream

Put pineapple in sherbet or other dessert glasses. Mix sour cream with sugar and pour over pineapple. Dust with nutmeg. Makes 2 servings.

Variation: Substitute 1 (1 lb. 4 oz.) can pineapple chunks for frozen pineapple. Put drained fruit in 4 dessert dishes. Top with sour cream, omitting sugar. Dust with nutmeg. Makes 4 servings.

PEACH ISLANDS

1 (3¼ oz.) pkg. coconut cream   1 (1 lb. 14 oz.) can peach
   pudding mix   halves
1 c. heavy cream, whipped

Prepare pudding mix as directed on package. Chill. Stir until smooth. Fold in whipped cream.

Put custard pudding in dessert dishes; top with drained, chilled peach half, rounded side up. Makes 6 servings.

Mapled Peaches—Unusual Combination Simmer together ½ c. syrup drained from canned peach halves (1 lb. can) with 2 tblsp. brown sugar and ¼ tsp. maple flavoring. Add the drained peach halves and serve topped with vanilla ice cream. Makes 6 servings.

Variations: Substitute canned pears for the peaches. Add a few drops of maple flavoring to your favorite fruit cup for elusive flavor.

QUICK PLUM PUDDING

1 (1 lb. 1 oz.) can purple plums   1 c. light raisins
Water   ½ c. chopped walnuts
½ tsp. salt   Plum Sauce (see Index)
1 (14 oz.) pkg. gingerbread
  mix

Drain plums. Reserve ½ c. juice for sauce. To remaining juice, add water to make amount of liquid specified in package directions for making gingerbread.

Pit plums and cut in small pieces. Add salt, plums and required liquid to gingerbread mix. Mix as directed on package. Stir in raisins and nuts.

Pour into 10 greased and floured 4 oz. custard cups set on a baking sheet. Bake in moderate oven (375°) 25 to 30 minutes. Allow to stand a few minutes after removing from oven. Then remove from cups and pour Plum Sauce over each. Makes 10 servings.

BAKED PRUNE WHIP

1 (7 or 7½ oz.) can or jar
    junior baby prunes
½ c. sugar

1 tblsp. lemon juice
3 egg whites
⅛ tsp. salt

Combine prunes, sugar and lemon juice. Beat egg whites with salt until stiff. Fold into prune mixture. Spoon into a greased 1½ qt. casserole.

Bake in moderate oven (325°) until firm, 25 to 30 minutes. Makes 6 servings.

CREAMY JELLIED STRAWBERRIES

1 (3 oz.) pkg. strawberry
    flavored gelatin
1 c. boiling water
1 (10 oz.) pkg. frozen
    strawberries

½ c. sour cream
1 medium banana, sliced

Dissolve gelatin in water. Add frozen berries and stir gently until they separate. Add sour cream; beat with rotary beater 1 minute. Stir in banana. Pour into sherbet or other dessert glasses and chill until firm. Makes 6 servings.

Strawberries with Sour Cream Serve ripe berries in dessert dishes and top with dairy sour cream. Sprinkle liberally with brown sugar. Or pass the sour cream and brown sugar in bowls. Allow 1 c. each brown sugar and sour cream to 1 qt. berries.

ROYAL PURPLE SUNDAE

1 qt. vanilla ice cream
1 (6 oz.) can frozen grape-juice
    concentrate, thawed

Pumpkin pie spice

Place a scoop of ice cream in each sherbet or other dessert

glass. Top each with 2 tblsp. grape juice and dust lightly with spice. Makes 6 servings.

Note: In the summer, garnish with seedless green grapes.

ICE CREAM COOKIE PIE

1 (1 lb. 2 oz.) roll refrigerator   1 qt. strawberry ice cream
  sugar cookies   Ice cream topping

Slice cookie dough ⅛″ thick, using about ¾ roll to make crust. Line side of ungreased 8″ or 9″ pie pan with slices, overlapping slightly to make scalloped edge. Line bottom with more slices.

Bake in moderate oven (375°) about 9 minutes, or until lightly browned. Cool.

Fill with ice cream scoops or balls, drizzle with peach or strawberry topping and serve at once. Or freeze ice cream in the baked crust and add topping at serving time. Makes 6 servings.

Variations: Substitute sugar or butterscotch-nut refrigerator cookie roll for toasted coconut cookies, and vanilla ice cream for strawberry ice cream. Use chocolate topping for Sugar Cookie Pie, and butterscotch topping for Butterscotch-Nut Cookie Pie.

CHOCOLATE ICE CREAM SANDWICHES

Chocolate graham crackers
Vanilla or peppermint ice
  cream

Spread cracker with ice cream and top with another cracker to make as many sandwiches as you need.

Serve at once if you like the crackers crisp. Or freeze and serve them when the occasion arises. Then crackers will be soft and moist like cake.

SHORT-CUT DESSERTS WITH PIE FILLINGS Give canned pie fillings a chance in your kitchen. Don't always bake these ready-to-use fruits between pastry crusts. They are versatile.

One farm woman spoons the bright red-cherry filling, chilled, on thick slices of angel food cake and tops the servings with fluffs of whipped cream. She heats raisin pie filling and takes it to the table as an accompaniment to baked ham and ham loaf. Sometimes she crowns simple cakes and puddings with berry and peach fillings.

Cherry pie filling walks away with honors as the favorite among farm women who shared their best short-cut recipes with us.

Here are some of the much praised desserts they make with colorful fruit fillings from the cupboard.

CLOVER-LEAF CHERRY TORTES

1 (1 lb. 2 oz.) roll refrigerator sugar cookies
1 (1 lb. 6 oz.) can cherry pie filling
¼ tsp. almond extract
½ c. heavy cream, whipped

Slice cookie dough ⅛″ thick. Arrange three slices with edges slightly overlapping, clover-leaf style, on ungreased baking sheet.

Bake in moderate oven (375°) until golden brown, 7 to 9 minutes. Cool 1 minute before removing from baking sheet.

Fold extract into cherry pie filling.

To serve, put cookie clover leaf on dessert plate. Top with 3 tblsp. cherry pie filling, then with another clover leaf, and 1 tblsp. cherry pie filling. Garnish each torte with whipped cream or vanilla ice cream. Makes 6 to 7 servings.

CHERRY PUDDING DESSERT

1 (3¼ oz.) pkg. vanilla pudding and pie filling mix
2 c. milk
1 (1 lb. 4 oz.) can cherry pie filling

Prepare pudding mix with milk as directed on package. Chill.

To serve, place cherries in 6 dessert dishes. Top with pudding. Makes 6 servings.

CHERRY-PEACH DUMPLINGS

½ c. water
2 tblsp. lemon juice
½ tsp. cinnamon
⅛ tsp. ground cloves
1 (1 lb. 8 oz.) jar cherry pie filling
1 (1 lb.) can peach halves, drained
Milk
1 egg, beaten
2 c. biscuit mix

Stir water, lemon juice, cinnamon and cloves into pie filling in 10″ skillet. Add peaches; bring to boil.

Add milk to egg to make ½ c.; stir into biscuit mix to form soft dough.

Drop dough by tablespoonfuls on top of boiling fruit. Cook over low heat 10 minutes; cover skillet and cook 10 minutes more. Serve warm (spooning fruit over dumplings), with cream. Makes 6 servings.

RASPBERRY CRUNCH

1 (1 lb.) can raspberry pie filling	½ c. flour
½ c. brown sugar	½ c. quick-cooking oatmeal
	⅓ c. butter or margarine

Place pie filling in greased 8″ square pan.

Combine brown sugar, flour and oatmeal. Cut in butter. Sprinkle on top of raspberries.

Bake in moderate oven (350°) 40 to 45 minutes. Serve hot or cold in dessert bowls with cream. Makes 6 servings.

Variation: Substitute other canned fruit or berry pie fillings for the raspberry filling.

BUTTERSCOTCH DESSERT WAFFLES

¼ c. butter or margarine	6 full-size frozen-waffle sections
½ c. brown sugar	Vanilla ice cream
½ c. flaked or shredded coconut	

Combine butter, sugar and coconut. Spread on waffles and broil until delicately browned. Top with ice cream. Makes 6 servings.

Note: If you bake waffles and freeze them, the amount of topping is correct. The frozen waffles you buy usually are smaller. You'll need 12 of them.

COCONUT CREAM PUDDING

2 (3¾ oz.) pkgs. instant coconut cream pudding mix	4 tsp. grated orange rind
3 c. milk	Orange sections or Rosy Rhubarb Sauce (recipe
1 c. light cream	follows)

Combine all ingredients in bowl.

Beat until well blended, about 1 minute. Pour into bowl or pan; let stand about 5 minutes.

Spoon into serving dishes. Garnish with orange sections or Rosy Rhubarb Sauce. Makes 8 servings.

Rosy Rhubarb Sauce Combine 1 (1 lb.) pkg. frozen rhubarb, ¼ c. light corn syrup and dash salt in a saucepan. Bring to a boil; reduce heat and simmer for 5 minutes or until rhubarb is tender. Cool; chill. Spoon over coconut cream pudding. Makes about 2 cups.

Rocky-Road Chocolate Pudding Make pudding from 1 pkg. regular chocolate pudding mix as directed on package. Cool about 10 minutes. Fold in 1 c. miniature marshmallows and serve, or chill before serving. Or substitute butterscotch pudding mix for chocolate pudding mix.

COFFEE-BUTTERSCOTCH CREAM

1 (4 oz.) pkg. butterscotch pudding mix and pie filling	1½ c. milk
⅓ c. sugar	2 egg yolks, slightly beaten
1 tblsp. instant coffee	½ c. heavy cream, whipped

Combine pudding mix, sugar, coffee and milk in saucepan. Cook and stir over medium heat until mixture begins to thicken. Pour a little of hot mixture into egg yolks and stir quickly to blend. Pour eggs into remaining pudding mixture and continue cooking until mixture comes to a full boil.

Cool and chill.

At serving time, fold whipped cream into pudding. Spoon into dessert glasses. Makes 6 servings.

Note: For a pretty trim, save out a little of the whipped cream and use to garnish pudding tops. For a touch of glamour, scatter on a sprinkling of tiny chocolate decorating candies.

Date Bar Desserts Make bars with date bar mix as directed on package. When cool, cut into 9 bars. Top with vanilla ice cream or whipped cream.

GREEN AND GOLD DESSERT

2 (3 oz.) pkgs. lime flavor gelatin	2 c. cold milk
1¾ c. boiling water	1 c. light cream
¾ c. cold water	½ tsp. vanilla
2 (10 oz.) pkgs. frozen sliced peaches	1 (3¾ oz.) pkg. instant vanilla pudding mix

Dissolve gelatin in boiling water; add cold water. Pour into pan, making layer about 1″ thick. Chill.

To serve, cut chilled gelatin in 1″ cubes with sharp knife. Run spatula under cubes to loosen; lift with spatula.

Alternate spoonfuls of gelatin cubes and partially thawed peaches in individual dessert dishes.

To make sauce, combine milk, cream and vanilla in bowl. Add pudding mix; beat slowly with rotary beater until thoroughly mixed—about 1 minute. Pour over dessert. Makes 6 servings.

ORANGE-BANANA TAPIOCA

¼ c. quick-cooking tapioca	1½ c. water
3 tblsp. sugar	2 medium bananas
Dash salt	
1 (6 oz.) can frozen orange juice	

Combine tapioca, sugar and salt. Blend in thawed orange juice and water. Let stand 5 minutes. Bring to a boil over medium heat, stirring frequently.

Pour into individual serving dishes and serve warm or chilled with garnish of sliced bananas. Makes 4 to 6 servings.

Note: For a change, top dessert servings with whipped cream or coconut, flaked or shredded, or serve with light cream.

PEACH FLIP-OVER

1 (1 lb. 14 oz.) can sliced peaches, well drained	2 tblsp. sugar
2 c. biscuit mix	½ tsp. cinnamon
	½ c. milk

Line 8″ square pan with foil; allow foil to extend over edge of pan. Spread peach slices on foil.

Combine biscuit mix, sugar and cinnamon. Add all the milk at once and stir with fork to make soft dough. Beat vigorously 20 strokes.

Turn out on surface floured with biscuit mix. Knead 8 or 10 times. Place dough between 2 sheets of waxed paper and pat to an 8″ square.

Place dough over peaches. Bake in very hot oven (450°) 15 to 18 minutes. Turn out on serving plate; remove foil while warm. Serve topped with whipped cream or ice cream. Makes 6 servings.

PUMPKIN PUDDING À LA MODE

1 c. canned pumpkin
¼ tsp. salt
¼ tsp. cloves
½ tsp. cinnamon
1 tblsp. molasses

1½ c. milk
1 (3¾ oz.) pkg. instant vanilla
  pudding mix
½ c. heavy cream, whipped

Combine pumpkin, salt, spices and molasses. Blend in milk. Add pudding; beat slowly until thick, about 1 minute.

Fold in whipped cream. Spoon into dessert dishes; chill. To serve, top with nut ice cream. Makes 6 to 8 servings.

CINNAMON-PEACH COBBLER

⅓ c. sugar
1 tblsp. cornstarch
⅔ c. water
6 fresh peaches, peeled and
  sliced

1 (9.5 oz.) pkg. refrigerator
  cinnamon rolls
Cream

Combine sugar and cornstarch in saucepan. Add water and bring to boil, stirring constantly. Add peaches and heat to boiling point. Pour into a 2 qt. casserole.

Lay cinnamon rolls on peaches, cinnamon side up. Bake in hot oven (400°) until rolls are browned, 25 to 30 minutes. Spread frosting from package over top of rolls. Serve warm with cream. Makes 6 servings.

OFF-THE-GRIDDLE SHORTCAKES

2 eggs
1 c. milk
2⅓ c. biscuit mix
2 tblsp. sugar

¼ c. salad oil
Strawberries, or other fruit
Heavy cream, whipped

Beat eggs until soft peaks form; blend in milk; add mix and sugar; stir until just blended; fold in oil.

Bake on preheated griddle, using ¼ c. batter for each. Stack; fill and top with fruit and cream. Makes 1 dozen (4") light, fluffy cakes.

Jiffy Toppings Just-thawed frozen strawberries and peaches in their own syrup; warm crushed pineapple; pineapple tidbits, blueberries or cherries stirred into dairy sour cream; whipped cream cheese with preserves blended in. For sauce- or syrup-topped pancakes, pass bowls of chopped nuts and flaked coconut, to add flavor and texture.

10-MINUTE DESSERTS The secret to these timesaving desserts is to keep the makings on hand in cupboard and freezer. Cooks vary in speed of working, but the average time spent on each dish in our Countryside Test Kitchens was 10 minutes. And all the desserts passed taste tests with high honors.

Company Torte Cut angel food cake (from your freezer) in 3 crosswise layers; put together and frost with Fruited Cream, made this way: combine 1 (1 lb. 4 oz.) can crushed pineapple with 1 (4 oz.) pkg. instant vanilla pudding. Fold into 2 c. heavy cream, whipped. Garnish top with canned mandarin-orange sections or coconut. Serve at once, or chill.

Honey-Nut Sundae Combine ¼ c. peanut butter with ¾ c. warm honey. Serve over vanilla ice cream.

Hot Jelly Cake Spread sides and top of white or yellow cake from freezer with jelly; sprinkle with flaked coconut and broil until jelly bubbles and coconut browns lightly. Serve hot.

Apricot Treat Top orange sherbet with cooked, dried apricots (chopped), or fill drained canned apricot halves with orange sherbet.

Fruit Fluff With rotary beater, blend 1 (4 oz.) pkg. instant lemon pudding with 1 c. apricot nectar and 1 c. dairy sour cream. Serve in dessert glasses.

Broiled Apples Broil canned pie-sliced apples 5 minutes; pour on thin butterscotch sauce, sprinkling top with flaked coconut. Broil a few minutes longer to toast coconut.

Maple-Cream Waffle Topping Slowly add 1 c. maple-blended syrup to 1 c. heavy cream, whipped. Fold to blend. Serve in pitcher with waffles made from packaged mix or with waffles from the freezer heated at the table in an electric toaster.

STRAWBERRY SHORTCAKE ROYALE

2½ c. biscuit mix
⅓ c. shortening
3 tblsp. sugar
1 tsp. vanilla
¾ c. milk

1 qt. strawberries, cut in half
⅓ c. sugar
Triple Cream Sauce (recipe
  follows)

Cut shortening into biscuit mix until crumbly. Combine sugar, vanilla, milk; stir into biscuit mixture; beat 15 strokes. Pat into two well-greased 8″ cake pans. Bake in a hot oven (425°) 12 to 15 minutes or until golden brown. Cool.

Meanwhile, sprinkle berries with sugar. Let stand 30 minutes. Spread half of the sweetened berries on a shortcake layer. Top with second layer. Add remaining berries. Spoon Triple Cream Sauce over shortcake. Makes 6 to 8 servings.

Triple Cream Sauce

1 c. ice cream, softened
½ c. sour cream
¼ c. sugar

1 tsp. vanilla
1 c. heavy cream

Combine softened ice cream, sour cream, sugar and vanilla.

Whip heavy cream until quite stiff. Thoroughly fold into ice cream mixture. Sauce can be made ahead and stored in refrigerator. Makes 3 cups.

Dessert Sauces

DESSERT SAUCES AND TOPPINGS Just plain cakes, puddings or ice creams turn into specials when you top them with fruit, sauce or cream. Here are some quick-to-do toppings with enough taste appeal to redeem even day-old cake. There's even an idea for using day-old cake to make a topping for ice cream!

Applesauce à la Mode Serve it on unfrosted spice cake or gingerbread. Spoon the applesauce on the dessert and top with a scoop of vanilla or nut ice cream. Sprinkle lightly with cinnamon.

Topping for Apple Pie Fold ¼ c. crushed peanut brittle and ½ tsp. grated orange rind into 1 c. lightly sweetened whipped cream. Top each serving of pie with spoonful of the topping. Also try this on pumpkin pie.

BLUEBERRY SAUCE

1 (10 oz.) pkg. frozen
   blueberries
½ c. unsweetened pineapple
   juice
¼ c. water

¼ c. sugar
1 tblsp. cornstarch
⅛ tsp. salt
¼ tsp. grated lemon rind
1 tsp. lemon juice

Combine all ingredients except lemon juice in 1 qt. saucepan. Cook, stirring, over medium heat until sauce thickens. Cool slightly; stir in lemon juice. Chill. Makes about 1¾ cups.

Cake Coconut Topping When you have a leftover slice of white cake, combine ¾ c. cake crumbs and ¼ c. shredded coconut. Spread on a baking sheet and toast in moderate oven (350°) until light golden brown. Serve over vanilla or chocolate ice cream.

EGGNOG FOR SAUCE

1 egg, beaten
1 c. milk

2 tsp. sugar
¼ tsp. vanilla

Combine ingredients thoroughly. Makes enough for 2 servings on cereal or puddings.

QUICK CARAMEL SAUCE

½ lb. (about 28) caramel candies
   candies
½ c. hot water

Place caramels and water in top of double boiler. Heat, stirring frequently, until caramels melt and make a smooth sauce. Makes 1 cup.

Note: Serve Quick Caramel Sauce, warm or cold, on vanilla ice

SOUTHERN SOFT CUSTARD

2½ c. evaporated milk
2½ c. cold water

1 (3¾ oz.) pkg. instant vanilla
   pudding mix

Combine milk and water in mixing bowl. Add mix; beat gently with rotary beater 1 minute, or until blended. Let set 5 minutes.

Serve immediately in dessert dishes, or pour into jar or pitcher, cover and refrigerate. Makes 5 cups.

Variation: For sweeter custard, add ½ c. sugar and 1 tsp. vanilla.

SHORTCAKE POUR-CREAM

1 c. heavy cream, whipped
2 egg yolks

3 tblsp. honey
2 tblsp. lemon juice

Whip cream until slightly thick. Add egg yolks one at a time and continue beating. Slowly drizzle in honey and lemon juice. Sauce will be thick and creamy. Pour over shortcakes. Makes about 1¼ cups.

CRANBERRY TOPPING

1 c. heavy cream, whipped
½ c. sugar
1 (8½ oz.) can crushed
  pineapple, drained

1½ c. Cranberry Relish (see Index), partly thawed and drained

Whip cream, adding sugar slowly, until stiff.

Fold in pineapple and relish, but do not blend completely. Serve on angel food cake slices or use as filling and topping for angel food and other cakes. Refrigerate frosted cakes until served. Makes about 1 quart.

Variation: To make Frozen Cranberry Salad, freeze Cranberry Topping in 1 qt. mold. Serve on lettuce.

EASY CUSTARD-TYPE DESSERT SAUCE

1 (3¼ oz.) pkg. vanilla pudding mix
2½ c. milk

Combine pudding mix and milk in saucepan. Heat, stirring constantly, until mixture comes to a full boil. Serve sauce warm. Makes 2¾ cups.

Variation: Add a few drops of almond flavoring after removing sauce from heat.

Note: If you chill this sauce, it thickens.

Ice Cream Sauce   Serve vanilla ice cream, softened until it resembles whipped cream, over desserts. Or stir a little chocolate, butterscotch or other ice cream topping you buy at your food store through vanilla ice cream for Rippled Ice Cream Sauce.

A farm woman in Nebraska sent us her favorite recipe for an ice cream topping. It has that wonderful molasses-butter-pecan flavor blend suggestive of New Orleans. You won't want to miss trying this topping for ice cream. It's good on cake and puddings, too.

NO-COOK PRALINE SAUCE

1 c. light corn syrup	⅔ c. chopped pecans
2 tblsp. molasses	2 tblsp. water
1 (4 oz.) pkg. instant butterscotch pudding mix	

Blend together syrup and molasses; stir in pudding mix. Add nuts and water. Chill ½ hour. Stir before using. Makes about 2 cups.

PEANUT-CHOCOLATE SAUCE

1 (4 oz.) pkg. chocolate pudding mix	¼ tsp. salt
¾ c. water	1 tblsp. butter or margarine
¾ c. corn syrup	⅓ c. peanut butter
	½ tsp. vanilla

Empty package contents into saucepan. Gradually add water, mixing until smooth. Add corn syrup and salt; mix well.

Cook over medium heat, stirring constantly until mixture comes to a boil.

Remove from heat and add butter, peanut butter and vanilla; stir until melted. Serve warm or cold over ice cream. Makes 1¾ cups.

Section 5
Snacks, Nibbles
and Beverages

You will be a relaxed and gracious hostess if you have an inventory of snacks, nibbles and beverages on hand that will be easy to assemble or ready to serve.

Then whether two or twenty unexpected guests drop in to visit, you will always be prepared. Ten minutes in the kitchen and you're free to enjoy the fun.

We have selected a wide assortment of snacks and sippers to meet just about every situation from morning to midnight. On a frosty winter day, late morning callers will be intrigued when you bring in mugs of steaming Clam Unique Chowder. Serve either Nippy Cheese or the nutty-flavored Swiss Cheese dip for dunking, along with a basket of toasted bread chunks.

Afternoon visitors will enjoy these sweet treats: Rich Buttery Pralines that melt on your tongue, and Chocolate Nut Drops that take only seconds to fix.

On sultry summer evenings surprise guests—or family—with a thick creamy Lemon Cooler or a chilly Raspberry Float. Both are tangy thirst quenchers. And dieters will be delighted with Lemon Iced Tea.

MEAL STARTERS The best way to get the company meal off to a good start is to serve a tasty, colorful appetizer. It's a forecast of what will follow. Here are some excellent choices.

FRUIT AND SHERBET COCKTAIL

1 (1 lb. 14 oz.) can pineapple   1 pt. lime sherbet
  chunks, chilled
1 (10 or 11 oz.) can mandarin
  oranges, chilled

Drain fruits. Half fill glasses with pineapple chunks; top with scoop of sherbet. Fill around sherbet with orange sections. Makes 6 servings.

3-IN-1 FRUIT JUICE COCKTAILS

Ruby Punch   Combine 4 c. cranberry juice cocktail, 1 c. pineapple juice and 1 c. orange juice. Garnish each drink with a quarter of thin slice of orange. Makes 8 (6 oz.) glasses.

Pineapple Glow   Combine 3 c. apple juice, 3 c. pineapple juice, ¼ c. maraschino cherry juice and ¼ tsp. almond extract. Garnish each drink with a maraschino cherry and a sprig of mint. Makes 8 (6 oz.) glasses.

Royal Ade   Combine 3 c. apple juice, 3 c. grape juice, 2 tblsp. fresh lime juice and ¼ tsp. nutmeg. Garnish with lime slices. Makes 8 (6 oz.) glasses.

MELON-BOAT COCKTAIL

1 large cantaloupe   1½ to 2 c. pineapple chunks
½ c. Fresh Mint Syrup (recipe   and sliced strawberries
  follows)

Cut cantaloupe into sixths; make a crisscross pattern in wedges. Spoon about 1 tblsp. Fresh Mint Syrup over each. Heap fruit in center. Makes 6 servings.

Fresh Mint Syrup

1 c. sugar   ¼ c. lemon juice
⅔ c. water   ½ c. orange juice
½ c. chopped mint leaves

Combine sugar and water in small saucepan. Boil 3 minutes. Add mint leaves; cool. Strain. Add lemon and orange juice. Chill. Makes 1½ cups.

Variations: Use honeydew melon instead of cantaloupe, or pour Fresh Mint Syrup over servings of melon cubes; a combination of fresh and frozen fruits like pineapple, orange and grapefruit; strawberries, raspberries or blueberries; drained, canned fruit cocktail or other fruits. To step up color and flavor, add scoops of lime, orange, lemon or raspberry sherbet.

CLAM CHOWDER UNIQUE

1 (10½ oz.) can New England style clam chowder

1 (10½ oz.) can cream of potato soup

½ c. finely shredded Cheddar cheese

Combine soups and prepare according to directions on cans. Ladle into serving bowls. Top with cheese and serve with crackers. Makes 4 to 6 servings.

Asparagus-Clam Soup   Combine 1 (5½ to 8 oz.) can of undrained minced clams, 1 (10½ oz.) can condensed cream of asparagus soup and 1 soup can of milk, light cream, or half milk and half cream. Mix well and heat. Makes 4 servings.

TOMATO BOUILLON

1 (16 to 17 oz.) can tomato juice

1 (10½ oz.) can condensed beef broth

¼ tsp. seasoned salt

Combine all the ingredients and heat. Serve piping hot with crisp crackers. Makes 6 servings.

PIZZA SNACKS

½ lb. Italian sausage

1 (6 oz.) can tomato paste

1 tsp. mixed Italian herbs

1 (8 oz.) pkg. buttermilk biscuits

1 c. shredded sharp cheese

¼ c. grated Parmesan cheese

Brown sausage; drain off fat. Stir in tomato paste and herbs.
Flatten biscuits on greased baking sheet with bottom of floured
custard cup. Leave rim cup makes.

Fill centers with sausage mixture. Top with shredded cheese;
sprinkle with Parmesan cheese. Bake in hot oven (425°) for 10
minutes. Makes 10 pizzas.

Variations: Use sliced frankfurters, chopped brown-and-serve sausages or hamburger for Italian sausage.

NIPPY CHEESE DIP

1 (8 oz.) pkg. cream cheese
¼ c. Basic Red Sauce (see Index)

Soften cream cheese at room temperature.

Whip cheese with electric mixer or wooden spoon. Add Basic Red
Sauce gradually, beating after each addition, until light and fluffy.

Serve with snack-style crackers, potato chips or corn chips. Makes
1½ cups.

HOT DIPS FOR DUNKING When friends drop in on a chilly
evening, serve them hot dips. Set the dip bubbling hot on the table
along with a plate of crusty bread cut in 1½" cubes. Be sure every
piece of bread has some crust. You can use French, Italian or
Vienna bread, or hard rolls. Provide everyone with a fork and plate.

Start the fun by spearing a piece of bread on your fork through
the soft part to the crust. Dunk the bread in the dip and transfer it
to your plate—then eat it. Ask everyone to join in.

Be sure to keep the dip piping hot. You can serve it in a chafing
dish or a heavy casserole over a candle warmer. Make it in a
double boiler. Or, still easier, make and serve the dip in an electric
skillet (see recipe for Swiss-Cheese Dip which follows). The skillet
will keep it at just the right heat.

You also can serve these dips in a meal—supper or lunch. Just
spoon them over toast.

SWISS-CHEESE DIP

1 tsp. salt	1 tblsp. vinegar
½ tsp. garlic salt	2 tsp. mustard
2 tblsp. flour	½ tsp. Worcestershire sauce
1½ c. milk	
1 lb. natural Swiss cheese, coarsely grated (about 4⅓ c.)	

Combine salt, garlic salt and flour. Add ¾ c. milk; blend well. Add remaining milk; blend. Pour into electric skillet; heat to simmering point (200°), stirring constantly.

Drop cheese by cupfuls into milk to melt; stir with fork after each addition.

Add remaining ingredients; stir well. Serve from skillet (do not reduce heat) or other cooking utensil. Makes 3 cups.

MUSHROOM-BACON SUPREME

2 tblsp. butter or margarine	1 tsp. lemon juice
2 tblsp. flour	½ tsp. Worcestershire sauce
1½ c. milk	1 c. crisp-fried bacon, crumbled
¼ tsp. salt	½ c. finely chopped mushrooms
¼ tsp. pepper	

Melt butter over low heat. Add flour; mix until smooth and bubbly. Remove from heat; stir in milk. Heat to boiling, stirring constantly, and let bubble 1 minute.

Add remaining ingredients and heat thoroughly. Makes 2 cups.

TUNA TREAT

2 (10½ oz.) cans cream of chicken soup	2 (7 oz.) cans tuna, drained and flaked
3 tblsp. lemon juice	¾ c. chopped stuffed olives
¾ c. coarsely grated process American cheese	

Heat soup; add lemon juice and cheese. Stir until cheese melts. Add tuna and olives. Heat thoroughly. Makes 4½ cups.

HOT DEVILED HAM

3 (4½ oz.) cans deviled ham
3 tblsp. cornstarch
1 tblsp. mustard
½ tsp. ground red pepper

3 tblsp. minced onion
3 tblsp. chopped green pepper
¾ c. dairy sour cream

Heat ham; drain off fat. Add cornstarch and thicken over low heat.
Add remaining ingredients, except sour cream, and heat thoroughly.

Fold in sour cream; heat just to simmering; serve hot. Makes about 2 cups.

JIFFY CHOCOLATE-NUT DROPS

2 (9¾ oz.) sweet chocolate bars
2 c. chopped walnuts

Melt chocolate over hot water. Stir in nuts. Drop by teaspoonfuls onto waxed paper. Makes 3 dozen.

Note: Chill the candy in the refrigerator when in a hurry.

CHOCOLATE-MARSHMALLOW CANDY

2 (9¾ oz.) sweet chocolate bars   2 c. chopped walnuts
3 c. miniature marshmallows

Melt chocolate over hot water. Stir in marshmallows and nuts.
Drop from teaspoon on waxed paper. Makes 4 dozen.

QUICK PRALINES

1 (4 oz.) pkg. butterscotch
   pudding mix
1 c. sugar
½ c. brown sugar, firmly packed

½ c. evaporated milk
1 tblsp. butter
1½ c. pecans

Combine pudding mix, sugars and milk in a saucepan. Add butter and cook, stirring frequently, over low heat until mixture reaches the soft-ball stage (236°). Add nuts and remove from heat.

Beat just until mixture begins to thicken. Drop by spoonfuls onto waxed paper. Makes 2 dozen pralines.

MILK STEAMERS AND COOLERS   Serve flavored milk hot in mugs or cups or frosty cold in glasses. These good-for-you drinks are refreshing either way. The weather often decides for the cook which one will have the greatest appeal at the moment.

SPICED STEAMER

2 qts. milk
1 c. Spiced Syrup (recipe follows)

⅛ tsp. salt
Marshmallows or whipped cream

Heat milk in double boiler, covering to prevent skin from forming. Stir hot milk into syrup. Add salt. Serve hot in mugs, topped with marshmallows. Makes 8 servings.

Spiced Syrup   Mix in saucepan 2 c. water, ¼ c. whole cloves, ½ c. red cinnamon candies and ½ c. sugar. Simmer 15 minutes, stirring occasionally. Strain. Use 2 tblsp. for a cup of milk.

Coffee-Cocoa   Mix 3 tblsp. instant coffee, 3 tblsp. instant cocoa and 1 tblsp. sugar. Stir into hot milk. Pour into mugs; top with whipped cream. Serve at once.

Butterscotch Steamer   Add ¼ c. butter and ½ c. dark brown sugar to hot milk. Blend; serve at once, sprinkled with cinnamon.

Note: You may use dry milk in steamers. Either reconstitute it and heat or slowly stir dry milk into hot water. If you prefer a sweeter drink, use whole milk with extra dry milk added.

CHOCOLATE-BANANA MILK

3 c. milk
3 medium, ripe bananas

½ c. instant chocolate mix

Blend half of ingredients in blender 1 minute. Pour into pitcher. Blend second half of ingredients 1 minute. Add to pitcher. Makes 4 servings.

Note: For a south-of-the-border touch, add ½ tsp. cinnamon to chocolate mix.

HONEY-PEANUT FOAM

1 tblsp. honey
2 tblsp. peanut butter

1 c. milk
2 tblsp. dry milk

Combine ingredients and whip in drink mixer or blender until well blended and foamy. Pour over frozen milk cubes. Makes 1 big (10 oz.) glass.

To make 4 servings: Blend ¼ c. honey and ½ c. peanut butter in your electric mixer. Slowly add 1 qt. milk, continuing to beat; scrape mixer bowl often. Add ½ c. dry milk and (for adults) 1 tsp. instant coffee; whip until foamy. Pour over frozen milk cubes. Makes 4 (10 oz.) glasses.

Frozen Milk Cubes Pour reconstituted dry milk into ice-cube tray and freeze.

LEMON COOLER

1 qt. milk	½ c. dry milk
1½ c. fresh lemon juice	Dash salt
¾ c. sugar	½ pt. vanilla ice cream

Combine ingredients. Whip until ice cream is well blended. Serve immediately. Makes 8 (8 oz.) glasses.

LOW-CALORIE PICKUP

¾ c. frozen pineapple juice concentrate	Green food color
1 qt. reconstituted dry milk, chilled	Frozen Milk Cubes (see Index)

Combine pineapple concentrate and milk; whip until foamy.
Add food color for a minty green tint.
Pour mixture over Frozen Milk Cubes. Serve at once. Makes 6 (8 oz.) glasses.

Variation: If you prefer, use half whole milk and half reconstituted dry milk.

CHERRY-APPLE DRINK

2 envelopes *unsweetened* cherry flavor instant soft drink mix	1½ qts. apple juice or apple cider
½ c. sugar	2¼ qts. ice water
1 (6 oz.) can frozen lemonade concentrate, thawed	

Combine ingredients; stir until sugar dissolves. Makes 1 gallon.

CITRUS REFRESHER

2 (6 oz.) cans frozen lemonade concentrate, thawed

1 (6 oz.) can frozen orange juice concentrate, thawed

1 pint pineapple juice

3½ qts. ice water

5 tblsp. instant tea (optional)

Combine ingredients in order given. Makes 4½ quarts.

HARVEST COOLER

1 (3 oz.) pkg. lime flavor gelatin

1 c. boiling water

1 qt. pineapple juice

Juice of 3 lemons

1¼ qts. ice water

Dissolve lime gelatin in boiling water. Stir in remaining ingredients; chill thoroughly. Shake before serving. Makes 2¾ quarts.

STRAWBERRY FROST

1 qt. milk

3 tblsp. strawberry instant soft drink mix

½ c. strawberry ice cream

Combine ingredients; beat until foamy. Makes 4 (10 oz.) glasses.

Variations: Substitute 3 tblsp. strawberry flavor rennet dessert powder for soft drink mix. If you do not have ice cream, fold ½ c. whipped dry milk into drink just before serving.

3-CITRUS FRUIT DRINK

1 (6 oz.) can frozen orange juice concentrate

1 (6 oz.) can frozen lemonade concentrate

1 qt. cold water

2 (7 oz.) bottles carbonated water

1 pt. lime sherbet

Blend together orange and lemonade concentrates and 1 qt. water. Pour over ice cubes in pitcher. Carefully pour in carbonated water; stir gently. When ice thoroughly chills mixture, fill glasses ¾ full. Top with spoonfuls of lime sherbet. Makes 6 servings.

Note: You may substitute 2 c. plain cold water for carbonated water.

EASY SPARKLING PUNCH

1 (6 oz.) can frozen orange
  juice concentrate
¼ c. lemon juice, fresh, frozen
  or canned

¼ c. corn syrup
1 qt. ginger ale

Prepare orange juice as directed on can. Stir in lemon juice and syrup. Slowly pour in ginger ale. Serve in ice-filled glasses. Makes about 2 qts.

JIFFY FRUIT PUNCH

1 (6 oz.) can frozen orange
  juice
2 (6 oz.) cans frozen limeade
1 (6 oz.) can frozen lemonade
1 (46 oz.) can pineapple juice
1 pt. cranberry juice cocktail

2 to 4 c. cold water
2 qts. ginger ale, chilled
1 qt. plain soda water, chilled
Ice cubes
Mint for garnish

Empty frozen juices, pineapple and cranberry juice and water into large container or bowl. Thaw; stir well.

Pour mixture into punch bowl. Add ice cubes. Just before serving, gently pour in ginger ale and soda water. Top with sprigs of mint. Makes 30 servings.

HOLIDAY FRUIT PUNCH

1 (6 oz.) pkg. or 2 (3 oz.)
  pkgs. lime flavor gelatin
1¼ c. sugar
3½ c. boiling water

2 (5¾ oz.) cans frozen lemon
  juice concentrate, thawed
1 (46 oz.) can pineapple juice
6 c. cold water

Dissolve gelatin and sugar in boiling water. Stir in lemon juice, then pineapple juice and cold water.

Pour over ice cubes in punch bowl. Serve in punch cups. Makes about 4½ quarts.

LEMON ICED TEA

12 tea bags
1 qt. boiling water
2 qts. cold water

1 (6 oz.) can frozen lemonade
  concentrate

Steep tea in boiling water 5 minutes. Remove tea bags. Stir in remaining water and lemonade concentrate. Serve in ice-filled glasses. Makes 12 servings.

LIME COOLER

1 (6 oz.) can frozen lemonade
concentrate
½ c. lime juice

1 (7 oz.) bottle ginger ale
Few drops green food color

Prepare lemonade as directed on can. Add lime juice, ginger ale and food color.

Serve over ice. Garnish with thin lime slices. Makes 6 servings.

RASPBERRY FLOAT

3 (3 oz.) pkgs. raspberry flavor
gelatin
4 c. boiling water
1½ c. sugar
4 c. cold water
½ c. lime juice

2¼ c. orange juice
1¼ c. lemon juice
1 qt. ginger ale
2 (10 oz.) pkgs. frozen
raspberries
Ice cubes

Dissolve gelatin in boiling water; add sugar, cold water and juices; cool, but do not chill or gelatin will congeal. (If you let it congeal, heat just enough to bring back to liquid state.)

When time to serve, pour punch into punch bowl. Add ginger ale and frozen raspberries. Stir until raspberries break apart and are partially thawed. Add ice cubes. Makes about 4 quarts.

SPICED TOMATO JUICE

1 (46 oz.) can tomato juice
6 tblsp. brown sugar
6 whole cloves

2 (2½″) sticks cinnamon
½ lemon, sliced

Combine all ingredients in saucepan. Bring to a boil; simmer 5 minutes. Strain; serve hot. Makes 5½ cups.

TIPS FROM A SMART COUNTRY COOK

Summer Orange Lemonade For the picnic or motor trip, slightly thaw 1 (6 oz.) can frozen concentrate for lemonade and 1 (6 oz.)

can frozen concentrate for orange juice. Pour into a 2 qt. jar, fill with ice cubes and add all the cold water jar will hold. Seal. Set jar in two paper bags, one inside the other, for insulation. You can carry this refreshing drink in your car for 4 to 6 hours. It still will be cold.

Winter Orange Lemonade Fill the jar as directed, seal, and let stand unrefrigerated until ready to serve.

Variations: Substitute frozen grape juice concentrate for the orange juice. Or substitute frozen concentrate for strawberry, raspberry or pineapple lemonade or canned frozen concentrate for limeade for the lemonade.

CHILDREN'S SPECIALS

Cocoa Float Make 4 c. hot cocoa with instant cocoa mix as directed on label. Serve in cups, topping each with a scoop of vanilla ice cream. Dust with cinnamon if desired. Serve at once. Makes 8 to 10 servings.

Ginger-Orange Float Put a scoop of orange sherbet in each glass and fill with chilled ginger ale.

Children's Root Beer Pour ¾ c. chilled, liquefied dry milk in each tall glass. Stir in ¼ c. chilled root beer. Add a big spoonful of vanilla ice cream to each glass.

PEACH MILK SHAKES

1 c. diced fresh peaches	1½ c. milk
¼ c. honey	1 pt. vanilla ice cream
½ tsp. vanilla	

Mix peaches and honey. (Honey keeps peaches from darkening as well as sweetening them.) Add remaining ingredients and mix in blender to a smooth cream. Serve in tall glasses. Makes 4 servings.

Variation: Substitute ice cream of other flavors for the vanilla ice cream. Try coffee ice cream.

Note: Never keep honey in refrigerator; cold temperatures encourage it to crystallize. When crystallized, set the container of it in warm water to liquefy it. Honey must be at room temperature to blend with milk.

CHERRY SODAS

1 (⅝ oz.) pkg. cherry flavor
  drink powder
1 c. sugar
2 c. milk

1 qt. carbonated water
Vanilla ice cream (about 1½
  pts.)

Blend together drink powder, sugar and milk. Slowly pour in carbonated water.

Put generous scoop of ice cream in each glass. Pour cherry beverage mixture over ice cream. Makes 6 servings.

COFFEE-BUTTERSCOTCH FOAM

4 tsp. instant coffee
½ c. boiling water
1½ c. cold water

¼ c. butterscotch topping
½ pt. (1 c.) vanilla ice cream

Dissolve coffee in hot water; add cold water. Combine with remaining ingredients in blender or large bowl of electric mixer. Blend or beat until frothy. Pour into tall glasses. Sprinkle with cinnamon if desired. Makes 3 servings.

Coffee, Swedish Style Here's how to fix coffee outdoors on the grill. Bring 2 qts. water to boil. Combine 1 c. regular grind coffee with ¼ c. cold water and 1 egg, beaten. Pour boiling water over coffee mixture; cover and let stand 12 to 15 minutes in warm spot on grill, but do not let boil. Makes 8 servings.

SPARKLING STRAWBERRY PUNCH

1 qt. strawberries
½ c. sugar
3 c. orange juice
¾ c. lemon juice

1½ qts. ginger ale, chilled
½ c. sugar
1 c. strawberries, sliced

Mash 1 qt. strawberries with ½ c. sugar. Let stand 1 hour. Force through strainer. Add orange and lemon juices, ginger ale and sugar to strained strawberry juice. Pour into large punch bowl. Add sliced strawberries. Makes about 3 qts.

Part II
Make-Ahead
Cooking

Introduction

For the woman who runs a household—and perhaps a job in addition—few days follow a predictable schedule. Often the time planned to prepare and serve a good meal disappears in thin air and good intentions. And, if unexpected company turns up . . . panic!

There are two ways to peace of mind in the kitchen: Buy time via partly prepared dishes or short-cut ingredients that can be combined at the last minute. Push time around by making dishes ahead and having them ready and waiting in the refrigerator, freezer—or soothingly simmering away without benefit of stirring or inspection.

This Make-Ahead Cookbook is designed to help you push time around and end up with more taste appeal and nutrition in both your everyday and company meals. Our recipes let you borrow an hour or two from a less busy day and put this time to work to free an equal amount for crisis days or the big-push period. Then you'll have a dividend or "extra" time when you need it most.

Many of our recipes can be completely prepared ahead and frozen. Others are partially prepared in advance and frozen, with a few ingredients added at the last minute. Take full advantage of the freezing space you have. It will substitute for a second pair of hands in the kitchen—and can give you an extra bonus day a week.

As we tested the fix-ahead recipes for this book, we plotted to help you make the most of your refrigerator, too. We found that many of the recipes that chill several hours in the refrigerator or simmer without watching for 3 hours, are perfect to prepare on days spent at home. Then when guests arrive most of your work is completed and you're free to enjoy them.

Many of our recipes originated in country kitchens, where they had been "use-tested" on family and friends. We sorted, tested and perfected these. Then we included some original recipes from our own Countryside Test Kitchens. We divided this Make-Ahead book into 5 sections for your easy use: Main Dishes: Meat, Poultry, Fish, Eggs and Cheese; Vegetables, Salads, Salad Dressings, Relishes and Sauces; Sandwiches and Breads; Desserts: Pies, Cakes, Frostings, Cookies and Other Desserts; Snacks, Nibbles and Beverages.

Section 1
Main Dishes

This section brings you mealtime magic in the form of basic main-dish recipes that can be prepared ahead of time. Some are geared to days when you are in the mood to cook and freeze; others are designed for day-before fixing to free your time on the day company arrives or your schedule is jam-packed.

When you are freezing main dishes, here are a few tips to give you perfect results: Slightly undercook any food that is to be frozen; this will prevent a soggy overdone result when the main dish is reheated for serving. Be sure to cool foods quickly after cooking and then package in the amounts that will be eaten in one meal. Some casserole dishes can be covered with freezer wrap, sealed with tape and frozen right in the containers in which they have been cooked (however, be sure to check manufacturer's directions before you bake and freeze). It is preferable to freeze in smaller-size casseroles—when you put a large-size frozen casserole in the oven it may burn around the edges while food in the center is still luke-warm. To prevent this, thaw a large-size casserole completely before baking.

You can also freeze casserole dishes in plastic freezer containers—pack them solidly. Cover foods with a sauce or gravy; this helps exclude air and prevents that warmed-over taste.

We believe you will find an exciting assortment of main dishes, with practical ideas. Our After-Church Stew requires no pot-watching, for instance. The thrifty and versatile Basic Beef Mix will make four different and tasty dishes.

And meat loaves with imagination: Mini Loaves, a hot and spicy Chili Meat Loaf, Sweet and Sour, Stuffed Meat Loaf and many others.

Wonderful buffet specialties too—crunchy and different Chicken Casserole that can be frozen before or after baking. Do try Ranch Style Chicken played up with spices!

Meat

BRAISED BEEF IN CREAM

1 (4 lb.) boneless pot roast
(sirloin tip, bottom round,
rump or chuck)
2 tblsp. melted shortening
Salt and pepper
½ c. water

½ c. butter or margarine
2 c. heavy cream
2 large cloves garlic
4 tblsp. fresh lemon juice
Watercress or parsley

In a Dutch oven or heavy casserole with cover, slowly brown meat on all sides in melted shortening. Season generously with salt and pepper. Add water; cover and simmer 2½ to 3 hours or until tender.

Remove meat from pan; allow to stand for 20 minutes; slice thinly. Pour off pan juices and save for another use.

Heat butter in pan until it bubbles and browns. Add cream, garlic, lemon juice, about 1½ tsp. salt and about ¾ tsp. pepper. Cook over medium heat, stirring constantly, for about 3 minutes.

Spoon half of the sauce over bottom of a shallow heatproof serving platter. Arrange meat slices, slightly overlapping, in sauce. Pour remaining sauce over top.

Near serving time, bake in a moderate oven (350°) for 10 minutes or until heated through. Spoon sauce over meat; sprinkle very generously with chopped watercress or parsley; garnish with watercress or parsley sprigs. Makes about 8 servings.

RANCHERO POT ROAST

3 lbs. bottom round roast
2 tsp. salt
¼ tsp. freshly ground pepper
¼ tsp. paprika
1 clove garlic, finely chopped

2 tblsp. shortening
1 c. beef broth
½ c. chopped onions
½ c. chili sauce

Rub salt, pepper, paprika and garlic into meat. Cover; refrigerate overnight.

Next day, brown meat slowly in hot fat to a deep brown.

Place meat on rack in deep pan. Add broth and onions; cover and simmer 1½ hours (add more broth if necessary). Add chili sauce and cook 30 minutes. Makes 6 servings.

Note: If you want to freeze for later use, cool quickly. Pack into containers, seal, label, date and freeze.

Recommended storage time: 3 to 4 months.

To serve, partially thaw and simmer until well heated and tender, about 1 hour.

DEEP-PEPPERED PORK

1 (4 lb.) boneless rolled pork
  roast
Coarsely ground black pepper
Salt
Fresh garlic (optional)

1 lemon
8 medium-size potatoes, peeled,
  halved, cooked just until
  tender and drained
Thin lemon slices

With a sharp knife, pierce surface of pork about 1½″ deep in about 10 places. With forefinger, press into each hole about ⅛ tsp. pepper, about 1/16 tsp. salt, ¼ clove garlic and a thin strip of lemon peel (yellow part only). Rub surface of roast with fresh lemon juice, salt and pepper.

Place pork on rack in open roasting pan and bake in a slow oven (300°), allowing about 40 minutes per pound or until meat thermometer registers 185°. Allow to stand 20 minutes or more; slice, saving meat juices. Loosen crusty drippings from roasting pan.

Arrange pork slices, slightly overlapping, in a deep platter or shallow casserole for serving; spoon on meat juices and enough roast drippings to moisten (avoid excess fat) and remaining juice from lemon.

Coat potatoes with roast drippings and arrange around pork slices. Bake in a slow oven (300°) for 20 to 30 minutes or until pork is heated through, basting once or twice with pan juices. Garnish with lemon slices. Serve very hot. Makes about 8 servings.

BEEF 'N' RIGATONI STEW

1 c. dried prunes
¼ c. flour
1 tsp. salt
1½ lbs. lean chuck beef, cut in
  1½″ cubes
2 tblsp. salad oil
1 medium onion, coarsely
  chopped
1 clove garlic, minced

2 tsp. salt
¼ tsp. pepper
½ tsp. oregano
4 drops Tabasco sauce
1 (8 oz.) can tomato sauce
Hot water
½ (1 lb.) pkg. rigatoni, or
  other large macaroni

To make pitting easier, stew prunes 5 minutes in 2 c. water. Drain and cool, then pit and set aside. (The pitted prunes now available do not require precooking.)

In a plastic bag containing flour and 1 tsp. salt, shake beef cubes, a few at a time, until they are well coated.

Brown beef in hot oil in deep 4 qt. Dutch oven. Add onion, garlic, 2 tsp. salt, pepper, oregano and Tabasco sauce.

Add tomato sauce and enough hot water to keep liquid 1" above meat (about 3 c.). Stir well.

Cover tightly and bake in slow oven (300°) 2 hours.

Add rigatoni and prunes. Add enough hot water to cover (about 2 c.). Bake 1 hour longer. Makes 6 servings.

AFTER-CHURCH STEW

1½ lbs. lean beef, cut in 1½" cubes (chuck, round or top sirloin)
2 tsp. salt
½ tsp. basil
¼ tsp. pepper
2 stalks celery, cut in diagonal slices

4 carrots, cut in halves lengthwise and crosswise
2 onions cut in ½" slices
1 (10½ oz.) can condensed tomato soup
½ soup can water
3 potatoes peeled and cubed

Place beef (no need to brown it) in 3 qt. casserole. Sprinkle with salt, basil and pepper. Top with celery, carrots and onions.

Combine soup and water. Pour over meat and vegetables, coating all pieces.

Cover tightly and bake in slow oven (300°) 3 hours.

Add potatoes and bake 45 minutes longer. Makes 5 servings.

SAVORY STEW

2 lbs. lean beef chuck, cut in 1½" cubes
⅓ c. flour
1 tsp. salt
4 slices bacon
12 small white onions, peeled
4 carrots, peeled and cut in halves crosswise and lengthwise
1 clove garlic, minced

1 (10½ oz.) can condensed beef bouillon
2 c. cranberry juice cocktail
1 tblsp. sugar
6 crushed peppercorns
4 whole cloves
1 bay leaf
1 tsp. salt
½ tsp. marjoram
¼ tsp. thyme

Dredge beef cubes in flour and salt.

Fry bacon. Cut in 1" pieces; place in heavy 3 qt. casserole.

Brown beef cubes quickly in bacon fat; place in casserole. Add onions and carrots.

Sauté garlic in drippings 2 or 3 minutes. Add bouillon; bring to a boil and stir from bottom to loosen particles. Add cranberry juice, sugar and seasonings; bring to boil again. Pour over meat and vegetables. Cover tightly and bake in slow oven (300°) 2 hours. Cool and refrigerate overnight.

Next day, lift congealed fat from top. Pour liquid into saucepan and heat. Make thin paste of ¼ c. flour and water; add slowly to hot liquid, stirring and cooking until mixture thickens and comes to a boil. Pour over meat and vegetables in casserole. Heat in slow oven (300°) 30 minutes. Makes 6 servings.

SWISS BLISS

2 lb. chuck steak, 1½" thick
1 (1 lb.) can tomatoes
1 pkg. onion soup mix
1 (4 oz.) can sliced
    mushrooms, drained

½ c. chopped green pepper
1 tblsp. steak sauce
1 tblsp. cornstarch
1 tblsp. chopped parsley

Cut steak in serving-size pieces and arrange in 3 qt. casserole. Drain tomatoes, reserving juice, and arrange over steak. Sprinkle soup mix, mushrooms and green pepper over tomatoes. Combine reserved juice with remaining ingredients and pour over all. Cover casserole and bake in moderate oven (350°) for 2 hours or until meat is tender. Makes 6 servings.

BARBECUED STEAK

1 c. ketchup
½ c. water
¼ c. vinegar
¼ c. chopped green pepper
¼ c. chopped onion
1½ tblsp. Worcestershire sauce

1 tblsp. prepared mustard
2 tblsp. brown sugar
½ tsp. salt
⅛ tsp. pepper
4 lbs. round steak, cut ½"
    thick

Combine all ingredients except round steak in a saucepan. Bring to a boil, then simmer gently for about 5 minutes over low heat. Keep barbecue sauce hot.

Pound round steak to break connective tissue. Cut into serving-size portions. Place pieces in a large roasting pan. Pour hot barbecue sauce over meat.

Cover tightly and bake in moderate oven (325°) for 1½ to 2 hours or until meat is fork-tender. Makes 8 to 10 servings.

ROUND STEAK

2½ lbs. top round steak (½"
   to ¾" thick)
2 tblsp. soy sauce
2 tblsp. water
2 tblsp. grated onion
1 tblsp. prepared mustard

1 tblsp. cider vinegar
1 tsp. ground ginger
½ tsp. sugar
½ tsp. salt
¼ tsp. pepper

Cut steak in 6 pieces; place in large shallow dish.

Combine remaining ingredients; pour over steak. Cover and store in refrigerator several hours or overnight.

Place steak and sauce in large skillet. Simmer, covered, 1½ hours or until tender, turning occasionally. Makes 6 servings.

SUNDAY SWISS STEAKS

½ c. flour
2 tsp. salt
¼ tsp. pepper
6 slices eye of round, 1½"
   thick

½ c. thinly sliced onion rings
¼ c. shortening
1 (8 oz.) can tomato sauce
1 c. pizza sauce

Combine flour, salt and pepper; pound into meat.

Brown onions lightly in hot fat in large skillet; remove onions and brown meat. Place onions on top of meat.

Add tomato and pizza sauces. Cover; simmer 1½ to 2 hours until tender. Serve sauce with meat. Makes 6 servings.

If you want to freeze meat for later use, package cooked steaks individually, with sauce, in small foil pie pans; wrap with foil. Seal, label, date and freeze. Easy to choose the number of servings you need from freezer.

Recommended storage time: 3 to 6 months.

To serve, heat in skillet.

BASIC BEEF MIX

¾ c. instant nonfat dry milk
1 c. quick rolled oats, uncooked
1 c. tomato juice
2 tblsp. minced onion
¼ tsp. pepper
½ tsp. monosodium glutamate
2 tsp. salt
2 lbs. ground beef

Combine all ingredients except ground beef. Add meat; mix well.

Freezing directions: For Hobo Knapsacks, shape half of mix into 6 patties. Place between squares of waxed paper; wrap with freezer paper or aluminum foil and freeze. For Meat Ball Stew or Sweet 'n Sour Meat Balls, shape half of mix into small balls. Place in a shallow pan; cover tightly with freezer paper or aluminum foil and freeze. When meat balls are frozen, remove from pan and store in freezer containers. For Spruced-up Meat Loaf, spread entire mix in aluminum foil-lined (13×9×2″) pan. Wrap and freeze. When mix is frozen, remove it from pan and wrap tightly with foil or freezer paper; return to freezer for storage.

Thaw mix before using in these recipes. The ideal way to thaw mix is to refrigerate overnight in freezer wrapper or container. If you are in a hurry, loosen wrapper, separate pieces and let stand at room temperature 40 to 50 minutes.

HOBO KNAPSACKS

½ recipe Basic Beef Mix, shaped into 6 patties
2 tblsp. butter or margarine
2 medium potatoes, sliced ½″ thick
2 large tomatoes, sliced ½″ thick
1 large onion, sliced ½″ thick
1 (10 oz.) pkg. frozen mixed vegetables, uncooked
1 (3 oz.) can sliced mushrooms, drained
1 tsp. salt
¼ tsp. pepper
½ tsp. ground thyme

Brown patties lightly in butter; reserve drippings.

Place each patty in center of a 12″ square of heavy-duty aluminum foil. Top with single slices of potato, tomato and onion; spoon on frozen vegetables and mushrooms. Sprinkle on seasonings. Pour drippings over the top.

Close foil around meat and vegetables, allowing ends to flare out like a knapsack. Place on baking sheet. Bake in moderate oven (350°) 1 hour. Makes 6 servings.

MEAT BALL STEW

½ recipe Basic Beef Mix,
   shaped into small balls
1 tblsp. salad oil
3 tblsp. flour
1 (1 lb.) can tomatoes
1 c. water
½ tsp. salt

2 tsp. sugar
1 tsp. basil
3 medium potatoes, diced
4 small carrots, diced
1 onion, coarsely chopped
1 stalk celery, sliced

Brown meat balls in salad oil.

Remove meat balls from skillet; pour off all fat except 3 tblsp. Blend in flour. Stir in remaining ingredients. Bring mixture to a boil; simmer for 10 minutes. Add more water if needed. Pour over meat balls in a 2 qt. casserole.

Bake, covered, in moderate oven (350°) 1 hour or until vegetables are tender. Makes 6 servings.

SPRUCED-UP MEAT LOAF

1 recipe Basic Beef Mix,
   shaped into 13×9″
   rectangle on aluminum
   foil or waxed paper

½ c. pizza flavor ketchup
1 c. shredded sharp Cheddar
   or mozzarella cheese

Spread beef mix with ketchup; sprinkle with cheese. Roll up meat jelly roll fashion.

Place meat loaf roll, open edge down, in greased shallow pan. Bake in moderate oven (350°) about 1¼ hours. Makes 8 servings.

SWEET 'N' SOUR MEAT BALLS

½ recipe Basic Beef Mix,
   shaped into small balls
1 (1 lb.) can tomatoes
¼ c. firmly packed dark
   brown sugar

2 tblsp. vinegar
¼ tsp. salt
1 tsp. grated onion
5 gingersnaps, crushed

Bake meat balls in shallow pan in very hot oven (450°) about 20 minutes or until browned.

Combine remaining ingredients and bring to a boil. Add meat balls; simmer 5 minutes. Serve. Will hold in a covered casserole in a very slow oven (250°). Makes 5 servings.

BUSY-DAY MEAT MIX

4 c. ground cooked meat	1 tsp. salt
½ lb. pork sausage	¼ tsp. pepper
2 c. bread cubes	1 tsp. monosodium
2 eggs, slightly beaten	glutamate
1 (4 oz.) can chopped	2 tsp. Worcestershire sauce
mushrooms	1 (10½ oz.) can condensed
¼ c. chopped parsley	cream of mushroom soup

Combine all the ingredients. Makes 3 pints.

Pack into freezer containers, seal, label, date and freeze.

Recommended storage time: 2 to 3 months.

To use, partially thaw and use to stuff cabbage leaves, green peppers or squash, or as a filling for biscuit rolls or pastry turnovers, which may be prepared and frozen. Or you can make individual meat loaves.

Individual Meat Loaves Shape Busy-Day Meat Mix in ½ cup measure. Makes 12 individual loaves.

Freeze on baking sheet; wrap individually in foil or saran, seal, label, date and return to freezer.

To serve, remove wrapping, place frozen meat loaves in baking pan. Bake in moderate oven (375°) 45 minutes.

MIXER-MADE MEAT LOAF

2 eggs	4 tsp. salt
1 (10½ oz.) can tomato purée	½ tsp. pepper
1 c. water	2 tsp. Worcestershire sauce
6 slices bread	3 lbs. lean ground beef
¼ c. dried or fresh minced	
onion	

Beat eggs until frothy in large bowl of electric mixer. Reduce speed to very low; blend in tomato purée and water. Tear bread into pieces and gradually drop into turning mixer bowl; mix thoroughly. Add onion and seasonings.

Slowly add beef. If mixture climbs beaters before all beef is added, add water, a tablespoonful at a time. Shape into a loaf in a 13×9×2″ baking pan. Bake in slow oven (300°) 1¼ hours, or until pink color in center disappears. Makes 15 servings.

Variations

Beef Patties   Measure meat loaf mixture into ½ c. portions. Flatten and pan-fry or broil until no longer pink in the center, about 15 minutes. Makes 18 generous patties. (Keep a supply, uncooked, in the freezer for quick dinners.)

Little Meat Loaves   Pack meat loaf mixture into muffin-pan cups. Bake in very hot oven (450°) 15 minutes. Makes about 30—count on at least 2 for each adult serving.

MINI MEAT LOAVES

2 eggs	1 tsp. celery salt
1 c. milk	¼ tsp. pepper
2 c. soft bread crumbs	6 tblsp. grated onion
2 tsp. salt	2 lbs. ground beef
1 tsp. dry mustard	

Beat eggs slightly in large bowl; blend in milk. Add remaining ingredients. Mix thoroughly.

Shape mixture into 12 small loaves. Makes 6 servings.

Place on baking sheet; freeze. When frozen, remove from freezer, package in foil or saran, seal, label and date. Return to freezer.

HOOSIER CHILI MEAT LOAF

2 lbs. ground beef	2 eggs, slightly beaten
3 tblsp. instant minced onion	½ c. cracker crumbs
2 tsp. salt	1 c. canned tomatoes
1 tsp. chili powder	1 (1 lb.) can red kidney
¼ tsp. pepper	beans, drained and mashed
¼ tsp. garlic powder	

Combine all ingredients and mix thoroughly.

Line a 9×5×3″ loaf pan with foil; let ends of foil extend over edges of pan. Press meat mixture into pan. Makes 10 to 12 servings.

Freeze. Remove from pan, wrap, seal, label, date and return to freezer. Recommended storage time; 6 to 8 weeks.

When ready to use, place frozen wrapped meat loaf on rack in shallow pan. Bake in moderate oven (350°) 2½ hours.

FROZEN STUFFED MEAT LOAF

1 lb. lean ground beef	⅛ tsp. pepper
1 lb. ground pork	1 (4 oz.) can mushrooms,
1 c. dry bread crumbs	drained and chopped
½ c. grated carrot	1 tblsp. finely chopped onion
¼ c. finely chopped onion	2 tblsp. butter
2 eggs, beaten	2 c. soft bread crumbs
½ c. milk	1 tblsp. chopped parsley
2 tsp. salt	½ tsp. poultry seasoning
1 tsp. Worcestershire sauce	¼ tsp. salt

Mix together the first six ingredients. Add milk, 2 tsp. salt, Worcestershire sauce and pepper. Mix lightly, but well.

Place on a double-thick square of greased aluminum foil. Shape into a 14×8″ rectangle.

Sauté mushrooms and 1 tblsp. onion in butter until golden. Add soft bread crumbs, parsley, poultry seasoning and ¼ tsp. salt.

Spread stuffing mixture over meat; roll up, starting with long side. Press overlapping edge into roll to seal. Bring foil edges together in a tight double fold on the top of the meat. Fold ends up, using tight double folds. Freeze.

When ready to use, place frozen wrapped meat loaf on rack in shallow pan. Bake in hot oven (450°) for 1½ hours. Open foil; continue baking for 15 minutes or until brown. Makes 6 servings.

MEAT BALLS IN BROWN GRAVY   A Tennessee reader shares her treasured recipe for Meat Balls in Buttermilk Sauce with us. Her specialty is truly delicious, but you need to allow about an hour to shape, brown and bake the balls and to make the sauce. But once the beef nuggets, swimming in smooth, thickened gravy, are tucked in the oven, you can forget them for 30 minutes.

MEAT BALLS IN BUTTERMILK SAUCE

2 lbs. ground beef	2 tsp. salt
1 c. bread crumbs	¼ tsp. pepper
½ c. diced onion	⅓ c. butter
1 c. milk	

Sauce

½ c. butter	2 tsp. salt
½ c. flour	¼ tsp. pepper
¼ c. sugar	4½ c. buttermilk
3 tblsp. dry mustard	2 eggs, beaten

For meat balls: Combine all ingredients, except butter; shape into large balls (about 16). Brown on all sides in butter; remove from skillet; keep hot.

For sauce: Add butter to drippings in skillet. Mix flour, sugar, mustard, salt and pepper; blend into fat.

Stir; gradually add buttermilk. Cook over low heat, stirring constantly, until sauce is smooth and thick.

Stir some hot sauce into eggs; return to skillet and cook 2 to 3 minutes more. Pour into greased 3 qt. casserole; add meat balls. Bake in slow oven (300°) 30 minutes. Makes 8 servings.

BEEF BALLS WITH BEAN SAUCE

2 lb. ground beef	½ tsp. garlic salt
½ c. instant minced onion	½ tsp. celery salt
1 c. fine bread crumbs	⅔ c. milk
2 eggs	2 tblsp. shortening
1 tsp. salt	Bean Sauce (recipe follows)

Combine beef, onion, bread crumbs, eggs, salts and milk; mix thoroughly. Shape into 20 balls about 1½" in diameter. Heat shortening in a large skillet and cook meat balls, shaking pan to cook them evenly and keep them round. Remove balls to hot platter. Drain off drippings, reserving 3 tblsp. for sauce. Makes 8 to 10 servings.

Bean Sauce

3 tblsp. pan drippings	¼ c. ketchup
3 tblsp. flour	1 tsp. salt
1 (8 oz.) can pork and beans in tomato sauce	½ tsp. chili powder
	¼ tsp. paprika
1¾ c. water	⅛ tsp. pepper

Combine pan drippings and flour in skillet. Add pork and beans; mash with fork to blend. Gradually stir in water. Bring to boil; reduce heat and simmer for 2 minutes. Stir in ketchup, salt, chili powder, paprika and pepper. Cook 1 minute. Makes about 2 cups.

GREEN BEAN—BURGER BAKE

4 slices bacon, diced	2 (10 oz.) pkgs. frozen green
1 lb. ground beef	beans
1 c. fine bread crumbs	1 (1½ oz.) pkg. onion soup
1 tsp. salt	mix
1 c. dairy sour cream	1 (10½ oz.) can condensed
1 egg	cream of mushroom soup

Cook bacon in skillet; remove and drain.

Combine ground beef, bread crumbs, salt, ½ c. sour cream and egg. Shape into 12 meat balls; brown in bacon drippings.

Cook green beans as directed on package, but do not season.

Combine onion soup mix, mushroom soup and remaining ½ c. sour cream in greased 2 qt. casserole. Mix in bacon and drained beans. Top with meat balls.

Bake covered, in moderate oven (350°) 20 minutes. Makes 6 servings.

TWO-STEP MEAT BALLS   A New Jersey hostess who likes to serve meat balls in gravy to guests divides their preparation into two steps. She browns the meat quickly in the broiling oven and makes a thin brown gravy with the drippings. Then she puts the meat balls in a casserole, pours on the gravy and refrigerates them, covered, for 2 or 3 days. She bakes them an hour before dinner is served.

SWEDISH MEAT BALLS

1 lb. ground beef	1 egg
½ c. fine bread crumbs	2 tblsp. flour
⅔ tsp. salt	2 tblsp. fat
⅛ tsp. pepper	Water
Dash nutmeg	1 beef bouillon cube
1 medium onion, finely	
chopped	

Thoroughly mix together beef, bread crumbs, salt, pepper, nutmeg, onion and egg. Shape lightly in 1½" balls.

Place meat balls on foil-lined baking sheet, turning up edges to catch fat, or on a shallow pan. Brown quickly on all sides in the broiling oven. Remove meat balls to a large casserole.

Make gravy using 2 tblsp. each flour and fat for every cup

of gravy desired. Brown flour in fat, add cold water and stir until gravy is smooth and thickened (thin gravy is desirable). Dissolve bouillon cube in gravy and pour over the meat balls. Cover and bake in a moderate oven (325°) 1½ hours. Or refrigerate 2 or 3 days, then bake. Makes 6 to 8 servings.

MEAT BALL CHOWDER

2 lbs. ground lean beef	6 beef bouillon cubes
2 tsp. seasoned salt	6 carrots, sliced (3 c.)
⅛ tsp. pepper	3 to 4 c. sliced celery
2 eggs, slightly beaten	2 to 3 potatoes, diced (2 to
¼ c. finely chopped parsley	3 c.)
⅓ c. fine cracker crumbs	¼ c. long grain rice
2 tblsp. milk	1 tblsp. sugar
3 tblsp. flour	2 tsp. salt
1 tblsp. salad oil	2 bay leaves
4 to 6 onions, cut in eighths	½ to 1 tsp. marjoram
6 c. water	(optional)
6 c. tomato juice	1 (12 oz.) can Mexicorn

Combine meat, seasoned salt, pepper, eggs, parsley, cracker crumbs and milk. Mix thoroughly. Form into balls about the size of a walnut (makes about 40). Dip in flour.

Heat oil in 8 to 10 qt. kettle. Lightly brown meat balls on all sides (or drop unbrowned into boiling vegetables).

Add remaining ingredients (except add corn last 10 minutes of cooking). Bring to boil; cover. Reduce heat and cook at slow boil 30 minutes, or until vegetables are tender. If dinner must wait, turn off heat at this point. Takes only minutes to reheat. Serve in big soup plates. Makes 6 to 7 quarts.

To freeze, cook until the vegetables are crisp-tender. Cool quickly. Ladle into freezer containers, cover, seal, label and date. Recommended storage time: 2 to 3 months.

To serve, partially thaw until chowder softens. Heat until piping hot, about 45 minutes.

HERB-STUFFED MEAT BALLS

2 lbs. ground beef	¼ c. dry bread crumbs
1 tsp. salt	½ c. milk
¼ tsp. pepper	Herb Stuffing (recipe follows)
1 egg	Spicy Gravy (recipe follows)

Combine ground beef, salt, pepper, egg, dry bread crumbs and milk. Shape into 12 (4″) patties.

Place a mound of stuffing in center of each pattie and press meat around stuffing ball. Evenly space meat balls, sealed side down, in 13×9×2″ pan. Bake in moderate oven (350°) for 30 minutes. Pour hot Spicy Gravy over meat balls, and bake an additional 30 minutes. Makes 6 servings.

Herb Stuffing

5 c. toasted bread crumbs	¼ tsp. pepper
¼ c. butter	1 tblsp. parsley
½ c. finely chopped onion	½ to 1 tsp. sage
½ c. chopped celery	¼ c. warm water
½ tsp. salt	

Combine all ingredients, mixing lightly but thoroughly.

Spicy Gravy

1 can (10¾ oz.) mushroom gravy	½ tsp. Worcestershire sauce
1 can (10¾ oz.) beef gravy	½ tsp. prepared mustard
1 bay leaf	½ tsp. bottled gravy sauce
	1 c. water

Blend all ingredients in 1 qt. saucepan. Heat to boiling.

BEEF-MACARONI CASSEROLE

1 lb. ground beef	¼ c. chopped green pepper
2 eggs	½ c. mayonnaise
½ c. ketchup	1 c. grated American cheese
⅓ c. milk	½ c. dry bread crumbs
¼ c. chopped onion	2 tblsp. melted butter or
1½ tsp. salt	margarine
8 oz. elbow macaroni, cooked	6 slices tomato
2 tsp. prepared mustard	

Mix beef, eggs, ketchup, milk, onion and salt.

Mix macaroni, mustard, green pepper and mayonnaise; spread in greased 2 qt. baking dish. Spread beef mixture over top; sprinkle with cheese; top with mixture of crumbs and butter.

Bake in moderate oven (350°) 20 minutes; place tomatoes on top and bake 10 minutes. Makes 6 servings.

BEEF-CHEESE CASSEROLE

1½ lbs. ground beef
1 medium onion, chopped
(about ¾ c.)
1 tsp. salt
⅛ tsp. pepper
2 (8 oz.) cans tomato sauce
1 c. cottage cheese

1 (8 oz.) pkg. cream cheese
¼ c. dairy sour cream
⅓ c. chopped green pepper
⅓ c. chopped green onion
8 oz. noodles, cooked and
drained

Combine ground beef and onion in skillet and cook until beef is browned. Add salt, pepper and tomato sauce and simmer slowly while preparing remaining ingredients.

Combine cottage cheese, cream cheese, sour cream, green pepper and green onion.

Place half the noodles in bottom of greased 3 qt. casserole. Top with cheese mixture, then remaining noodles. Pour meat mixture over top.

Bake in moderate oven (350°) 30 minutes. Makes 8 to 10 servings.

Note: You can use 2 (1½ qt.) casseroles.

MAZETTI

2 lbs. ground beef
½ bunch celery and leaves,
finely chopped (2½ c.)
2 large onions, chopped
2 cloves garlic, finely chopped
8 oz. fine noodles
2 (10½ oz.) cans condensed
tomato soup

1 (6 oz.) can mushrooms and
liquid
2 tsp. salt
½ tsp. pepper
½ lb. grated sharp Cheddar
cheese

Brown meat in a skillet. Add celery, onion and garlic with 1 tblsp. water. Cover; steam until vegetables are tender. Remove from heat.

Cook noodles according to package directions and drain. Add to beef mixture; mix in remainder of ingredients except cheese. Spread mixture in 3 qt. casserole or two 1½ qt. casseroles. Top with cheese. (If you wish, refrigerate up to 24 hours or freeze.)

Place dish in cold oven set at 250°. Bake uncovered until bubbly, about 1 hour. Makes about 10 servings.

CONFETTI CASSEROLE

2 lbs. ground beef
½ c. chopped onion
2 tsp. salt
¼ tsp. pepper
½ tsp. dry mustard

2 tblsp. brown sugar
1 (8 oz.) pkg. cream cheese
2 (8 oz.) cans tomato sauce
2 (10 oz.) pkgs. frozen mixed
vegetables, defrosted

Brown meat in skillet; add onion and cook until tender. Add seasonings, sugar and cream cheese; stir until cheese melts. Add tomato sauce and defrosted vegetables.

Turn into a 3 qt. casserole. Sprinkle crushed corn chips over the top. Cover and bake in moderate oven (375°) 40 minutes. Uncover; bake 10 minutes longer. Makes 10 to 12 servings.

TAGLIARINI CASSEROLE

1 lb. ground beef
½ lb. bulk pork sausage
1 c. chopped onion
1 medium green pepper,
chopped
1 (12 oz.) can whole kernel
corn, well drained
1 (10½ oz.) can condensed
tomato soup
1 (8 oz.) can tomato sauce

⅓ c. sliced, pimiento-stuffed
green olives
1 clove garlic, minced
1 tsp. salt
1 (8 oz.) pkg. sharp Cheddar
cheese, shredded
1 (8 oz.) pkg. wide noodles,
cooked 5 minutes and
drained

Brown meat; skim off fat. Add onion, green pepper, corn, tomato soup, tomato sauce, olives, garlic and salt.

Reserve ½ of cheese. Stir remaining cheese and noodles into vegetable-meat mixture. Turn into a 3 qt. casserole.

Sprinkle reserved cheese on top. Cover and bake in moderate oven (350°) 35 minutes. Uncover; bake 10 minutes longer. This casserole makes 10 to 12 servings.

PLANTATION STUFFED PEPPERS

1 lb. ground beef
1 c. chopped onion
1 clove garlic, chopped
2 tsp. chili powder
1 tsp. salt
½ tsp. pepper

2 (10½ oz.) cans condensed
tomato soup
½ lb. sharp process cheese,
shredded or sliced
1½ c. cooked converted rice
8 medium green peppers

Cook ground beef, onion and garlic in skillet until meat is browned. Add seasonings and tomato soup; simmer, covered, 10 minutes.

Add cheese. Cook slowly, stirring occasionally until cheese melts. Stir in rice. Cool.

Cut peppers in halves lengthwise. Remove membranes and seeds. Cook in boiling salted water to cover until barely tender, about 3 minutes. Drain and cool.

Place peppers on baking sheet or in shallow pan. Stuff with rice mixture. Makes 8 servings.

To freeze, place in freezer until peppers are frozen. Remove, wrap frozen peppers in foil or saran. Seal, label, date and return to freezer.

Recommended storage time: 2 to 3 months.

To serve, remove wrapping, place partially thawed peppers in shallow pan. Cover with foil. Bake in hot oven (400°) 30 to 45 minutes.

MEXICAN BEEF HASH

1 c. chopped onion	2 tsp. salt
1 c. chopped green pepper	¼ tsp. pepper
1 lb. ground beef	1 c. uncooked rice
3 to 4 tsp. chili powder	2 (1 lb.) cans tomatoes (4 c.)

Sauté onion and green pepper with ground beef until beef is browned.

Add remaining ingredients, except tomatoes, and mix well.

Line 2 (1½ qt.) casseroles with aluminum foil. Divide mixture evenly between the 2 casseroles. Pour 1 can tomatoes over each casserole and mix lightly to blend. Cover and bake in moderate oven (350°) 20 minutes. Remove from oven, leave covered, and cool quickly to room temperature. Each casserole makes 4 to 6 servings.

Place casseroles in freezer. When hash is frozen, lift foil from casserole. Wrap in moisture-vapor-proof paper, seal, label, date and return to freezer. Recommended storage time: 3 to 6 months.

To serve, take package from freezer, remove wrappings and place in casserole. Cover and bake in moderate oven (350°) 1 hour.

STUFFED PORK CHOPS

6 pork chops, at least 1"
   thick for stuffing
2 tblsp. butter or margarine
2 tblsp. finely chopped onion
¼ tsp. sage
¼ tsp. crushed basil

1 tblsp. dried or chopped
   fresh parsley
1½ c. small dry bread cubes
¼ c. dry onion soup mix
½ c. water

Cut pork chops along the bone, about halfway through, then cut toward outside to make a pocket.

Melt butter; add onion, sage, basil and parsley. Sauté until onion is golden. Toss with bread cubes. Stuff mixture into pork chop pockets.

Brown chops in small amount of fat; place in 13×9×2" casserole or baking pan. Sprinkle dry onion soup mix over chops. Pour on ½ c. water and cover.

Bake in moderate oven (325°) about 1 hour, or until chops are tender. Makes 6 servings.

SWEET AND SOUR PORK CHOPS

6 pork chops
Salt and pepper
1 (4 oz.) can mushrooms,
   drained
2 medium onions, sliced
½ c. chopped green pepper

2 tblsp. vinegar
2 tblsp. soy sauce
2 tblsp. molasses
2 tsp. cornstarch
2 tblsp. water

Sprinkle pork chops with salt and pepper. Brown on both sides in a large skillet.

Drain mushrooms, reserving liquid. Add enough water to liquid to make 1 cup. Arrange onions, green pepper and mushrooms on top of chops. Combine vinegar, soy sauce, molasses and water; pour over vegetables. Bring to a boil; reduce heat, simmer covered for 1 hour or until tender.

Remove chops. Combine cornstarch with water. Stir gradually into boiling liquid, stirring constantly. Boil 1 minute. Serve over chops. Makes 6 servings.

BARBECUED PORK CHOPS

8 loin or shoulder pork chops, 1″ thick	1 tsp. celery seeds
1 (8 oz.) can tomato sauce	⅛ tsp. cloves
½ c. ketchup	½ tsp. Tabasco sauce
½ c. water	1 tblsp. prepared mustard
¼ c. vinegar	1 medium onion, sliced
1 tsp. salt	1 clove garlic, crushed (optional)

Cut a little fat from pork chops, heat in skillet, then brown meat in it (about 10 minutes). Place meat in shallow baking dish (13×9×2″) one layer deep.

Pour fat from skillet. Combine remaining ingredients; mix with browned particles in skillet. Pour over chops.

Bake uncovered in moderate oven (350°) 1 hour and 15 minutes. Turn once during baking. Adjust time for thicker or thinner chops. Makes 8 generous servings. If someone is late to dinner, these chops will taste good rewarmed.

Note: If your family likes more "bite" in sauce, sprinkle chops with a little red pepper before baking.

MEAT AND POTATOES Many busy women resist giving up some of the great all-American dishes even if they do require considerable time for proper cooking. Hearty pork chops and scalloped potatoes are a splendid example.

In the recipe for this favorite that follows, the potatoes and pork bake 1½ hours for perfection. But you need pay no attention to them while they cook. And when you take them, hot and neatly browned on top, from the oven, getting the rest of the meal is quick.

There are short cuts in fixing the dish. The pork chops are browned only on one side. Canned soup provides seasoning as well as liquid and eliminates adding flour. It also prevents curdling of the cheese sauce that makes itself around the meat and potatoes.

Here's a dish to fix when you want to give your attention to work about the house, but not in the kitchen.

SCALLOPED POTATOES WITH PORK CHOPS

6 pork chops, ½" thick
1 tblsp. fat
5 c. sliced, peeled raw
   potatoes
6 (1 oz.) slices process
   American cheese

1 tsp. salt
¼ tsp. pepper
½ c. chopped green onions
1 (10½ oz.) can condensed
   cream of celery soup
1¼ c. milk

Brown chops on one side in hot fat.

Place half of potatoes in greased baking pan (13×9×2"). Top with cheese slices. Add remaining potatoes. Place pork chops, browned side up, on potatoes. Sprinkle with salt and pepper.

Cook onions in drippings in skillet until tender, but do not brown. Add soup and milk. Heat; then pour over the pork chops.

Cover with foil or a baking sheet and bake in moderate oven (350°) 1 hour. Remove cover and continue baking 30 minutes. Makes 6 servings.

Variations: Use condensed cream of mushroom soup for the celery soup and slices of ham for the pork chops. Or use process pimiento cheese instead of American cheese.

PORK CHOP CASSEROLE

6 pork chops
Salt and pepper
3 c. sliced potatoes
2 c. sliced carrots
½ c. chopped celery

1 medium onion, sliced
1 (10½ oz.) can condensed
   cream of celery soup
½ c. water
¼ tsp. thyme

Season pork chops with salt and pepper. Brown on both sides in a skillet.

Arrange potatoes, carrots, celery and onion in a 13×9×2" glass ovenware casserole. Pour soup over vegetables.

Remove fat from skillet, reserving 2 tblsp. Add water to fat and scrape particles from bottom of skillet. Pour over vegetables. Sprinkle with thyme. Place pork chops on top.

Bake in moderate oven (325°) for 1 hour or until chops are tender. Makes 6 servings.

SKILLET CHOP SUEY

2 c. finely diced fresh pork	3 tblsp. cornstarch
3 tblsp. salad oil	1 tblsp. molasses
3 c. chopped celery	½ c. water
2 c. chopped onion	1 (1 lb.) can bean sprouts
2 tblsp. soy sauce	1 (4 oz.) can mushroom
2 chicken bouillon cubes	pieces
1 c. boiling water	

Brown pork in hot oil; add celery, onion and 1 tblsp. soy sauce; cook 10 minutes.

Dissolve bouillon cubes in boiling water. Add to pork along with cornstarch mixed with remaining soy sauce, molasses and ½ c. water. Stir in bean sprouts and mushrooms with their liquids. Cook, stirring until thickened. Makes 8 servings.

To serve at once, cook 5 minutes longer.

To freeze, cool quickly, place in freezer containers, seal, label, date and freeze.

Recommended storage time: 2 to 3 months.

To serve, partially thaw at room temperature and quickly heat in skillet.

SOUTHWESTERN PORK SKILLET

3 tblsp. salad oil	1 tsp. chili powder
1 medium onion, sliced	2 tsp. sugar
1 stalk celery, diced	2½ c. canned tomatoes
½ green pepper, diced	¾ lb. cooked pork roast, cut
1 tsp. salt	in thin strips
⅛ tsp. pepper	6 corn muffins or corn sticks
1 tblsp. flour	

Heat oil in skillet. Sauté onion, celery and green pepper until barely tender. Add salt, pepper, flour, chili powder and sugar. Stir to make a smooth paste.

Gradually stir in tomatoes and bring to a boil. Reduce heat and simmer for 15 minutes, stirring occasionally. Add pork strips and continue to simmer for 5 minutes.

Serve over corn muffins, broken into halves. Makes 6 servings.

PORK CURRY

4 tblsp. butter or margarine
1 medium onion, finely
chopped
1 tart apple, peeled and diced
¾ tsp. salt
⅛ tsp. pepper

1 tblsp. curry powder
3 tblsp. flour
2 c. chicken broth
¾ lb. cooked pork roast, cut
into thin strips
2 tblsp. raisins

In a heavy saucepan over medium heat melt butter and sauté onion and apple until golden. Stir in salt, pepper and curry powder and simmer a few minutes. Stir in flour to make a smooth paste. Gradually stir in chicken broth. Cook and stir over medium heat until sauce is thickened. Add pork pieces and raisins. Cook for 5 minutes more or until pork is heated through. Makes 5 to 6 servings.

SWEET AND SOUR PORK

¾ lb. cooked pork, cut into
thin strips
1 tsp. salt
1 tblsp. cornstarch
1 egg
½ tblsp. flour
½ c. salad oil
1 tblsp. sugar
2 tblsp. cornstarch
1 c. water

½ c. pineapple juice
¼ c. ketchup
1 tsp. soy sauce
¼ c. vinegar
1 green pepper, cut into
wedges
1 large onion, coarsely diced
1 (1 lb. 4½ oz.) can pineapple
chunks, well drained
(reserve juice)

Toss pork strips with salt and 1 tblsp. cornstarch. Mix egg and flour to make a batter. Dip pork pieces into batter with slotted spoon. Fry in hot oil until nicely browned. Drain on paper towel.

In a deep skillet, mix sugar and cornstarch; stir in water, pineapple juice, ketchup, soy sauce and vinegar. Bring to boil, stirring constantly; then cook over medium heat until thickened.

Add green pepper and onion and cook in sauce for 5 minutes. Add pineapple chunks and pork pieces and simmer uncovered for 10 minutes until green pepper is tender and pork pieces are heated through. Serve with rice. Makes 5 servings.

PORK CABBAGE ROLLS

1 large head cabbage
2½ c. ground or finely
 chopped cooked pork
 roast
½ c. fine bread crumbs
⅓ c. finely chopped onion
1 egg, slightly beaten
1 tblsp. chopped parsley

1 tsp. caraway seeds
1½ tsp. salt
¼ tsp. freshly ground pepper
1 (8 oz.) can tomato sauce
½ c. water
1 tsp. cornstarch
½ tsp. sugar
1 tblsp. lemon juice

Discard wilted outer leaves of cabbage and remove core. Carefully remove 12 to 14 large whole leaves. Steam leaves for 3 minutes in a small amount of boiling, salted water, covered. Drain and cool.

Mix pork, bread crumbs, onion, egg, parsley, caraway seeds, salt and pepper. Put a heaping tablespoonful of pork mixture near the stem end of each cabbage leaf. Fold in the two sides, then roll leaf.

Place cabbage rolls close together in a large skillet. Mix tomato sauce, water, cornstarch, sugar and lemon juice; pour over rolls. Cover tightly and simmer for 25 to 30 minutes, until leaves are tender. Makes 10 to 12 rolls.

POTLUCK HAM CASSEROLE

½ c. milk
1 (10½ oz.) can condensed
 cream of mushroom soup
1 c. dairy sour cream
2 tsp. prepared mustard
1 tsp. instant minced green
 onion

⅛ tsp. pepper
4 oz. noodles, cooked and
 drained
2 c. thin pieces cooked ham
¼ c. toasted slivered almonds

Gradually add milk to mushroom soup, stirring over low heat to make smooth sauce. Blend in sour cream, mustard, onion and pepper.

Arrange half of noodles, ham and sauce in greased 2 qt. casserole. Repeat layers. Top with toasted almonds.

Bake in moderate oven (325°) 25 minutes. Makes 6 servings.

HAM AND BROCCOLI ROYALE

3 c. cooked rice
2 (10 oz.) pkgs. frozen
  broccoli spears, cooked and
  drained
6 tblsp. butter
2 c. fresh bread crumbs
2 c. chopped onion
3 tblsp. flour

½ tsp. salt
¼ tsp. pepper
3 c. milk
4 c. cubed ham (about 1½
  lbs.)
1 (8 oz.) pkg. sliced process
  American cheese

Spoon cooked rice into a greased 3 qt. casserole. Layer broccoli over rice. Melt butter; remove 2 tblsp. and sprinkle over bread crumbs in a bowl; set aside.

Sauté onion in remaining butter. Blend in flour and seasonings. Slowly stir in milk. Cook, stirring constantly, until thickened. Add ham; heat until bubbly. Pour into casserole. Layer cheese over ham mixture.

Sprinkle on buttered crumbs. Bake in moderate oven (350°) for 45 minutes or until top is golden brown. Makes 8 to 10 servings.

HE-MAN HAM CASSEROLE

½ c. chopped onion
½ c. chopped green pepper
6 tblsp. butter
6 tblsp. flour
⅛ tsp. pepper
1½ c. milk
1 c. chicken broth

4 c. cubed ham
1 (10 oz.) pkg. frozen peas,
  thawed and drained
4 c. hot seasoned mashed
  potatoes
1 egg, beaten
1 c. shredded Cheddar cheese

Sauté onion and green pepper in butter. Add flour and pepper; stir until smooth. Gradually stir in milk and broth. Cook, stirring, until thickened. Combine with ham and peas in a 3 qt. casserole.

Combine mashed potatoes, egg and cheese. Drop by spoonfuls onto mixture in casserole.

Bake in moderate oven (375°) for 45 minutes or until golden brown and bubbly. Makes 10 servings.

ROAST VEAL WITH SWEET ONIONS

1 (4 lb.) boneless veal roast (rolled shoulder or leg)	1½ tsp. salt
⅔ c. salad oil	½ tsp. pepper
6 tblsp. wine vinegar	1 sweet onion, very thinly sliced

Place meat on rack in roasting pan; insert meat thermometer. Roast in moderate oven (325°) until meat thermometer registers 170° or about 40 minutes per pound. Remove from oven and allow to stand about 20 minutes, then slice, saving juices.

Shake or beat together oil, vinegar, salt and pepper. Remove any excess fat and burned drippings from roasting pan; loosen drippings. Add meat juices and the oil-vinegar mixture; stir to blend.

Arrange meat slices, slightly overlapping, in roasting pan; spoon on juices to moisten well. Cover with foil. Before serving, place in moderate oven (350°) 10 minutes, or until heated through. Arrange meat slices on a warm serving platter; top with onions separated into rings.

Quickly heat remaining roasting pan juice mixture; pass as a sauce. Makes 8 servings.

Variation

Roast Lamb with Sweet Onions Follow recipe for the roast veal, substituting 1 (4 lb.) boneless rolled leg of lamb for the veal. Roast until meat thermometer registers 160°, about 35 minutes per pound. The lamb will make about 8 generous servings.

MARINATED LAMB ROAST

4 to 5 lb. presliced square shoulder of lamb	½ tsp. dried oregano
1 medium onion, sliced	1 bay leaf, crushed
1 lemon, sliced	¼ c. salad oil
2 cloves garlic	¼ c. water
1 tblsp. salt	½ c. vinegar
½ tsp. pepper	1 (8 oz.) can tomato sauce
	2 drops Tabasco sauce

Have meatman cut lamb shoulder into 1″ chops with hand saw; then tie together with cord into original shape.

Tuck onion and lemon slices in between chops. Crush garlic into salt; add remaining ingredients; pour over lamb in a large shallow bowl.

Cover and marinate at least 6 hours, or overnight, in refrigerator, turning occasionally.

Roast on rack in shallow pan in moderate oven (325°), allowing 30 minutes per pound. Baste with marinade during last hour of roasting. Cut string to serve. Makes 8 servings.

Note: Try our marinade with a boned and rolled shoulder roast —perfect for rotisseries. Follow range manufacturer's directions. Insert meat thermometer to get correct degree of doneness: 175° for medium, 180° for well done.

BARBECUED LAMB SHANKS

8 lamb shanks	½ tsp. salt
½ c. flour	½ tsp. pepper
1 tsp. salt	1 c. ketchup
½ c. salad oil or shortening	2 tblsp. vinegar
½ c. brown sugar	1 (1 lb.) can tomatoes
2 tsp. dry mustard	

Roll lamb shanks in mixture of flour and 1 tsp. salt. Brown several at a time in salad oil in large Dutch oven or kettle. When browned, remove from kettle and brown other shanks. Pour off all fat.

Meanwhile combine brown sugar, dry mustard, ½ tsp. salt and pepper. Stir in ketchup and vinegar. Pour over lamb shanks in Dutch oven. Then pour tomatoes over.

Cover and bake in moderate oven (350°) 1½ to 2 hours, until meat is tender. Or simmer gently on top of range. Makes 8 servings.

PENNSYLVANIA LIVER PASTE

1 lb. frozen pork liver	1 c. milk
6 slices bacon	2 eggs
1 medium onion	1 tsp. salt
¼ c. flour	½ tsp. pepper

Put liver, bacon and onion through food chopper two or three times, using finest blade. Liver is easier to handle if partially frozen. Blend in remaining ingredients.

Spread mixture in greased (9×5×3″) loaf pan. Bake in moderate oven (325°) about 1 hour and 35 minutes or until done. Makes 1 loaf.

Cool, turn out of pan, wrap, seal, label, date and freeze.

Recommended storage time: 6 to 8 weeks.

To serve, thaw in refrigerator. Makes delicious sandwiches.

Note: You can serve the Liver Paste warm like a meat loaf.

TIMBALLO WITH CHEESE SAUCE

1 lb. spaghetti (break strands in half)
⅓ c. butter
1 lb. pork sausage
1 (4 oz.) can sliced mushrooms, drained
3 tblsp. finely chopped onion
⅓ c. sliced stuffed olives
½ c. grated Parmesan cheese

2 tblsp. chopped parsley
½ tsp. salt
¼ tsp. pepper
2 eggs, well beaten
¼ lb. mozzarella cheese, shredded
¼ c. dry bread crumbs
Cheese Sauce (recipe follows)

Cook spaghetti for 10 minutes in boiling salted water. Drain; toss with butter; coat well.

Sauté sausage until almost done. Pour off all fat except 2 tblsp. Add mushrooms and onion. Sauté in fat until tender.

Toss together spaghetti, sausage mixture, olives, Parmesan cheese, parsley, salt and pepper.

Coat a buttered 9″ spring-form pan with bread crumbs; reserve some for top. Place half the spaghetti mixture in pan; pour eggs evenly over all. Sprinkle with mozzarella cheese; put remaining mixture on top. Sprinkle with remaining crumbs. Cover with foil; bake in moderate oven (375°) 40 minutes. Let stand 5 minutes. Serve with Cheese Sauce. Makes 6 to 8 servings.

Cheese Sauce

2 c. medium cream sauce
¼ c. Parmesan cheese

1 tblsp. chopped parsley

Combine all ingredients. Makes 2 cups.

TWIN SAUSAGE CASSEROLES

1 (6 oz.) can sliced or chopped mushrooms	1 c. chopped green pepper
6 chicken bouillon cubes	½ c. grated Parmesan cheese
1 lb. pork sausage	1 tsp. salt
1 lb. ground beef	½ tsp. marjoram leaves
2 c. chopped celery	⅛ tsp. pepper
	2 c. uncooked rice

Drain mushrooms and add enough water to liquid to make 5 c. Add bouillon cubes and heat to dissolve.

Brown meat and drain off fat and liquid. Combine meat with remaining ingredients except bouillon.

Line 2 (2 qt.) casseroles with aluminum foil. Divide mixture evenly between the 2 casseroles. Pour half of hot bouillon over each casserole. Stir lightly to blend. Cover and bake in moderate oven (350°) 15 minutes. Remove from oven, leave covered, and cool quickly to room temperature. Each casserole makes 4 to 6 servings.

Freeze. When frozen, lift foil from casserole. Wrap each in moisture-vapor-proof freezer paper, seal, label, date and return to freezer.

Recommended storage time: 1 month.

To serve, take package from freezer, remove wrappings and place in casserole. Cover and bake in moderate oven (350°) 1½ hours.

LASAGNE CASSEROLE

8 oz. broad noodles	1 tblsp. instant minced onion
1 tblsp. salad oil	1 tsp. mixed Italian herbs
1 (8 oz.) pkg. heat-and-serve sausages	1 c. drained cottage cheese
	¼ c. grated Parmesan cheese
1 (1 lb.) can tomatoes	1 (6 or 8 oz.) pkg. mozzarella
1 (6 oz.) can tomato paste	cheese, cut in ½″ strips

Cook noodles as directed on package and drain. Return to same saucepan. Toss with salad oil to prevent sticking.

Meanwhile, dice sausages and brown, stirring often, in medium skillet. Stir in tomatoes, tomato paste, onion and herbs. Heat to boiling and simmer, stirring occasionally, 5 minutes.

Layer half the noodles, cottage cheese, Parmesan cheese, tomato mixture and mozzarella cheese in greased 2 qt. casserole. Repeat, trimming the top by crisscrossing mozzarella cheese strips.

Bake in moderate oven (350°) 30 minutes, until cheese is browned. Makes 6 servings.

Poultry

CHICKEN IN PAPRIKA SAUCE

4 lbs. frying chicken pieces	¾ c. dairy sour cream
¼ c. butter or margarine	½ (10½ oz.) can condensed
2 green peppers, cut in large pieces	cream of mushroom soup
	1 tblsp. paprika
10 small white onions, peeled	⅛ tsp. red pepper
4 large tomatoes, cut in wedges or 12 whole cherry tomatoes	2 tsp. salt
	¼ tsp. Worcestershire sauce
	1 to 2 tblsp. cornstarch
4 celery stalks, cut in pieces	2 tblsp. cold water (about)

Brown pieces of chicken in butter in a large skillet or Dutch oven. Add green pepper, onions, tomatoes and celery. Simmer, covered, for 15 minutes.

Combine remaining ingredients, except cornstarch and water, in a small saucepan. Heat just to boiling point over moderate heat, stirring constantly.

Pour sauce over chicken and vegetables. Cover and continue cooking over low heat for about 1 hour, or until chicken is fork-tender. If sauce is thin, thicken with cornstarch dissolved in cold water. Makes 6 to 8 servings.

CHICKEN CURRY

1 (3 to 4 lb.) broiler-fryer, cut in pieces	3 c. chicken broth
	6 tblsp. flour
1 large onion, chopped	1 tsp. to 1 tblsp. curry powder
¼ c. butter	Cooked rice

Drop chicken pieces into boiling salted water to cover. Simmer, covered, until tender. Remove from broth and cool. Strain and reserve broth.

Remove chicken from bones and cut in bite-size pieces.

In a large saucepan, sauté onion in melted butter until clear (do not brown). Add 2 c. strained chicken broth; heat.

Make a thin paste of flour and 1 c. cold broth or water, and slowly add to heated chicken broth, stirring constantly until smooth. Continue cooking and stirring until sauce is of medium thickness.

Place curry powder in a small bowl. Gradually stir in a cup of the thickened broth, then return it to the saucepan. Add chicken and heat.

To serve, spoon chicken curry over rice. Let people help themselves to condiments such as raisins, finely chopped almonds or peanuts, chopped hard-cooked egg, chopped sweet pickles, chutney, chopped fresh tomatoes or sliced green onions. Makes 6 generous servings.

Note: You can double this recipe to make 12 servings.

ARIZONA CHICKEN-STUFFED CREPES

1⅓ c. milk	2 whole chicken breasts,
2 tblsp. butter	cooked and cut in strips
2 eggs, beaten	½ lb. cooked ham, cut in
½ c. sifted flour	strips (1¼ c.)
1 tsp. baking powder	¼ c. canned sweet chili
½ tsp. salt	peppers (cut in strips)
1 pt. dairy sour cream	½ c. grated Gruyère cheese

Heat 1 c. milk and butter in saucepan until butter is melted; cool.

Beat in eggs, then flour, baking powder and salt, sifted together; beat until smooth and well blended.

To bake, lightly grease 4″ or 5″ skillet; heat and pour in 3 tblsp. batter for each crepe; tilt skillet to cover evenly. Cook about 1 minute to brown, flip and brown other side.

Spread one side of all crepes with sour cream (takes about 1 c.); place several strips of chicken, ham and chili peppers on crepes, roll and place in 7×11″ baking dish. Makes 10 crepes.

Wrap, seal, label, date and freeze.

Recommended storage time: 1 month.

To serve, let thaw in refrigerator. Mix ⅓ c. milk with 1 c. sour cream and pour over crepes. Sprinkle with cheese. Bake, uncovered, in moderate oven (350°) 20 minutes, just to melt cheese.

Note: If you do not freeze stuffed crepes, let dish stand in refrigerator up to 24 hours, then bake and serve.

Frozen Crepes Bake crepes, cool, stack, placing foil between each crepe.

Wrap, seal, label, date and freeze.

Recommended storage time: 2 months.

CHICKEN IN BARBECUE SAUCE

1 egg, beaten	2 lemons, thinly sliced
1 c. water	2 onions, thinly sliced
2 stewing hens, cut up	Barbecue Sauce (recipe
2 c. flour (about)	follows)
½ c. fat	

Beat together egg and water. Dip chicken in egg, then shake in flour in plastic bag. Brown all sides in hot fat; cool on rack; do not stack.

Place chicken, skin side up, in large roasting pan; do not stack. Top each piece with half slices lemon and onion. Pour cooled Barbecue Sauce over chicken. Makes 6 to 8 servings.

Cover, seal, label, date and freeze in pan.

Recommended storage time: 3 to 6 months.

To serve, partially thaw chicken in pan at room temperature or in refrigerator overnight. Bake, covered, in moderate oven (350°) about 3 hours, basting occasionally. Remove cover during last ½ hour.

Note: For fryers, bake about 2½ hours.

Barbecue Sauce

4 (6 oz.) cans tomato paste	1 tblsp. vinegar
3 c. water	1 tblsp. salt
1½ c. chopped celery	1 clove garlic, minced
1 c. ketchup	¼ tsp. chili powder
⅓ c. Worcestershire sauce	⅛ tsp. pepper
2 tblsp. brown sugar	⅛ tsp. Tabasco sauce
1½ tblsp. liquid smoke	1 bay leaf, crushed

Combine all ingredients in a large saucepan. Bring to a boil; reduce heat and simmer for 10 minutes. Cool.

RANCH-STYLE CHICKEN

6 tblsp. shortening or cooking oil	1 (8 oz.) can tomato sauce
½ c. flour	1 (1 lb.) can tomatoes
3 tsp. salt	½ c. pitted, sliced ripe olives and juice
¼ tsp. pepper	1 (3½ to 4 oz.) can sliced mushrooms
2 (2 to 3 lb.) frying chickens, cut in serving pieces	1 tsp. salt
1 onion	¼ tsp. mixed Italian herb seasoning
8 sprigs parsley	⅛ tsp. pepper
1 clove garlic	
2 tblsp. olive oil	

Line 2 (12×8×2") baking dishes with aluminum foil. Melt 3 tblsp. shortening in each dish.

Combine flour, salt and pepper in paper bag. Shake chicken pieces to coat with flour. Lightly moisten chicken pieces in melted fat. Arrange in one layer, skin side up in baking dishes. Bake in very hot oven (450°) 30 minutes.

Chop onion, parsley and garlic. Sauté in olive oil. Add tomato sauce, tomatoes, olives, mushrooms and juice, and seasonings. Pour sauce evenly over the 2 dishes of chicken. Cool. Makes 4 to 6 servings.

Cover and place in freezer. When frozen, lift foil from baking dish. Wrap in moisture-vapor-proof freezer paper, seal, label, date and return to freezer.

Recommended storage time: 3 to 6 months.

To serve, take foil package from freezer, remove wrapping and place in baking dish. Bake, uncovered, in moderate oven (350°) 1 hour and 15 minutes.

CHICKEN CASSEROLE

1 stewing chicken, 3½ lbs. or larger	1 c. mayonnaise
1 c. chopped celery	2 tblsp. lemon juice
1 c. chopped walnuts, pecans or almonds	¾ tsp. salt
2 tblsp. minced onion	¼ tsp. pepper
1 (10½ oz.) can condensed cream of chicken soup	Fine buttered bread crumbs or crushed potato chips
	Paprika

Steam chicken until very tender. Remove meat from bones and cut into bite-size pieces. Mix with remainder of ingredients except potato chips and paprika.

Turn chicken mixture into greased 2 qt. casserole. Top with buttered bread crumbs or crushed potato chips. Sprinkle with paprika.

Bake uncovered in moderate oven (350°) until bubbly, about 30 minutes. Makes 6 to 8 servings. (Freeze casserole before or after baking.)

BROILED CHICKEN

2 (2 to 2½ lb.) broiler-fryer   1½ tsp. salt
  chickens   ⅛ tsp. pepper
Italian salad dressing

Cut chickens in halves. Break wing, hip and drumstick joints so chicken will stay flat while cooking. Brush both sides generously with salad dressing. Cover and chill in refrigerator overnight (or 4 to 5 hours).

Season chicken with salt and pepper. Place skin side up on rack in broiling pan.

Broil 7″ from heat 25 minutes, or until lightly browned, basting occasionally with Italian salad dressing. Turn, brush again with salad dressing and continue broiling 30 minutes longer, or until chicken is golden brown. (Chicken is cooked when drumstick cuts easily and no pink color shows.) Makes 4 servings.

TERIYAKI CHICKEN

½ c. soy sauce   1 clove garlic, finely chopped
2 tblsp. oil   1 (2 to 2½ lb.) broiler-fryer
½ c. chopped onion   chicken, cut up
1 tsp. sugar

Combine soy sauce, oil, onion, sugar and garlic. Marinate chicken in this mixture for 2 hours.

Arrange chicken on rack in shallow pan. Brush with marinade. Bake in moderate oven (325°) for 1½ hours, basting occasionally, until tender. Makes 4 servings.

DEEP-PEPPERED PORK—The roast is cooked and carved ahead. When company arrives just reheat in delectable meat juices. Easy and elegant entertaining. Recipe page 161.

SLAW-STUFFED PEPPERS will be the highlight of the buffet table. Crisp "biting" cole slaw tucked into a green pepper shell marinates in a nippy marinade for at least a week. Recipe page 233.

CHICKEN CASSEROLE SUPREME

1 (10½ oz.) can condensed
cream of vegetable soup
1 (14½ oz.) can asparagus
spears
1 (8 oz.) pkg. noodles, cooked
and drained
1⅓ c. cubed, cooked chicken
or 2 (5 oz.) cans boned
chicken

⅓ c. sliced, stuffed green
olives
½ c. corn flake crumbs
1 tblsp. butter

Heat soup blended with liquid drained from asparagus.

Place thick layer of noodles in bottom of a greased 2 qt. casserole. Top with half the chicken, asparagus and olives. Repeat layers ending with noodles. Pour heated soup mixture over noodles.

Top with corn flake crumbs. Dot with butter.

Heat in moderate oven (350°) 20 minutes. Makes 6 to 8 servings.

CHICKEN-CORN CASSEROLE

⅓ c. butter or margarine
⅓ c. flour
¾ tsp. salt
¼ tsp. pepper
½ tsp. celery salt
2 c. milk

2 c. cubed cooked chicken
1 (1 lb.) can cream style corn
¼ c. bread or cracker
crumbs
1 tblsp. butter

Melt butter over low heat. Stir in next 4 ingredients; cook until smooth and bubbly. Remove from heat. Add milk; boil for 1 minute.

Combine sauce, chicken and corn. Pour into 1½ qt. casserole. Top with crumbs; dot with butter.

Bake in moderate oven (350°) 25 to 30 minutes, until browned on top. Makes 6 to 8 servings.

Note: If you don't have cooked chicken in the freezer to use in this dish you can substitute canned chicken.

CHICKEN CRUNCH

½ c. chicken broth or milk
2 (10½ oz.) cans condensed
cream of mushroom soup
3 c. diced cooked chicken
1 (7 oz.) can tuna, drained
and flaked
¼ c. minced onion

1 c. diced celery
1 (5 oz.) can water chestnuts,
thinly sliced
1 (3 oz.) can chow mein
noodles
⅓ c. toasted almonds
(optional)

Blend broth into soup in 2 qt. casserole. Mix in remaining ingredients except almonds.

Bake in slow oven (325°) 40 minutes. Just before serving, sprinkle with almonds. Makes 8 servings.

Variation: Omit water chestnuts and use ⅓ c. more celery.

CHICKEN-NOODLE HOT DISH

4 oz. broad noodles
1 (10½ oz.) can condensed
cream of chicken soup
1 c. milk
1 (5 oz.) can boned chicken,
chopped, or ⅔ c. chopped
cooked chicken

½ c. shredded Cheddar cheese
½ c. pimiento-stuffed olives
½ tsp. salt
½ c. toasted, slivered almonds

Cook noodles in boiling, salted water as directed on package.

Blend together soup and milk. Add chicken and cheese and heat to boiling. Add olives, salt and noodles. Place in greased 1½ qt. casserole. Top with almonds.

Bake in moderate oven (350°) 30 minutes. Makes 6 servings.

CHICKEN FOR SUNDAY DINNER

What to do on Saturday: Cook chicken. You will cut cooking time in half by using a pressure cooker. Electric ones are handy. Assemble casserole of chicken (recipe follows), cover and refrigerate it.

Pressure-cooked Chicken Disjoint and cut up a 5½ lb. (dressed weight) stewing fowl. Place in pressure pan. Add 2 c. water, 4 tsp.

salt, 1 small onion, quartered, 1 small carrot, quartered, 3 celery tops, 1 whole clove and 2 peppercorns. Place lid on pressure pan and secure. Cook at 10 lbs. pressure, 40 to 50 minutes. Reduce pressure and remove cover as manufacturer of pressure pan recommends. Remove chicken, strain broth, cool; remove meat from bones in large pieces. If meat and broth will not be used immediately, cover and refrigerate at once. If you have no pressure pan, simmer chicken until thickest pieces are fork-tender in water to cover. This takes 2½ to 3½ hours. Use broth and meat in Chicken-Noodle Casserole.

CHICKEN-NOODLE CASSEROLE

1 (8 oz.) pkg. broad noodles	¼ c. cold water
3 qts. boiling water	2 (10 oz.) pkgs. frozen peas
1 tblsp. salt	4 to 5 c. cubed cooked
4½ c. chicken broth	chicken
Salt and pepper	1 (3 oz.) can chow mein
½ c. chicken fat (or part	noodles
butter or margarine)	2 cooked carrots (optional)
½ c. flour	

Cook broad noodles 5 minutes in boiling salted water. Drain; cover with paper towel to prevent drying.

Heat broth; season with salt and pepper. Blend fat, flour and cold water. Add to broth, stirring. Boil 2 to 3 minutes.

Pour boiling water over peas to separate them; drain. Reserve ½ c. peas for garnish.

Arrange noodles, peas, chicken and gravy in layers in a 4 qt. greased casserole for buffet service (or covered-dish supper) or in two 2½ qt. casseroles for easy passing at sit-down family meal. Mound peas in center of casserole and cover. Refrigerate overnight.

On Sunday, bake casserole in moderate oven (375°) 40 to 50 minutes or until bubbly hot (15 minutes less for casseroles not refrigerated).

Sprinkle band of chow mein noodles around rim of casserole. Slice carrots on the slant to make flower petal garnish; arrange around peas on casserole. Return to oven and bake 5 minutes. Serve at once. Makes 8 to 10 servings.

CHICKEN NEWBURG

6 tblsp. butter or margarine
2 tblsp. flour
1 tsp. salt
⅛ tsp. nutmeg
Dash red pepper
2 egg yolks (slightly beaten)

1 c. undiluted evaporated milk
1 c. milk
1 tblsp. lemon juice
2 c. diced cooked chicken
6 toast slices

Melt butter in saucepan; blend in flour and seasonings.

Combine egg yolks and milks; stir into flour mixture. Place over medium heat, stirring constantly, until mixture comes to a boil and thickens.

Gently stir in lemon juice and chicken. Serve at once on toast. Makes 6 servings.

Fish

SHRIMP ALMOND

1 (6 to 7 oz.) pkg. shell
  macaroni
1 (3 oz.) can chopped
  mushrooms
⅓ c. slivered almonds
¼ c. butter
1 tblsp. chopped pimiento
2 tblsp. flour
1 tsp. salt

⅛ tsp. pepper
1 (10½ oz.) can condensed
  cream of vegetable soup
2 c. milk
1 lb. shrimp, cooked and
  cleaned
1 c. bread crumbs
3 tblsp. butter, melted

Cook macaroni as directed on package.

Cook mushrooms and almonds in ¼ c. butter about 1 minute. Stir in pimiento, flour and seasonings. Add soup and milk gradually. Cook over medium heat, stirring constantly, until sauce comes to a boil.

Combine macaroni, shrimp and sauce in a greased 2 qt. casserole.

Toss bread crumbs with 3 tblsp. melted butter. Sprinkle over shrimp mixture. Cover and refrigerate.

When preparing meal, bake casserole, uncovered, in moderate oven (350°) 30 minutes. Makes 6 servings.

COMPANY TUNA CASSEROLE

1 (3 oz.) can chow mein
  noodles
1 (10½ oz.) can condensed
  cream of mushroom soup
¼ c. water
1 (6½ oz.) can tuna, drained
  and flaked

1 (1¼ lb.) pkg. salted
  cashews, chopped
1 c. finely chopped celery
¼ c. minced onion
1 tblsp. soy sauce

Combine one-half can noodles with remaining ingredients in greased 1½ qt. casserole. Sprinkle on remaining noodles.

Bake in moderate oven (350°) 40 minutes. Makes 5 servings.

MUSTARD-GLAZED TUNA CUPS

2 (7 oz.) cans tuna, drained
  and flaked
2 eggs, slightly beaten
½ c. milk
¼ c. ketchup
1 tblsp. melted butter
1 c. rolled oats

½ tsp. salt
¼ tsp. pepper
3 tblsp. chopped parsley or
  celery
¼ c. finely chopped onion
Mustard Sauce (recipe follows)

Mix all ingredients. Pour into buttered muffin or custard cups; top with Mustard Sauce.

Bake in moderate oven (350°) 25 minutes. Makes 6 servings.

If you wish to freeze for later use, cool quickly; remove from cups. Wrap individually; label, date and freeze in plastic bags.

Recommended storage time: 4 to 6 weeks.

To serve, put back in cups; bake unthawed and covered in moderate oven (350°) 55 minutes (uncover last 30 minutes).

Mustard Sauce

1½ tblsp. butter
1 tblsp. flour
½ c. chicken broth
1 tsp. prepared mustard

½ tsp. horse-radish
¼ tsp. salt
⅛ tsp. pepper

Melt butter in a small saucepan. Stir in flour. Gradually add chicken broth, stirring constantly, until mixture thickens. Add mustard, horse-radish, salt and pepper. Cook 1 minute.

TUNA TOMATO SAUCE

¼ c. chopped onion
¼ c. chopped green pepper
½ tsp. finely chopped garlic
¼ c. oil
1 (2 lb. 3 oz.) can plum
   tomatoes
1 (6 oz.) can tomato paste
⅔ c. water
1 tsp. salt

½ tsp. oregano
½ tsp. basil
¼ tsp. nutmeg
¼ tsp. pepper
¼ tsp. sugar
1 (7 oz.) can solid pack tuna,
   drained and flaked
1 lb. pasta, cooked and
   drained

Sauté onion, green pepper and garlic in oil until tender. Press tomatoes through sieve. Combine all ingredients except tuna. Bring mixture to boil; simmer for 35 minutes. Add tuna; simmer for 10 minutes. Serve over cooked pasta. Makes 6 to 8 servings.

PARTY CRAB BAKE

6 oz. shell macaroni
1 (8 oz.) pkg. cream cheese
½ c. dairy sour cream
½ c. cottage cheese
¼ c. sliced green onions and
   tops
1 (7½ oz.) can crab meat,
   flaked

2 medium tomatoes, peeled
   and sliced
¼ tsp. salt
1½ c. shredded sharp Cheddar
   cheese

Cook macaroni as directed on package.

Combine cream cheese, sour cream, cottage cheese and onions.

Arrange half of macaroni in bottom of greased 2 qt. casserole. Dip half of cream-cheese mixture by spoonfuls over macaroni. Spread to cover. Top with half of crab meat. Repeat these layers. Top crab meat with sliced tomatoes. Sprinkle with salt and with shredded cheese.

Bake in moderate oven (350°) 30 minutes. Makes 4 to 6 servings.

SALMON POTATO LOAF

1 (1 lb.) can salmon, drained
and flaked
1 c. grated cooked potato
1 c. grated carrot
2 tblsp. finely chopped onion
2 eggs, well beaten

½ c. scalded milk
2 tblsp. melted butter
3 tblsp. lemon juice
1 tsp. salt
Dash pepper

Combine salmon, potato, carrot, onion, eggs, milk, butter, lemon juice, salt and pepper. Toss together lightly.

Turn into a lightly buttered 8½ ×4½ ×2½″ loaf pan. Bake in moderate oven (350°) for 45 minutes or until loaf is set in the center. Makes 4 to 6 servings.

Eggs

SUNDAY-SUPPER DEVILED EGGS

½ c. chopped onion
¼ c. butter or margarine
2 c. precooked rice (or 4 c.
cooked regular rice)
1 tsp. salt
2 c. boiling water
1 (12 oz.) can pork luncheon
meat

⅛ tsp. pepper
3 tblsp. chopped parsley
⅔ c. mayonnaise
2 tblsp. light cream
3 tblsp. ketchup
12 Deviled Egg halves (see
Index)

Sauté onion in melted butter over low heat until golden. Add rice, salt and water. Cover; let stand 5 minutes.

Cut meat into 3 or 4 slices; mash with fork. Add to rice mixture with pepper and parsley.

Blend together mayonnaise, cream and ketchup. Add half this sauce to rice mixture. Spread in bottom of greased shallow baking dish (12×7½″).

With back of spoon make depressions in rice to hold Deviled Egg halves. Spoon remaining sauce over indentations. Put eggs in place. Cover; bake in moderate oven (350°) 20 minutes. Makes 6 servings.

DEVILED EGGS

6 hard-cooked eggs
1 tsp. vinegar
¼ tsp. salt
Dash pepper
½ tsp. prepared mustard
1 tblsp. melted butter or margarine
1½ tblsp. mayonnaise

Cut eggs in halves lengthwise. Remove yolks; put through sieve, or mash with fork.

Add remaining ingredients to yolks; whip until smooth and fluffy. Heap into white halves. Crisscross tops with tines of fork. Refrigerate. Makes 12 halves.

Variations: Follow egg-yolk recipe above and add 1½ to 2 tblsp. of cream or grated cheese, deviled or chopped ham, mashed cooked chicken livers or crisp bacon bits. Or, put bits of any of these in hollow of egg white halves before adding yolk mixture.

Cheese

NEAPOLITAN LASAGNA

Sauce

⅓ c. oil
2 tblsp. finely chopped onion
½ tsp. minced garlic
1 (2 lb. 3 oz.) can plum tomatoes, sieved
2 beef bouillon cubes
1 c. water
1 (6 oz.) can tomato paste
½ bay leaf
2 whole cloves
½ tsp. basil
½ tsp. oregano
½ tsp. salt
¼ tsp. pepper
¼ tsp. sugar

Filling

1 lb. cream-style cottage cheese
1 (9 oz.) pkg. frozen spinach, cooked, drained and chopped
2 eggs, slightly beaten
½ c. grated Parmesan cheese
¼ tsp. salt
¼ tsp. nutmeg
⅛ tsp. pepper
1 (1 lb.) pkg. lasagna noodles, cooked and drained
¼ lb. mozzarella cheese, shredded
Grated Parmesan cheese

Sauté onion and garlic in oil. Stir in remaining sauce ingredients. Bring to boil; simmer 1 hour. Stir occasionally. Remove bay leaf and cloves.

Blend together cottage cheese and next six ingredients. Set aside.

Spread 1 c. sauce in 13×9×2″ baking dish. Lay ⅓ of noodles in single layer on top. Spread with sauce; spoon on ½ spinach mixture; sprinkle with ⅓ of mozzarella cheese. Repeat layers, topping with sauce. Add remaining noodles; cover with remaining sauce. Sprinkle with mozzarella and Parmesan cheeses. Cover loosely with foil. Bake in moderate oven (350°) 40 minutes. Makes 12 servings.

DOUBLE CHEESE BAKE

1 c. elbow macaroni	1 tblsp. minced onion
¼ c. butter	1 tblsp. chopped parsley
1 c. soft bread crumbs	¼ tsp. salt
1 c. shredded Cheddar cheese	⅛ tsp. pepper
½ c. shredded Swiss cheese	1½ c. milk, scalded
½ c. slivered ham	Paprika
3 eggs, well beaten	

Cook macaroni according to package directions; drain. Add butter; toss until coated.

Add remaining ingredients except paprika; mix well. Turn into greased 2 qt. casserole. Sprinkle with paprika. Bake in moderate oven (325°) 40 to 45 minutes. Makes 6 servings.

Section 2
Vegetables, Salads, Salad Dressings, Relishes, Sauces

These recipes for vegetables, salads, dressings, relishes and sauces were chosen with the busy cook in mind. They'll remove the last-minute pressure.

Many of the vegetable combinations can be prepared the day before and refrigerated until ready to be cooked the next day. We feature recipes for just about every vegetable in the garden patch or supermarket. Examples: Spanish Lima Beans, a tasty and colorful combination of limas and canned tomatoes; Potato Cheese Balls, coated with golden crumbs with a hidden nugget of melted cheese in the center, pretty enough for company; delicious short-cut recipes for home-baked beans. Then for frosty winter days, a potpourri of hearty vegetable chowders that taste garden fresh.

Most salads don't take kindly to freezing, but we have several that do—they actually mellow in flavor when frozen. You'll serve the Frozen Sherbet Salad proudly when company drops in unexpectedly. We also have an exciting batch of overnighters—salads that improve in flavor and texture when made the day before, such as Sauerkraut Slaw and Overnight Fruit Salad.

We star Main Dish Salads, too—an Onion-Macaroni with a tangy sour cream dressing and a unique Chicken Salad brightened with nuts, green grapes and mandarin orange sections.

To dress up the salads, we include a grand collection of dressings—blue cheese, orange honey, fruit juice French and others, plain and fancy.

Then for a little touch that adds a lot, there's a great variety of relishes. Some add sparkle to a main dish, others are delicious serve-alongs with buffet meals. And don't miss our fruit honeys to spread on hot breads and lift a meal out of the ordinary.

NEW-STYLE CREAMED ASPARAGUS

1 (10½ oz.) can condensed
cream of mushroom soup
½ c. milk
2 (1 lb.) cans whole asparagus,
drained

⅔ c. cheese-cracker crumbs
1 tblsp. butter

Blend together soup and milk in saucepan. Heat to boiling.

Place half of asparagus in bottom of greased 1½ qt. casserole. Top with half of soup and cracker crumbs. Repeat layers. Dot with butter.

Bake in moderate oven (350°) 20 minutes. Makes 6 to 8 servings.

ITALIAN GREEN BEANS WITH SOUR CREAM

3 (9 oz.) pkgs. frozen Italian
green beans
1 (3½ oz.) can mushroom
pieces
¼ c. sliced green onion

2 tblsp. butter or margarine
2 tblsp. flour
½ tsp. salt
1 c. dairy sour cream
Pimiento (optional)

Cook green beans as directed on package; drain.

Drain mushrooms, reserving liquid.

Cook mushrooms and onion in melted butter 1 minute. Stir in flour and salt. Add mushroom liquid and sour cream and heat to boiling, but do not boil.

Add cream mixture to green beans and toss gently. Serve hot, garnished with pimiento strips. Makes 8 servings.

Note: You can prepare this dish in advance. Store it in refrigerator in a 2 qt. casserole. Heat, covered, in moderate oven (350°) just until hot, about 20 to 30 minutes. You can substitute regular green beans for the broad Italian ones.

BROCCOLI CASSEROLE

1 (12 oz.) pkg. frozen broccoli
1 (10½ oz.) can condensed
cream of celery soup
⅔ c. shredded Cheddar cheese

2 slices bread
2 tblsp. butter or margarine,
melted

Cook broccoli as directed on package until barely tender. Place in greased 1 qt. casserole. Top with soup, then cheese. Quickly tear bread in tiny pieces, toss in melted butter and sprinkle over top.

Bake in moderate oven (350°) 30 minutes. Makes 4 to 5 servings.

Variations: Substitute green beans, lima beans, cauliflower or asparagus for broccoli.

CABBAGE CASSEROLE

1 medium head cabbage, shredded	½ c. milk
	⅓ c. buttered bread crumbs
2 c. diced ham	
1 (10½ oz.) can condensed cream of mushroom soup	

Steam cabbage in covered saucepan with small amount of water until tender-crisp. Drain if necessary.

Arrange cabbage and ham in alternate layers in greased 2 qt. casserole.

Blend soup and milk; pour over over cabbage-ham mixture. Top with crumbs.

Bake in moderate oven (350°) 30 minutes. Makes 8 servings.

BAKED LIMA BEANS

3 (10 oz.) pkgs. frozen lima beans	¾ c. ketchup
	½ c. water
6 bacon slices, cut in ½″ pieces	2 tblsp. prepared mustard
	¾ tsp. salt
½ c. chopped onion	¾ tsp. smoke salt
⅔ c. molasses	¼ tsp. pepper

Cook beans as directed on package until barely tender; drain.

Pan-fry bacon in skillet until partly cooked. Add onion and continue cooking until bacon is browned.

Mix together molasses, ketchup, water, mustard, salts and pepper in a 2 qt. casserole. Stir in beans, bacon and onion with bacon drippings.

Bake in moderate oven (350°) 1 hour. Makes 8 servings.

Note: The beans are quite sweet. Reduce amount of molasses if you want less sweetening. For a peppy note, add 1 tblsp. prepared horse-radish with the seasonings.

SPANISH LIMAS

1 medium onion, chopped
1 green pepper, chopped
2 tblsp. butter or margarine
1 c. cooked or canned tomatoes
1 tsp. Worcestershire sauce
1 tsp. salt

¼ tsp. pepper
⅛ tsp. cayenne pepper
2 c. cooked frozen or canned
   lima beans
1½ c. grated process American
   cheese

Fry onion and pepper slowly in butter until golden. Add tomatoes; simmer 10 minutes. Add seasonings and well-drained beans.

Alternate layers of bean mixture and cheese in greased 1 qt. casserole.

Bake in moderate oven (350°) 30 minutes. Makes 6 servings.

CURRIED ONIONS

2 (1 lb.) cans onions, drained
1 (10½ oz.) can condensed
   cream of chicken soup
2 tblsp. mayonnaise
¼ tsp. curry powder

½ c. cracker crumbs
2 tblsp. butter or margarine,
   melted
2 tblsp. parsley flakes

Place onions in greased 1½ qt. casserole. Combine soup, mayonnaise and curry powder. Spoon over onions. Top with crumbs tossed in butter and parsley.

Bake in moderate oven (375°) until hot and bubbly, about 30 minutes. Makes 8 servings.

POTATO AND MUSHROOM CASSEROLE

1 (1½ lb.) pkg. frozen whole
   potatoes
1 (10½ oz.) can condensed
   cream of mushroom soup
⅓ c. milk
1 (4 oz.) can sliced mushrooms,
   drained

1 tblsp. chopped parsley
1½ tsp. instant minced onion
½ c. shredded Cheddar cheese
Paprika

Cook potatoes according to package directions until almost tender. Put potatoes in 1½ qt. casserole.

Combine soup and milk. Stir in next 3 ingredients. Pour over potatoes; toss gently. Top with cheese. Sprinkle with paprika.

Bake in hot oven (400°) for 15 minutes. Makes 6 servings.

POTATO-CHEESE BALLS

½ pkg. instant mashed potatoes	2 tblsp. butter or margarine
6 (½") cubes process America cheese	½ c. corn flake crumbs

Prepare potatoes as directed on package. Divide into 6 equal portions. Put a cheese cube in each portion of potatoes and form ball around it.

Melt butter in skillet. Roll potato balls in butter, then in crumbs. Bake in skillet or greased shallow pan in hot oven (400°) 15 minutes, or until browned. Makes 6 servings.

Note: You can get potato balls ready for baking and refrigerate them. Bake 5 minutes longer.

Church-Supper Potatoes   A group of Minnesota church women use packaged instant mashed potatoes, making them as directed on package. They heap the fluffy potatoes in an electric roaster pan, lightly oiled, and keep them warm. They serve the potatoes from the roaster, or from the chafing dishes and casseroles with candle warmers. By experience they found that people like their potatoes piping hot. The economy of using the packaged kind comes in avoiding the waste of leftovers. More potatoes may be fixed in a jiffy if the supply runs low—just enough to satisfy appetites.

BAKED CREAMED POTATOES

1 c. dairy sour cream	⅛ tsp. pepper
½ c. milk	5 c. sliced cooked potatoes
1 tblsp. instant minced onion	(5 or 6 medium potatoes)
1 tsp. instant parsley flakes	½ c. grated Cheddar cheese
1 tsp. salt	

Mix together sour cream, milk, onion, parsley, salt and pepper. Place half the potatoes in a greased baking dish (10×6×1½"). Top with half the sauce. Repeat layers. Sprinkle cheese over the top.

Bake in moderate oven (350°) 20 to 25 minutes. Makes 6 servings.

TWO-STEP POTATOES

12 medium red potatoes
1 tsp. salt
¼ tsp. pepper
½ tsp. onion or garlic salt

½ lb. mild Cheddar cheese,
grated
1 c. heavy cream

Cook unpeeled potatoes in water until almost tender, but still firm. Cool, peel and grate, using wide grater (makes about 4½ c.).

Grease baking dish (9×9×1½″) with butter; cover bottom with half the potatoes. Sprinkle with half the seasonings; top with half the cheese. Repeat for top layer.

Pour cream over top. Bake in moderate oven (350°) until browned, about 1 hour. Makes 6 servings.

SWEET POTATO BONBONS

3 lbs. sweet potatoes, peeled
and cooked
¼ c. butter
½ c. brown sugar
1 tsp. salt

½ tsp. grated orange rind
6 marshmallows, halved
4 c. corn flakes, crushed
⅓ c. melted butter
12 pecan halves

Mash sweet potatoes until light and fluffy. Beat in butter, sugar, salt and orange rind. Let cool. Divide into 12 portions. Press potatoes around each marshmallow half, being careful to keep marshmallow in center. Shape into ovals.

Coat each with melted butter. Roll in crushed corn flakes, top with pecan half and place on lightly greased baking sheet. Bake in very hot oven (450°) for 7 to 8 minutes. Serves 6 to 8.

BAKED WHOLE TOMATOES

6 medium tomatoes
1 tsp. salt
⅛ tsp. pepper

¾ c. salad dressing
3 tblsp. grated sharp process
cheese

Cut stem ends from tomatoes. Cut thin slice from top of each. Place tomatoes in shallow pan; make a cross about ½″ deep in top of each.

Sprinkle tomatoes with salt and pepper; spread with salad dressing and sprinkle with cheese.

Bake in moderate oven (375°) until tomato is thoroughly heated, about 20 minutes. Makes 6 servings.

BAKED GREEN TOMATOES

8 medium green tomatoes	⅛ tsp. pepper
1 c. small bread cubes, toasted	3 tblsp. butter or margarine
1½ tsp. salt	⅓ c. grated Parmesan cheese

Cut tomatoes a little under ½" in thickness and arrange half of them in a single layer in greased baking dish. Scatter on half the bread cubes, salt and pepper; dot with half of the butter. Repeat, making a second layer. Sprinkle cheese on top.

Bake uncovered in moderate oven (350°) until tender, 45 to 50 minutes. Makes 6 servings.

MIXED VEGETABLES MORNAY

2 (10 oz.) pkgs. frozen mixed vegetables	½ c. shredded sharp Cheddar cheese
3 tblsp. butter or margarine	½ c. grated Parmesan cheese
3 tblsp. flour	2 slices bread, torn in tiny pieces
1½ c. milk	
½ tsp. salt	2 tblsp. butter or margarine, melted
⅛ tsp. pepper	

Cook vegetables as directed on package until barely tender.

Melt 3 tblsp. butter; blend in flour (do not brown). Add milk and cook over low heat, stirring constantly, until mixture thickens. Add seasonings and cheese, stirring until cheese melts.

Place drained vegetables in greased 1½ qt. shallow casserole. Cover with sauce. Toss bread in remaining butter and scatter on top.

Bake in very hot oven (450°) about 10 minutes, or until browned. Makes 6 to 8 servings.

HAVE A HEAD START WITH CANNED BAKED BEANS

Some of the great American dishes depend on long, slow cooking to maintain their fame. Boston Baked Beans is a classic example.

The New England woman who gave us her short-cut recipe for baking the brown beauties often serves them to company. Frequently a guest exclaims, "One reason we like to come to your house for bean suppers is that you bake beans the good, old-fashioned way." Clever hostess that she is, she keeps the secret—she doesn't want to dampen the enthusiasm of her guests.

She neither soaks the beans overnight nor cooks them slowly for eight hours. Here's how she does it.

BOSTON BAKED BEANS

2 (1 lb. 11 oz.) jars New
   England-style baked beans
½ c. maple blended syrup, or
   maple syrup

Combine beans and syrup in 2 qt. bean pot or casserole. Bake in moderate oven (325°) 3 hours. Makes 8 servings.

Note: To cut the baking time in two, heat the beans, with syrup added, to the boiling point before pouring into the bean pot. If you have a freezer, double or triple this recipe; bake and freeze the extra supply of beans.

PRESSURE-COOKER BAKED BEANS

1 lb. navy beans	3 tblsp. ketchup
Water	½ c. chopped onion
⅓ lb. bacon, cut in pieces	1½ tsp. salt
3 tblsp. brown sugar	½ tsp. prepared mustard
3 tblsp. molasses	2 c. water

Wash and sort beans. Soak overnight in water to cover. Rinse and drain beans.

Sauté bacon in 4-qt. pressure cooker. Add remaining ingredients. Close cover securely. Cook beans at 15 lbs. pressure (following manufacturer's directions for your pressure cooker) for 50 minutes. Let pressure drop of own accord. Makes about 6 servings.

Oven Method: Soak beans (as above) overnight. Rinse and drain. Add enough water to cover beans. Bring to a boil; reduce heat. Cook for 20 minutes.

Put beans and liquid in a 2 qt. bean pot or casserole. Add remaining ingredients. Cover. Bake in slow oven (300°) for 6 to 8 hours, adding more water as needed to keep beans moist. Uncover for last 30 minutes of baking. Beans should be tender and not mushy. Makes 6 servings.

CORN CHOWDER

4 bacon slices, chopped	¼ tsp. pepper
2 tblsp. instant minced onion	1 (10½ oz.) can condensed
½ (9 oz.) pkg. quick	tomato soup
hash-brown potatoes	1 (1 lb. 1 oz.) can
4½ c. water	whole kernel corn
1 tsp. salt	1 (6 oz.) can evaporated milk

Cook bacon in large saucepan until crisp. Pour off excess fat. Add onion, potatoes, water and seasonings. Bring to a boil; simmer until potatoes are tender, 15 to 20 minutes.

Add soup and corn; simmer a few minutes. Stir in milk and heat. Makes 8 servings.

Variation: It takes longer to make this chowder with raw onions and potatoes. Cook bacon and 2 medium onions, chopped, until bacon is crisp; drain off excess fat; add 3 medium potatoes (3 c.), peeled and cubed, 3 c. water; add salt and cook until potatoes are tender. Add tomato soup and corn, simmer a few minutes, stir in the milk and heat.

PASTA AND BEAN SOUP

1 lb. dry Great Northern beans	1 (1 lb.) can stewed tomatoes
2 qts. water	½ bay leaf
2½ tsp. salt	½ tsp. oregano
1 large whole carrot	½ tsp. salt
6 strips bacon	¼ tsp. pepper
½ c. chopped onion	¼ c. water
½ c. chopped celery	1 c. ditalini or small elbow
1 small clove garlic, minced	macaroni

Soak beans 8 hours or overnight. Rinse and drain. Combine beans, water, salt and carrot; simmer in a 6 qt. pot 2 hours or until beans are tender.

Fry bacon until crisp. Remove bacon. Reserve ¼ c. bacon drippings. Add onion, celery and garlic. Sauté. Stir in tomatoes, bay leaf, oregano, salt, pepper and ¼ c. water. Bring to a boil; simmer 30 minutes. Remove bay leaf.

Cook macaroni according to package directions. Drain.

Purée half of the beans. Cube carrot. Crumble bacon. Combine all ingredients and heat through before serving. Makes 3½ qts.

Salads

FARM-FAVORITE SALADS They brighten country meals Good cooks know that molded salads with two layers of different colors are decorative on the table. Clever short-cut cooks are on the look-out for salads that make their own layers as they chill. A knowledge of fruits and foods that float and those that sink in gelatin mixtures helps achieve the layered effects.

Examples of fine floaters are: marshmallows, sliced bananas, grapefruit sections, canned mandarin oranges, raspberries, strawberry halves, broken nuts, fresh peaches and pears, and diced apples.

Among the dependable sinkers are: canned apricots, pineapple, peaches, pears, orange sections, grapes, prunes and plums.

The size of the pan or mold used affects the top layering. If it is deep, rather than shallow with large surface, the top has the best chance of becoming an over-all layer.

The following salads make their own two-tone effects.

FROZEN CRANBERRY SALAD

1 (1 lb.) can jellied cranberry sauce	1 tblsp. lemon juice
1 (8¾ oz.) can crushed pineapple	1 c. heavy cream, whipped
1 c. miniature marshmallows	¼ c. mayonnaise
	¼ c. confectioners sugar

Combine cranberry sauce, pineapple, marshmallows and lemon juice. Spread in bottom of ice-cube tray.

Combine whipped cream, mayonnaise and sugar. Spread over cranberry mixture. Freeze. Cut in squares and serve on lettuce. Makes 6 servings.

ORANGE-MARSHMALLOW SALAD

1 (3 oz.) pkg. orange flavor gelatin	2 (11 oz.) cans mandarin oranges
1 (3 oz.) pkg. lemon flavor gelatin	1 (13 oz.) can pineapple tidbits
2 c. boiling water	2 c. miniature marshmallows

Mix gelatins and dissolve in boiling water. Drain oranges and pineapple. Add cold water to orange and pineapple syrups to make 2 cups. Stir into gelatin mixture.

Add orange segments, pineapple and marshmallows. Pour into a shallow pan (9×9×2″) and chill until firm. Makes 12 servings.

SPRING-FLING FRUIT SALAD

1 (12 oz.) can apple juice	1 (1 lb.) can pear halves,
1 (3 oz.) pkg. lemon flavor	drained
gelatin	2 medium bananas, sliced

Heat 1 c. apple juice to boiling. Dissolve gelatin in hot liquid. Add water to remaining juice to make 1 c. Add to gelatin mixture. Arrange pear halves in bottom of loaf pan (9×5×3″). Add bananas to gelatin and pour over pears. Chill. Makes 6 servings.

Note: This makes a white-topped or layered salad with the bananas on top. You can chill salad more quickly in an 8″ square pan, but then the bananas will not completely cover the top.

RASPBERRY-APPLESAUCE SALAD

2 c. thick, smooth applesauce or	1 tsp. grated orange rind
1 (1 lb. 1 oz.) can applesauce	3 tblsp. orange juice
1 (3 oz.) pkg. raspberry flavor	1 (7 oz.) bottle lemon-lime
gelatin	carbonated beverage

Heat applesauce to boiling. Dissolve gelatin in hot applesauce. Add remaining ingredients. Chill until firm. Makes 6 servings.

FROZEN SHERBET SALAD

1 (6 oz.) pkg. or 2 (3 oz.)	1 c. hot water
pkgs. raspberry flavor gelatin	1 c. cold fruit juice
2 c. hot water	1 (13½ oz.) can pineapple
1 pt. raspberry flavor milk	tidbits, drained
sherbet	Greens
1 (3 oz.) pkg. lime flavor	
gelatin	

Dissolve raspberry gelatin in hot water. Add sherbet; stir until melted (may be necessary to heat slightly). Pour into 2 qt. mold; freeze.

The day you serve the salad, dissolve lime gelatin in hot water;

add juice and tidbits. Pour over frozen layer; refrigerate (will set in about 30 minutes). Unmold on greens. Makes 8 to 12 servings.

Note: You can freeze the sherbet mixture in paper liners in muffin-pan cups. When frozen, empty into plastic bags and store in freezer. Serve as dessert with a fluff of whipped cream.

Variations

Lime Lemon-Orange Combine lime gelatin and lemon sherbet; use orange gelatin for second layer, adding 1 c. fresh or 1 (11 oz.) can mandarin orange sections, drained.

Lime-Lime Combine lime gelatin and lime sherbet; use lime gelatin for second layer, adding 1 c. fresh or 1 (1 lb.) can grapefruit sections, drained.

Lemon Lemon-Cherry Combine lemon gelatin and lemon sherbet; use cherry gelatin for second layer, adding 1 (1 lb. 1 oz.) jar dark, sweet cherries, drained.

Orange Orange-Strawberry Combine orange gelatin and orange sherbet; use strawberry flavor gelatin for second layer, adding 1 (10½ oz.) pkg. frozen strawberries, thawed and drained.

GREEN GAGE PLUM SALAD

1 (1 lb. 4 oz.) can green gage plums	½ tsp. salt
1 (3 oz.) pkg. lemon flavor gelatin	¾ c. slivered toasted almonds
Juice of 1 lemon	Crisp lettuce cups
	Salad dressing

Drain juice from plums; add water to make 2 c. liquid. Heat to boiling, and pour over gelatin. Add lemon juice and salt; stir to dissolve. Cool until thickened.

Pour 2 tblsp. gelatin mixture into 6 baking cups or individual molds. Chill quickly until firm.

Pit and chop plums. Fold with almonds into remaining gelatin. Spoon over clear gelatin in molds. Chill until firm.

Serve in lettuce cups with dressing. Makes 6 servings.

MINT MIST

1 (20 oz.) can crushed pineapple	⅓ c. mint flavored apple jelly
1 pkg. unflavored gelatin	1 c. heavy cream, whipped

Drain pineapple, reserving juice.

Soften gelatin in ½ c. reserved pineapple juice. Place over low heat, stirring constantly, until gelatin is dissolved. Remove from heat; add jelly and stir until melted. Add pineapple and rest of juice.

Chill until thick and syrupy. Fold cream into gelatin mixture. Turn into a lightly oiled 1 qt. mold. Chill until set. Makes 6 servings.

RUSSIAN CREAM MOLD

1 (3 oz.) pkg. lemon flavor
  gelatin
1 c. boiling water
1 c. sour cream

1 (1 lb.) can peaches, drained
  and diced
⅓ c. flaked coconut
1 c. sliced strawberries

Dissolve gelatin in boiling water. Chill until thick and syrupy. Fold in sour cream and remaining ingredients. Turn into lightly oiled 1 qt. mold. Chill until set. Makes 4 to 6 servings.

MOLDED FRUIT MEDLEY

2 (3 oz.) pkgs. lemon flavor
  gelatin
2 c. boiling water
1 c. cold water
1 (9 oz.) can crushed pineapple
⅓ c. lemon juice
¼ c. sugar

2 tblsp. cornstarch
2 eggs, beaten
1 c. heavy cream, whipped
1 (1 lb. 14 oz.) can fruit
  cocktail, drained
12 marshmallows, cut in
  quarters

Dissolve gelatin in boiling water. Stir in cold water. Chill until thick and syrupy.

Meanwhile, drain pineapple, reserving juice. Combine pineapple juice, lemon juice, sugar and cornstarch in a small saucepan. Cook over medium heat, stirring constantly, until mixture thickens. Stir some of the hot mixture into the eggs; then gradually stir into remaining hot mixture. Cook, stirring for 1 minute. Remove; let cool.

Whip syrupy gelatin until light and fluffy. Fold in cooled custard and cream. Add fruit cocktail, marshmallows and pineapple.

Turn into a lightly oiled 10 c. mold. Chill until set. Makes 12 to 15 servings.

WHIPPED STRAWBERRY DELIGHT

1 (9 oz.) can crushed pineapple
1 (3 oz.) pkg. strawberry flavor
  gelatin
1 c. boiling water

1 pkg. whipped topping mix
½ c. milk
⅔ c. chopped nuts

Drain pineapple, reserving juice. Add enough cold water to juice to make 1 c.

Dissolve gelatin in boiling water. Stir in juice and water. Chill until thick and syrupy.

Whip topping mix with milk until soft peaks form.

Whip gelatin until fluffy. Beat in whipped topping. Add pineapple and nuts. Turn into a lightly oiled 5 c. mold. Chill until set. Makes 4 to 6 servings.

BLUEBERRY LIME IMPERIAL

1½ c. reconstituted frozen
  limeade
1 (3 oz.) pkg. lime flavor
  gelatin

1 c. heavy cream, whipped
1 c. frozen blueberries, thawed
  and drained

Bring 1 c. limeade to a boil. Dissolve gelatin in hot limeade. Stir in remaining ½ c. limeade. Chill until thick and syrupy.

Beat with electric mixer until light and fluffy. Fold in cream and blueberries.

Turn into a lightly oiled 5 c. mold. Chill until set. Makes 4 to 6 servings.

APRICOT SALAD

2 (12 oz.) cans apricot nectar
  (3 c.)
1 (6 oz.) pkg. or 2 (3 oz.)
  pkgs. lemon flavor gelatin
¼ c. lemon juice

1 (8¾ oz.) can crushed
  pineapple, drained
2 bananas, diced
Lettuce

Heat nectar to boiling. Add to gelatin and stir until dissolved. Add remaining ingredients. Chill until firm. Serve on lettuce. Makes 8 to 10 servings.

MOLDED CRANBERRY-RELISH SALAD

2 c. hot water
1 (6 oz.) pkg. or 2 (3 oz.)
  pkgs. lemon flavor gelatin
1½ c. cold water

3 c. Cranberry Relish
  (see Index)
1 c. chopped walnuts
1 c. chopped celery

Pour boiling water over gelatin; stir to dissolve. Add cold water and Cranberry Relish.

Chill until mixture starts to thicken. Fold in walnuts and celery. Chill in a 2 qt. mold until set. Makes 6 to 8 servings.

OVERNIGHT FRUIT SALAD

1 (1 lb. 13 oz.) can fruit
  cocktail, drained
2 c. miniature marshmallows

1 c. dairy sour cream
Lettuce
½ c. coarsely chopped nuts

Combine the fruit cocktail, marshmallows and cream. Cover and chill overnight. Serve on crisp lettuce. Sprinkle with nuts just before serving. Makes 6 servings.

AUTUMN FRUIT SALAD

2 (3 oz.) pkgs. lemon flavor
  gelatin
2 c. hot water
1½ c. cold water
1 (8 oz.) can crushed
  pineapple, undrained

1 (1 lb.) can whole cranberry
  sauce, chilled
2 apples, cut in small pieces
1 c. diced celery (optional)
Greens
Mayonnaise

Dissolve gelatin in hot water. Add cold water and pineapple; chill.

When mixture starts to thicken, add cranberry sauce, apples and celery. Pour into pan (12×7½"). Chill until firm. Serve on greens, topped with mayonnaise. Makes 8 to 10 servings.

WALDORF VARIATION SALAD

4 oranges, peeled and cut into
   sections
4 unpared red apples, cut into
   wedges
1 c. sliced celery

1 (13½ oz.) can pineapple
   chunks, drained
1 (6 oz.) can frozen lemonade,
   slightly thawed

Toss all ingredients. Chill well. Makes about 8 servings.

SUNSHINE FRUIT SALAD

1 (1 lb.) can grapefruit
   segments
1 (11 oz.) can mandarin
   oranges
1 (3 oz.) pkg. lemon flavor
   gelatin

1 c. Tokay or green grapes,
   halved and seeded, or seedless
   green grapes

Drain grapefruit and oranges. Add water to fruit syrups to make
2 c. Heat 1 c. syrup mixture to boiling.

Dissolve gelatin in hot syrup. Add cold syrup mixture and the
fruit.

Pour into pan (8×8×2″). Chill until set. Makes 9 servings.

Garnish for Fruit Salads Crush peanut brittle and sprinkle over
salads.

MANDARIN ORANGE SALAD

1 (11 oz.) can mandarin
   oranges, drained
1 (13½ oz.) can pineapple
   tidbits, drained
1 c. miniature marshmallows

½ c. flaked or shredded coconut
⅓ c. maraschino cherries
1 c. dairy sour cream
Lettuce

Mix all the ingredients. Chill about 2 hours. Serve in lettuce
cups. Pretty garnished with extra cherries. Makes 6 servings.

JEWELED SALAD EGG

1 (1 lb. 15 oz.) can apricots
1 (1 lb. 15 oz.) can sliced
  pineapple
2 (3 oz.) pkgs. orange flavor
  gelatin
2 c. boiling water

1 c. orange juice
1 tblsp. lemon juice
½ c. chopped nuts
Fluffy Fruit Dressing (recipe
  follows)
Emerald Grass (recipe follows)

Drain apricots and pineapple; combine fruit syrups and reserve 1 c. for the dressing. Dice fruit.

Dissolve gelatin in boiling water. Add orange and lemon juices. Chill until mixture begins to thicken. Fold in fruits and nuts. Pour into lightly oiled 1½ qt. melon mold or a heat-resistant 6-cup glass bowl. Chill salad until firm.

Unmold onto shallow platter. Decorate with Fluffy Fruit Dressing piped through a cake decorator tube and surround with Emerald Grass. Makes 8 to 10 servings.

Fluffy Fruit Dressing

¼ c. sugar
2 tblsp. cornstarch
1 c. reserved pineapple and
  apricot juice

1 egg, slightly beaten
2 tblsp. butter
1 c. heavy cream, stiffly whipped

Combine sugar and cornstarch in a 1 qt. saucepan. Gradually stir in reserved pineapple and apricot juice, egg and butter. Cook over medium heat, stirring constantly, until mixture is thickened.

Cool well. Beat cornstarch mixture until smooth. Fold into whipped cream. Makes 3½ cups.

Emerald Grass

2 (3 oz.) pkgs. lime flavor
  gelatin

2 c. boiling water
1 c. cold water

Dissolve gelatin in boiling water. Stir in cold water. Pour into a 8×8×2″ cake pan. Chill until firm, then put through a ricer or flake with a fork.

PINEAPPLE-CHEESE MOLD

1 (3 oz.) pkg. lime flavor gelatin
1 c. boiling water
1 c. evaporated milk
1 c. cottage cheese
1 (1 lb. 4½ oz.) can crushed
pineapple, well drained

½ c. mayonnaise
¼ c. chopped celery
¼ c. chopped nuts (optional)

Dissolve gelatin in water. Stir in remaining ingredients and pour into 1½ qt. mold; chill until firm. Makes 8 servings.

OLIVE WREATH MOLD

1 (3 oz.) pkg. lime flavor
gelatin
1 c. boiling water
⅔ c. cold water
2 tblsp. lemon juice
1 c. heavy cream, whipped
⅓ c. sliced stuffed olives
1 (8 oz.) can crushed pineapple,
drained

½ c. shredded American cheese
½ pimiento, chopped
½ c. finely chopped celery
½ c. chopped walnuts
½ tsp. salt
24 slices of stuffed olives

Dissolve gelatin in boiling water. Add cold water and lemon juice. Chill until syrupy. Stir in whipped cream; fold in the ⅓ c. sliced olives, pineapple, cheese, pimiento, celery, walnuts, salt.

Arrange the 24 olive slices in a circle around the bottom of an oiled 9" ring mold. Pour mixture into mold. Chill until firm. Makes 8 servings.

OVERNIGHT BEAN SALAD

1 (1 lb.) can French-cut green
beans, drained
1 (1 lb.) can wax beans, drained
1 (1 lb.) can kidney beans,
drained
½ c. chopped green pepper
½ c. chopped onion

½ c. salad oil
½ c. vinegar
¾ c. sugar
1 tsp. salt
½ tsp. pepper
Lettuce

Combine beans, green pepper and onion. Blend together remaining ingredients except lettuce. Pour over bean mixture.

Chill in refrigerator overnight or at least 6 hours. Serve in lettuce cups. Makes 8 to 10 servings.

Variations: Omit green pepper, salad oil, vinegar and sugar and add ½ c. sweet pickle relish, 1 tsp. celery seeds and 1 c. mayonnaise. When green onions are in season, use them sliced, instead of chopped onion.

CAROLINA AUTUMN SALAD

1 c. chopped cabbage	¼ tsp. salt
1 c. chopped celery	¼ c. mayonnaise or salad
1 large unpeeled red apple,	dressing
diced	Lettuce
½ c. seedless raisins	

Combine all ingredients. Serve in lettuce cups or on green cabbage leaves. Makes 4 servings.

Country-style Cucumber Salad Peel cucumbers and slice thin. Cover with cold, salted water (1 tsp. salt to 1 c. water). Let stand 10 to 20 minutes; drain and pour over French dressing with celery seeds added (¾ tsp. to ½ c. French dressing). Snip parsley with scissors and scatter over the cucumbers for a cool-looking garnish.

BEET-RELISH SALAD

2 c. finely chopped cooked or	1 tsp. seasoning salt
canned beets	⅛ tsp. pepper
1 c. finely chopped onion	½ c. mayonnaise
2 c. finely shredded cabbage	Green cabbage leaves

Combine all ingredients and serve on green cabbage leaves. Makes 6 servings.

Relish Salad Drain 1 (1 lb.) can red kidney beans and 1 (1 lb. 4 oz.) can garbanzos. Pour into two glass jars. Add ½ c. bottled Italian dressing or garlic French dressing to each. Cover and chill overnight or several hours. Mix and serve on lettuce.

Variations: Substitute 1 (15 oz.) can black-eye peas, drained, for the garbanzos. Heat the beans and garbanzos or peas and serve as a vegetable. Or serve the beans, garbanzos or peas on a relish tray along with cottage cheese, spiced crab apples, and other relishes.

TIPS FROM A COUNTRY COOK

Tossed Salad in a Hurry   Tear the washed greens in bite-size pieces. Place them in a garlic-rubbed bowl. Sliced cucumbers and green pepper may be added. Put bowl in a large plastic bag (size for freezing turkeys) and close tightly. Refrigerate several hours or until mealtime. At the last minute before serving, add dressing and toss. For a potluck supper, carry bowl of greens and bottled dressing. Toss to serve.

COUNTRY SALAD BOWL

5 large tomatoes, ripe but firm	Pepper
2 cucumbers	¼ c. French dressing
1 green pepper	Creamy Cheese Dressing (see
1 large sweet onion	Index)
Salt	

Chill vegetables.

Slice unpeeled tomatoes. Peel cucumbers; score with tines of fork; slice. Slice pepper and onion in rings.

Arrange vegetables in bowl. Cover tightly and refrigerate.

When ready to serve, sprinkle with salt and pepper (freshly ground if you have it). Drizzle lightly with French dressing. Serve with Creamy Cheese Dressing, passed in separate bowl. Makes 6 to 8 servings.

CUCUMBER-EGG SALAD

1 large head lettuce	⅓ c. French-type salad dressing
2 cucumbers, sliced	Grated Parmesan cheese
3 or 4 hard-cooked eggs, sliced	
1 or 2 sweet peppers, cut in rings	

Cut lettuce into 8 wedges; arrange in salad bowl.

Add cucumbers, eggs and peppers.

When ready to serve, add salad dressing. Sprinkle generously with cheese. Makes 6 to 8 servings.

Grapefruit-Beet Salad Team canned or fresh grapefruit sections with drained and diced pickled beets for a colorful relish salad. Add French or Italian dressing.

Lettuce Slaw Shred a head of iceberg lettuce. Toss in a bowl with 3 chopped green onions or 6 chopped pimiento-stuffed olives and French or Italian salad dressing. Makes 6 servings.

Louis Salad Toss 2 c. cooked and chilled green beans with crisp lettuce and 1 c. cooked or canned chilled shrimp or crab meat. Serve with ½ c. mayonnaise blended with ¼ c. chili sauce, 1 tblsp. chopped green onion and 1 tblsp. lemon juice. This makes a whole meal in a bowl.

SAUERKRAUT SLAW

1 (1 lb. 11 oz.) can sauerkraut	2 tblsp. sugar
¾ c. shredded carrots	1 tsp. salt
½ c. chopped stuffed olives or diced cucumber	½ tsp. dry mustard
2 tblsp. minced parsley	1 tsp. celery seeds
1 tblsp. chopped onion	2 tblsp. French dressing
	Salad greens

Chill sauerkraut. Open can and drain. Combine kraut with remaining ingredients; mix well. Cover and chill. Serve on crisp salad greens or outer cabbage leaves. Makes 8 servings.

Men's Special: Top frankfurters or hamburgers in buns with this slaw.

TOSSED SALAD

1 (8 oz.) can green beans, drained	½ c. bottled blue-cheese French dressing
1 (8 oz.) can cut asparagus, drained	1 c. sliced cauliflower flowerets
2 tblsp. chopped green onion or chives	1 qt. salad greens

Combine beans, asparagus, green onion and salad dressing. Chill 1 to 2 hours (or several hours) to blend flavors. Add cauliflower and greens. Toss lightly. Makes 6 to 8 servings.

MIXED VEGETABLE SALAD

1 head lettuce
2 c. raw cauliflower flowerets
2 large tomatoes, peeled and
  cut in wedges
½ large Bermuda onion, sliced
  and separated into rings

3 tblsp. crumbled blue cheese
⅔ c. bottled Italian salad
  dressing

Tear lettuce in bite-size pieces. Combine with cauliflower, tomato, onion rings and cheese. Add dressing and toss until blended. Makes 8 to 10 servings.

FIESTA VEGETABLE SALAD

Lettuce
4 tomatoes, peeled and sliced
1 sweet onion, thinly sliced
1½ c. cooked whole green
  beans, or 1 (1 lb. 1 oz.) can
  whole green beans

1 large cucumber, unpeeled,
  but sliced
French dressing

Line platter or chop plate with lettuce. Arrange tomatoes, onion, beans and cucumber on lettuce in separate sections. Serve with French dressing. Makes 6 servings.

Leftover Egg Yolks Poach the yolks in hot water until hard-cooked. Chill and slice or crumble over potato, lettuce and other vegetable salads.

FROSTY TOMATO CUP

3 (1 lb. 12 oz.) cans tomatoes,
  drained, or 5 medium-size
  fresh tomatoes, chopped
1½ c. green pepper strips
1 medium onion, cut into rings
⅓ c. oil

2 tblsp. vinegar
1 tsp. salt
¾ tsp. oregano
¾ tsp. basil
¼ tsp. pepper

Combine all ingredients. Chill. Makes 8 servings.

TOMATO COTTAGE-CHEESE SALAD

1 (12 oz.) carton cottage cheese,   3 medium to large tomatoes,
   or about 1½ c.   peeled and sliced
1 tsp. mixed dry herbs   Lettuce
½ tsp. onion salt

Combine cottage cheese, herbs and onion salt. Arrange 3 tomato slices on lettuce for each salad. Top with mound of cottage cheese. Makes 6 servings.

Chicken-Apple Salad Add 1½ c. diced cooked chicken or 2 (5 oz.) cans to your favorite Waldorf salad, made with 2 c. diced and cored but unpeeled apples. A good proportion of other ingredients to add is: 1 c. diced celery, 3 tblsp. mayonnaise or salad dressing, 1 tblsp. lemon juice and ¼ c. chopped pecans. Season with ½ tsp. salt. Serve on lettuce. Makes 4 servings.

Chicken Salad Just before serving your favorite chicken salad, fold in a sliced banana; or add cubes of jellied cranberries. In strawberry season, garnish chicken salad with a few berries.

Hot Potato Salad Put ⅔ c. bottled Italian-style salad dressing in your electric skillet. Heat slowly. Add 5 c. cooked, diced potatoes, 3 tblsp. chopped onion and 7 slices crisp, crumbled bacon. Toss lightly and heat. Garnish with chopped parsley or green pepper. Makes 6 servings.

ONION MAC

8 oz. elbow macaroni, cooked   ⅓ c. chopped pimiento
2 c. dairy sour cream   1 tsp. salt
1 c. chopped green onion

Mix macaroni with remaining ingredients. Chill. Stir before serving. Makes 8 servings.

The CREAM PUFF HEART, the basic cream puff gone fancy (recipe page 296), is a delicious and festive centerpiece for Valentine's Day, engagement announcement parties, showers and wedding anniversaries.

HAMBURGER-HOT DOG BAKE—Main dish sandwiches like this are hearty supper favorites. You can get them ready to bake and refrigerate them. Require no attention while they bake and brown in oven. Recipe page 243.

BEST-EVER CHICKEN SALAD

5 c. cubed cooked chicken
2 tblsp. salad oil
2 tblsp. orange juice
2 tblsp. vinegar
1 tsp. salt
3 c. cooked rice
1½ c. small green grapes

1½ c. sliced celery
1 (13½ oz.) can pineapple
 tidbits, drained
1 (11 oz.) can mandarin
 oranges, drained
1 c. toasted slivered almonds
1½ c. mayonnaise

Combine first 5 ingredients; let stand while preparing remaining salad ingredients. Gently toss together all ingredients. Makes 12 servings.

GOLDEN MACARONI SALAD

1 (8 oz.) pkg. shell macaroni,
 cooked and drained
6 c. chopped cabbage
½ c. chopped celery
½ c. green pepper strips
¼ c. minced onion
2 (1 lb.) cans red kidney beans,
 drained

3 eggs, slightly beaten
½ c. sugar
1 (9 oz.) jar prepared mustard
3 tblsp. butter
½ tsp. salt
¼ tsp. pepper

Toss together macaroni, cabbage, celery, green pepper, onion and kidney beans. Blend together remaining ingredients in top part of double boiler. Cook over simmering water for about 5 minutes or until mixture thickens slightly. Cool. Pour over vegetables; toss. Makes 10 to 12 servings.

DANISH POTATO SALAD

¼ c. vinegar
¼ c. water
¼ c. sugar
¼ tsp. salt
Dash pepper
1 tsp. prepared mustard
2 eggs, well beaten

1 c. salad dressing
4 c. cubed, cooked potatoes
 (about 2 lbs.)
2 hard-cooked eggs, chopped
½ c. chopped cucumber
1 tblsp. minced onion
1 tblsp. chopped green pepper

Combine vinegar, water, sugar, salt, pepper and mustard. Bring to a boil. Reduce heat; gradually beat in well-beaten eggs. Cook, stirring constantly, until slightly thickened, about 5 minutes. Beat in salad dressing.

Toss together remaining ingredients. Pour on dressing; toss gently. Adjust seasoning if it's necessary. Makes 6 servings.

To make a larger quantity For dressing: Use 1 c. each vinegar, water and sugar; 1 tblsp. mustard; 1 tsp. salt; ½ tsp. pepper; 5 eggs; and 1 qt. salad dressing.

Toss with 10 lbs. diced, cooked potatoes; 6 hard-cooked eggs; 2 c. cucumber; ½ c. each onion and green pepper. Makes about 6 qts.

TUNA-TOMATO SALAD

1 (1 lb.) can tomatoes	1 tblsp. chopped onion
1 (3 oz.) pkg. strawberry flavor gelatin	2 tblsp. chopped green pepper
	½ c. chopped celery
3 tblsp. vinegar	½ tsp. salt
1 (7 oz.) can tuna, drained and flaked	Greens

Heat tomatoes to boiling; add gelatin; stir to dissolve. Add remaining ingredients; spoon into 1 qt. mold. Chill until firm. Unmold and serve on greens. Makes 6 servings.

TURKEY SALAD SUPREME

3 c. diced cooked turkey	½ c. mayonnaise or salad dressing
½ c. French salad dressing	
1½ c. diced celery	½ c. heavy cream, whipped
½ tsp. salt	Lettuce

Combine turkey and French salad dressing; cover and chill several hours or overnight.

Add celery, salt, mayonnaise, and fold in whipped cream for a fluffy salad. Serve on crisp lettuce. Makes 4 servings.

Variations: Add ½ c. coarsely chopped salted pecans or 1 c. seedless green grapes. Serve salad on chilled and drained canned pineapple slices.

BLUE-CHEESE SALAD DRESSING

1 c. mayonnaise or salad
dressing
1 c. buttermilk
¼ tsp. salt

¼ tsp. pepper
1 tsp. grated onion
2 oz. blue cheese
Lettuce wedges

Combine mayonnaise, buttermilk, salt, pepper and onion. Crumble in half of cheese. Beat with rotary beater until well blended. Break remainder of cheese in larger pieces and stir in. Serve over lettuce wedges or tomato salad. Makes 2 cups.

CREAMY CHEESE DRESSING

1 c. cottage cheese
¼ lb. blue or Roquefort cheese
½ tsp. grated onion

½ tsp. Worcestershire sauce
½ c. dairy sour cream

Combine ingredients in blender; blend until smooth. Or force cottage and blue cheese through a sieve; add remaining ingredients; mix until smooth. (For thinner dressing, add a little sour cream, milk or light cream.) Makes 1¼ cups.

DAISY'S SALAD DRESSING

1 c. mayonnaise
½ c. sweet pickle juice

1 tsp. celery seeds

Combine ingredients. Store in refrigerator. Makes about 1½ cups.

FRUIT-SALAD DRESSING

1½ tblsp. flour
1¼ tsp. paprika
1 tsp. salt
1 tsp. dry mustard

1 tsp. celery seeds
⅓ c. lemon juice
¾ c. strained honey
1 c. salad oil

Combine all ingredients except honey and oil; add to honey in top of double boiler. Cook over hot water, stirring occasionally, until thickened.

Cool; then, using a fork, gradually beat in oil. Keep refrigerated. To serve, drizzle over fruit. Makes about 2 cups.

ORANGE-HONEY DRESSING

¼ tsp. paprika
½ tsp. dry mustard
1 tsp. salt
½ tsp. celery salt
½ c. honey

3 tblsp. lemon juice
2 tblsp. cider vinegar
3 tblsp. orange juice concentrate
1 c. salad oil

Combine dry ingredients in 1 qt. mixer bowl. Add honey, lemon juice, vinegar and orange concentrate; blend well. Beating constantly, slowly add oil; beat 5 minutes longer at medium speed. (Or blend all ingredients in blender for 20 seconds at high speed.) Chill. Shake before serving. Store in refrigerator; storage time, 1 month. Makes 1 pint.

FRUIT-JUICE FRENCH DRESSING

1 (6 oz.) can frozen orange-
    grapefruit juice concentrate,
    thawed

¾ tsp. salt
Dash paprika
1½ c. salad oil

Combine juice concentrate and seasonings. Beat in oil, a small amount at a time. Makes 2 cups.

RED FRENCH DRESSING

½ c. vinegar
1½ c. salad oil
2 tsp. salt
⅛ tsp. pepper
1 tsp. dry mustard

⅓ c. chili sauce
1 tblsp. prepared horse-radish
    (optional)
1 tsp. paprika

Mix all the ingredients with a rotary beater or electric mixer or shake in a quart fruit jar with tight lid. Store in refrigerator. Makes about 2 cups.

Variations

Lemon Use lemon juice instead of vinegar. Excellent on fruits.

Garlic Add 1 garlic clove, crushed.

Olive To 1 c. Red French Dressing, add ⅓ c. finely chopped pimiento-stuffed olives. Good on lettuce.

ITALIAN TOMATO DRESSING

½ c. oil
⅓ c. cider vinegar
1 (8 oz.) can tomato sauce
½ tsp. salt
2 tblsp. sugar
1 tsp. dry mustard
1 tsp. paprika

½ tsp. oregano
2 tsp. Worcestershire sauce
½ clove garlic, finely chopped
2 tsp. finely chopped onion
1 tblsp. finely chopped celery
2 tblsp. salad dressing

Combine all ingredients in 1 qt. mixing bowl. Beat at medium speed 2 minutes. (Or blend ingredients in blender for 15 seconds on high speed.) Chill. Store in refrigerator; storage time, 1 month. Makes 1 pint.

PEANUT SALAD DRESSING

2 tblsp. chunk-style peanut
  butter
2 tblsp. honey

½ c. mayonnaise or salad
  dressing

Blend peanut butter and honey; stir in mayonnaise. Makes about ⅔ cup.

RANCH-HOUSE SALAD DRESSING

1 c. mayonnaise
¼ c. vinegar
¼ c. ketchup
¼ c. chili sauce

2 tblsp. finely chopped onion
¼ tsp. salt
¼ tsp. paprika

Combine all ingredients. Serve with vegetable salads. Makes 1¾ cups.

CREAMY THOUSAND ISLAND

½ c. salad dressing
½ c. chili sauce
1 tsp. Worcestershire sauce
Dash Tabasco sauce
½ tsp. salt
¼ tsp. paprika

2 tblsp. chopped celery
2 tblsp. pickle relish
2 tblsp. chopped stuffed olives
1 tsp. minced onion
1 hard-cooked egg, chopped
½ c. sour cream

Combine salad dressing, chili sauce, Worcestershire, Tabasco, salt and paprika in 1 qt. bowl. Stir in celery, relish, olives, onion and egg; mix well. Fold in sour cream. Chill. Store in refrigerator; storage time, 1 month. Makes 1 pint.

SWEET/SOUR BACON DRESSING

4 slices bacon	3 tblsp. white vinegar
2 tblsp. chopped onion	½ c. water
3 tblsp. sugar	1⅓ c. salad dressing

Fry bacon until crisp and brown. Drain bacon and crumble into small pieces. Set aside.

Sauté onion in bacon drippings until tender. Add sugar, vinegar and water; bring to boiling point. Cool. Combine mixture with salad dressing; beat until smooth. Stir in bacon chips. Chill. Store in refrigerator; storage time, 1 month. Makes 1 pint.

SOUR-CREAM DRESSING

½ c. sour cream	⅛ tsp. pepper
1 tblsp. sugar	1 tblsp. lemon juice
¼ tsp. salt	1 tblsp. vinegar

Combine ingredients and pour over vegetables. Makes about ⅔ cup.

CHIVE SOUR CREAM DRESSING

½ c. dairy sour cream	2 tblsp. minced chives
½ c. mayonnaise	

Combine sour cream and mayonnaise. Stir in chives. Serve on sliced cucumbers, tomatoes, lettuce or mixed chopped vegetables. Makes 1 cup.

CELERY SOUR CREAM DRESSING

½ c. dairy sour cream	¾ tsp. salt
¼ c. minced onion	½ tsp. celery seeds
1 tblsp. vinegar	

Combine all ingredients. Serve on lettuce or mixed chopped vegetables. Makes about ⅔ cup.

Relishes

PICKLED BEANS

2 (15½ oz.) cans whole green
  beans
1 c. sweet pickle juice

1½ tsp. celery seeds
½ c. sweet pickle relish
1 hard-cooked egg, chopped

Drain beans. Spread them in a dish.

Combine remaining ingredients and pour over the beans. Cover and let stand in refrigerator overnight or 8 hours. Makes 8 servings.

COLORFUL CRANBERRIES THE YEAR ROUND   Cranberries harvested in autumn match the season's leaves in brilliant color. Then many country women take a day off to make ruby-red relish to freeze for use throughout the year. Partly thawed, it tastes just right in summer with fried chicken or cold sliced ham.

CRANBERRY RELISH

4 medium oranges, seeded
2 lbs. cranberries
4 medium unpeeled apples,
  cored

4 c. sugar

Peel the yellow rind from orange; trim off and discard white part. Put orange pulp and yellow rind, cranberries and apples through food grinder. Add sugar and mix well.

Cover and refrigerate. Or pour into glass jars, leaving ½″ head space. Seal and freeze. Makes 4 pints.

Note: Cranberry Relish has many uses in the kitchen. It is an ingredient in the following recipes in this cookbook (see Index): Cranberry Coffee Cake, Fruited Fantan Rolls, Molded Cranberry-Relish Salad, Cranberry Mincemeat Pie, Cranberry Nut Bread and Cranberry Topping.

GLISTENING CRANBERRY SAUCE   An Oregon farm woman sent her prized cranberry sauce recipe to us with this comment: "The berries stay almost whole and they have a pretty, glazed look."

OREGON CRANBERRY SAUCE

1 lb. cranberries (4 c.)	2 tblsp. water
2 c. sugar	Dash salt

Wash cranberries. Combine cranberries, sugar, water and salt in a large saucepan. Stir to mix sugar and berries.

Cover saucepan and set on heat. Cook only until berries start to pop. Remove lid and lightly stir. Cook 2 minutes. Let the mixture boil up; boil 1 minute longer. Makes about 3½ cups.

Note: The chilled cranberry sauce, served in dessert glasses and topped with puffs of whipped cream, a little grated orange rind folded in, makes a delightful, colorful dessert.

CRANBERRY CHUTNEY

1 (1 lb. 14 oz.) can fruit cocktail	½ tsp. salt
½ c. orange juice	2 c. cranberries
½ c. sugar	1 c. chopped, unpeeled apples
¼ c. light brown sugar	1 tblsp. finely chopped candied ginger
¼ c. cider vinegar	1 small clove garlic, minced
½ tsp. ground cloves	¾ c. seedless raisins
¼ tsp. red pepper	

Drain fruit cocktail. Measure 1¼ c. syrup; reserve fruit.

Combine syrup, orange juice, sugar, brown sugar, vinegar, cloves, red pepper and salt in a heavy 3 qt. saucepan. Bring to a full boil, stirring often. Add cranberries and remaining ingredients. Cook until berries pop, about 5 minutes. Stir in fruit cocktail. Simmer, stirring often, until mixture thickens slightly, about 15 minutes.

Pour into hot, sterilized jars. Seal immediately or store in refrigerator. Chutney will thicken as it cools. Makes about 2½ pints.

GOLDEN GLOW RELISH

2 qt. cucumbers, peeled and seeded	3 c. water
2½ c. ground carrots	2 tblsp. salt
2 c. ground onions	3 c. cider vinegar
1 c. ground red peppers	2 c. sugar
1½ c. ground green peppers	½ tsp. turmeric
1 (4 oz.) jar pimientos, chopped	1 tsp. dry mustard

Grind cucumbers; combine with carrots, onions, peppers, pimientos, water and salt; let stand 3 hours. Drain off brine and discard.

Combine vegetables with remaining ingredients in a 6 qt. pan. Bring to a boil; simmer 10 minutes. Ladle into hot, sterilized jars; process in hot water bath for 10 minutes. Makes 6 pints.

SLAW-STUFFED PEPPERS

12 whole green peppers	5¼ c. sugar
4 qt. water	6 c. water
¼ c. salt	6 c. cider vinegar
2 medium heads cabbage, finely shredded	1½ tsp. whole cloves
	5 sticks cinnamon
¼ c. salt	1½ tblsp. whole allspice
1 (4 oz.) jar pimientos, diced	1½ tsp. salt

Slice tops off peppers and remove seeds. Soak overnight in solution of 4 qt. water and ¼ c. salt.

Combine cabbage and ¼ c. salt; let stand overnight. Drain well. Mix pimientos and cabbage; fill peppers with mixture. Tie tops on with thread; put in 8 qt. crock.

Combine sugar, water, vinegar and spices in 6 qt. pan. Bring to a boil; cook 10 minutes. Pour hot solution over peppers and weight them down. Marinate at least one week. To serve, cut peppers in quarters. For smaller amount, halve recipe and use 4 qt. crock. Makes 12 peppers.

TANGY BEET RELISH

4 c. chopped raw beets	2 c. sugar
4 c. chopped cabbage	3 c. vinegar
1 c. chopped onion	1 tblsp. salt
1½ c. chopped red peppers	
1 (4 oz.) jar prepared horse-radish	

Combine beets, cabbage, onion, peppers, horse-radish, sugar, vinegar and salt in 4 qt. saucepan; simmer 10 minutes. Ladle into hot, sterilized jars; process in hot water bath 10 minutes. Makes 6 pints.

HEIRLOOM RELISH

8 c. peeled, ground cucumbers   2 c. sugar
3 c. ground onions   1 tblsp. mustard seed
5 c. ground cabbage   1 tblsp. celery seed
1 c. ground green peppers   ½ c. sifted flour
1 c. ground red peppers   2 tblsp. dry mustard
1 qt. water   ½ tsp. turmeric
2 tblsp. salt   Water
3½ c. cider vinegar

Combine cucumbers, onions, cabbage, peppers, water and salt, let stand overnight. Drain well; discard brine.

In a 6 qt. pan, combine vegetables, vinegar, sugar, mustard and celery seed; simmer 30 minutes. Combine flour, mustard, turmeric and enough water to make a paste; add to relish and cook 10 minutes. Pack in hot, sterilized jars; process in hot water bath 10 minutes. Makes 7½ pints.

COTTAGE-CHEESE RELISH

1 large peeled cucumber   ½ tsp. salt
½ c. mayonnaise   1 qt. small-curd cottage cheese
1 tsp. celery seeds

Cut cucumber into small cubes (about ¼") and mix it and all the other ingredients into cottage cheese. Chill in refrigerator.

Serve as relish, garnished with diced cucumber or parsley. Makes 10 to 12 servings.

Variations: Substitute dairy sour cream for mayonnaise. Add a few sliced green onions if they are in season. And if your cucumber is fresh out of the garden, wash it, but do not peel. The green of the cucumber rind adds attractive color.

Garlic Olives Almost fill a pint jar with drained, canned ripe olives. Add 5 garlic cloves, sliced, and 2 thin lemon slices. Pour on enough olive or salad oil to cover, put lid on jar and chill 1 to 2 days. Drain to serve (strain oil and use to make French dressing for tossed salads).

4-VEGETABLE RELISH

3 large tomatoes, peeled and
    cut in wedges
½ c. chopped green pepper
½ c. pared, grated cucumber

1 tblsp. grated onion
½ tsp. seasoned salt
½ tsp. salt
⅛ tsp. pepper

Combine tomatoes, green pepper, cucumber, onion, seasoned salt, salt and pepper in a large bowl. Chill ½ hour or longer to blend flavors. Makes 6 servings.

WINTER JELLIES Choose a day when there's frost on the kitchen windowpanes to make jelly. When the day's over, you'll find that everyone will enjoy looking at your display and tasting the summertime flavors they hold.

Jelly-making in January is easier than in June. No picking of fruit or berries and no washing, peeling, coring, chopping or straining. And no stained jelly bags to empty and wash! That's because you start with bottled or canned fruit juices.

Delicate, coral-pink apple jelly can be varied in many ways. We give you a few favorites of good country cooks.

JANUARY APPLE JELLY

1 qt. bottled or canned apple
    juice
5 drops (about) red food color

1 (1¾ oz.) pkg. powdered-
    fruit pectin
5½ c. sugar

Combine juice, color and pectin in large saucepan; bring to a full boil.

Add sugar; stir until dissolved. Return to boil; boil 2 minutes.

Remove from heat; skim. Pour into hot, sterilized jars; seal. Makes about 7 pints.

Variations

You can start with the January Apple Jelly recipe and make seven wonderful jellies. Omit the food color. Then follow these directions.

Cinnamon-Apple Add ⅓ c. red cinnamon candies with sugar.

Cranberry-Apple Use equal parts bottled cranberry and apple juices.

Spiced-Minted Apple Add about 5 drops green food color to apple juice; tie 1 tblsp. whole cloves in muslin bag; add to juice with pectin. Remove after cooking; add ½ tsp. peppermint extract.

Geranium Lay a washed rose geranium leaf in each jar before pouring in the hot jelly mixture.

Grape Use bottled grape juice for apple juice.

Grapefruit-Lemon Use unsweetened canned grapefruit juice for apple juice; add juice of 3 lemons and about 10 drops yellow food color.

Cranberry Use bottled cranberry juice for apple juice.

CITRUS HONEY

3 medium-size lemons	2 c. honey
1 medium-size orange	½ c. water
1 c. sugar	½ bottle fruit pectin

Pare rind from fruit; reserve fruit sections. Cut rind into ½" thin strips. Combine rind, sugar, ½ c. honey and water in a small saucepan. Bring to a boil. Cover. Simmer 10 minutes, stirring occasionally.

Meanwhile, remove all membrane from fruit sections; dice fruit. Add fruit and juice to cooked mixture; bring to boil. Simmer, covered, 20 minutes. You should have 2 cups of fruit mixture; if not add enough water to make 2 cups.

Turn into large saucepan; stir in 1½ c. honey. Bring to a rapid boil, stirring constantly. Boil 1 minute. Remove from heat.

Add pectin; stir and skim 5 minutes. Pour into sterilized jelly glasses. Seal. Makes 4 (6 oz.) glasses.

CRANBERRY HONEY

2 c. cranberry cocktail	1 c. honey
3 c. sugar	½ bottle fruit pectin
1 tsp. grated orange rind	

Bring cranberry cocktail, sugar and orange rind to a boil; simmer

10 minutes. Add honey. Bring to a rapid boil; boil 1 minute. Remove from heat.

Add pectin; skim. Pour into sterilized jelly glasses. Seal. Makes 5 (6 oz.) glasses.

SPICY PEACH PICKLES

1 (1 lb.) can peach halves
1 (3") stick cinnamon
1 tsp. whole cloves

1 tsp. whole allspice
¼ c. white vinegar

Drain syrup from peaches into saucepan. Add spices and vinegar. Simmer 5 minutes.

Pour over peaches, cover and refrigerate overnight, at least 8 hours. Serve as relish with chicken or meats. Makes 6 to 8 servings.

Note: Save the syrup after peaches are served. Heat and pour over more drained canned peaches, apricots, pears or pineapple. Chill.

Sauces

CHUNKY CIDER APPLESAUCE

9 c. pared, sliced apples
½ c. apple cider
1 tblsp. lemon juice

½ c. sugar
⅛ tsp. salt
½ tsp. nutmeg

Combine apples, cider and lemon juice in 3 qt. saucepan. Bring to boil over medium heat and simmer until apples are tender; about 20 minutes.

Add sugar, salt and nutmeg; cook 1 minute longer. Break up apples into chunks. Makes about 1 qt.

BLUEBERRY SAUCE

1 (10 oz.) pkg. frozen
  blueberries
½ c. unsweetened pineapple
  juice

¼ c. water
⅔ c. sugar
2 tsp. cornstarch
Dash salt

Combine all ingredients in saucepan. Cook, stirring, over medium heat until sauce thickens. Cool and chill. Makes about 2 cups.

Note: Substitute 1½ c. fresh blueberries for the frozen ones.

HONEYED CRANBERRY TOPPING

2 oranges, quartered   1 c. honey
4 c. cranberries (1 lb.)

Put unpeeled oranges, seeds removed, and cranberries through food chopper. Fold in honey. Cover and place in refrigerator. May be made several days ahead. Makes about 4 cups.

For dessert, spoon cranberry-orange mixture over vanilla ice cream.

CHOCOLATE SAUCE

1 (15 oz.) can sweetened   ⅛ tsp. salt
  condensed milk   1 c. hot water
2 (1 oz.) squares unsweetened   ½ tsp. vanilla
  chocolate

Place condensed (not evaporated) milk, chocolate and salt in top of double boiler. Cook over rapidly boiling water, stirring frequently, until thick, about 10 minutes. Remove from heat.

Slowly add hot water, beating with a rotary beater.

Cool, add vanilla and chill. Serve over ice cream, cake or pudding. Makes about 2½ cups.

HARD SAUCE

½ c. butter or margarine   ½ tsp. vanilla
1 c. sifted confectioners sugar

Beat butter and sugar with electric mixer until fluffy and creamy. Beat in vanilla. Chill or freeze. Makes 1 cup.

Variations: Shape Hard Sauce in balls and roll in grated lemon or orange rind. Or sprinkle Hard Sauce with a touch of nutmeg before serving.

LEMON HARD SAUCE

¼ c. heavy cream   1 tsp. grated lemon rind
½ c. butter or margarine   1 tblsp. lemon juice
1¼ c. confectioners sugar

Whip cream; set aside.

Cream butter with same beaters. Add sugar; beat until light and fluffy. Add lemon rind and juice.

Fold in whipped cream. Chill. Serve spoonful on each square of gingerbread or on spice cakes. Makes 2 cups.

Melba Sauce Blend 1 cup frozen red raspberries, thawed, 1 tsp. sugar and 1 tsp. cornstarch. Cook over low heat, stirring, until clear. Strain through a sieve. Cool. Serve over vanilla ice cream; or, for the Classic Peach Melba, serve over drained, canned peach halves, their centers filled with vanilla ice cream. Professional chefs add ½ cup currant jelly to the sauce to enhance its flavor and to add sparkle.

PLUM SAUCE

Boil ½ c. plum juice and ¼ c. Basic Sugar Syrup (see Index) together 5 minutes.

FRESH STRAWBERRY SYRUP

1 qt. fresh strawberries
¾ c. sugar
½ c. sugar
3 tblsp. lemon juice
¼ tsp. salt
2 tblsp. butter
½ tsp. vanilla

Mash berries and the ¾ c. sugar together. Force through strainer. Add water, if necessary, to make 2½ c. juice.

In a saucepan combine strained strawberry juice with the ½ c. sugar, lemon juice and salt. Bring to a boil, stirring constantly.

Boil 4 minutes. Remove from heat; skim off foam. Stir in butter and vanilla. Makes 2½ cups.

SAUCES FOR MEAT, FISH, VEGETABLES

APPLE-HORSE-RADISH SAUCE

2 c. applesauce or 1 (1 lb.) can
¼ c. prepared horse-radish
⅛ tsp. basil (optional)
½ tsp. salt
⅛ tsp. pepper

Combine applesauce, horse-radish, basil, salt and pepper in a bowl; mix well. Chill. Makes 2¼ cups.

SPICY TOMATO SAUCE

1 (10½ oz.) can condensed
    cream of tomato soup
1 tblsp. prepared mustard

2 tblsp. prepared horse-radish
⅛ tsp. pepper

Combine tomato soup, mustard, horse-radish and pepper in a saucepan. Heat and serve over meat loaf. Makes about 1½ cups.

TARTAR SAUCE

1 c. mayonnaise
2 tblsp. pickle relish
1 tblsp. chopped onion

1 tblsp. chopped parsley
1 tblsp. chopped pimiento

Combine all ingredients. Serve with fish. Makes about 1¼ cups.

HOT MUSTARD

1⅓ c. dry mustard
2 tblsp. sugar
2 tsp. salt

¼ c. oil
½ c. wine vinegar
½ c. water

Combine all ingredients; blend well. Refrigerate. Makes 1⅔ cups.

SPREADS FOR BREADS

ORANGE HONEY BUTTER

½ c. butter or margarine
⅔ c. honey

1 tblsp. orange juice
1 tsp. grated orange rind

Combine ingredients and beat until blended. Makes about 1¼ cups.

Variation: Add 1 tsp. lemon juice with orange juice.

Blender Butter Pour 1 c. heavy cream into blender's container. Blend at high speed 15 seconds or until cream is whipped and starts to thicken around blades. Add ½ c. cold water and 1 crushed ice cube. Blend at high speed 2 minutes. Spoon sweet butter into small bowl; work with a wooden spoon to extract liquid (save to use in baking, as in making biscuits). Salt butter if you wish. Makes 6 ounces.

Note: Peel a small clove of garlic. Add with cold water and crushed ice cube to Blender Butter. Spread on top of sizzling steaks.

Whipped Butter Let ½ lb. butter (unsalted, if available) stand at room temperature until soft, about 1 hour. Beat with electric mixer on low speed until smooth. Then beat on high speed until light and fluffy, about 10 minutes. The butter takes on a lighter color. Store in refrigerator. Let whipped butter soften at room temperature before serving with hot breads, pancakes and waffles. Makes about 1½ cups.

HERB FLAVORED BREAD

½ c. soft butter or margarine
½ tsp. salt
¼ tsp. paprika
¼ tsp. savory or 2 tsp.
  chopped parsley

½ tsp. thyme
Few grains red pepper
1 (13 to 16 oz.) loaf French
  bread

Cream butter with salt, paprika, savory, thyme and red pepper. Cut French bread diagonally, almost through to bottom crust, in 12 equal slices. Spread herb butter between slices. Wrap loaf in aluminum foil. Heat in hot oven (400°) for 15 minutes. Makes 6 servings.

SEASONED BUTTERS FOR FRENCH BREAD

Soften ½ c. butter or margarine by creaming in mixing bowl. (Makes enough to spread one loaf French bread.) Add and mix well:

Onion-Parsley 4 tblsp. each minced onion and parsley.

Chili-Ketchup ½ tsp. chili powder, 2 tblsp. ketchup and 2 crushed garlic cloves. (Garlic press may be used.)

Mustard 2 tblsp. prepared mustard.

Garlic Crush 3 or 4 peeled garlic cloves. Add to butter or margarine. Let stand at room temperature 1 or 2 hours, stirring occasionally.

Curry ½ tsp. curry powder.

Smoke ½ tsp. smoke salt.

Blue-Cheese ¼ c. crumbled blue or Roquefort cheese.

Swiss-Cheese ½ c. coarsely shredded Swiss cheese.

Sage ½ tsp. powdered dry sage.

Thyme ½ tsp. powdered dried thyme.

Sage and Thyme ¼ tsp. each.

Section 3
Sandwiches and Breads

When you're asked "What's for lunch?" and you bring one of these delicious sandwiches to the table you are sure to be voted best cook of the week by your family. Out-of-the-ordinary sandwiches and breads brighten up meals and menus. Our assemble-and-refrigerate sandwiches are sure winners. Make them in the morning; bake them in the evening. The Hamburger-Hot-Dog Bake will make a hit with the children.

Sandwiches you fill and stack into a loaf, such as our sturdy Cheese Rye Loaf or Baked Egg Sandwich Loaf are hearty enough for supper. These too can be fixed in the morning and baked at your leisure. Just add a tossed green salad and the meal is complete.

We think you'll like our Ladle-Over-a-Bun specials, such as the Barbecue Sandwich or the hefty corned beef mixture that is made ahead, ready to be reheated.

Make-and-freeze-ahead hot breads include the Spicy Pizza with several variations and Onion Mustard Buns—good when just thawed but very special when toasted and spread with cream cheese or used as a base for creamed salmon or eggs.

HAMBURGER—HOT-DOG BAKE

12 slices bread	6 frankfurters
Butter or margarine	2 medium onions, sliced
1 lb. lean ground beef	6 slices process American cheese
¼ c. ketchup	2 eggs, beaten
1 tsp. salt	1 c. milk

Spread 6 bread slices with butter; arrange in bottom of greased pan (13×9×2″). Toast in moderate oven (350°) about 15 minutes.

Combine beef, ketchup and salt; spread over toast (⅓ c. per sandwich). Top with frankfurters, cut almost in half lengthwise, onion and cheese slices. Cover with remaining bread slices.

Combine eggs and milk; pour over bread.

Bake in moderate oven (350°) about 50 minutes. Makes 6 servings.

Variations

Baked Tuna Sandwiches Omit ground-beef mixture and frankfurters. Spread toast with mixture of 2 (7 oz.) cans tuna, flaked, ¼ c. chopped celery, ¼ c. chopped apple and ¼ c. mayonnaise. Bake as directed.

Baked Luncheon-Meat Sandwiches Omit frankfurters. Substitute 1 (12 oz.) can luncheon meat, ground, for beef. Bake as directed.

Baked Ham and Chicken Sandwiches Omit ground-beef mixture, frankfurters and onions. Spread toast with mixture of 2 c. diced cooked chicken and ¼ c. mayonnaise. Top with 6 slices boiled ham and 6 process American cheese slices. Bake as directed.

ITALIAN HAMBURGERS

1 lb. ground beef	⅓ c. water
1 tblsp. instant minced onion	⅛ tsp. oregano
1 (10½ oz.) can condensed minestrone soup	1 (6 oz.) pkg. sliced mozzarella cheese
⅓ c. ketchup	6 hamburger buns

Brown ground beef in skillet. Pour off excess fat. Add onion, soup, ketchup, water and oregano. Simmer 5 to 10 minutes.

Spread mixture on split, toasted buns; top with cheese and broil until cheese melts. Makes 12 open-faced sandwiches.

CHEESE RYE LOAF

1 round loaf rye bread	2 (4½ oz.) cans deviled ham
¼ c. soft butter	1 (8 oz.) pkg. process pimiento cheese slices
¼ tsp. onion salt	

Slice bread in 12 (¾″) slices. Combine butter and onion salt. Divide bread as for 6 sandwiches; spread surfaces with butter, then deviled ham. Divide cheese between the 6 "sandwiches," cutting up 2 slices to fill in wider bread slices. Stack bread back in loaf shape. Wrap loaf in foil; bake in hot oven (425°) until cheese melts, about 25 minutes. To serve, cut through slits that have no cheese to make hot cheese sandwiches. Makes 6 servings.

CHEESE-SANDWICH FILLING

1 (3 oz.) pkg. cream cheese	¼ c. soft butter
⅓ c. shredded smoked cheese	

Blend together cream cheese, smoked cheese and butter. Makes about 1 cup.

EASY-DO BARBECUED SANDWICHES

1 (12 oz.) can luncheon meat	½ c. bottled barbecue sauce
½ c. ketchup	8 hamburger buns

Chop luncheon meat. Combine in saucepan with ketchup and barbecue sauce. Bring to boiling and simmer 5 minutes.
Serve between split hamburger buns. Makes 8 sandwiches.

CORNED BEEF SANDWICHES

1 small onion, chopped	1 c. ketchup
3 tblsp. butter or margarine	8 sandwich buns
1 (12 oz.) can corned beef, shredded	

Cook onion in butter until soft. Stir in corned beef and ketchup. Cook over low heat, stirring frequently, 15 minutes. Serve in hot, split buns. Makes 8 sandwiches.

BAKED EGG SANDWICH LOAF

1 tblsp. prepared mustard	⅔ c. salad dressing
1½ tsp. Worcestershire sauce	4 slices crisp-cooked bacon, crumbled
1 tsp. minced onion	
1 tblsp. lemon juice	10 hard-cooked eggs, minced
4 drops Tabasco sauce	1 (1 lb.) loaf stale white bread
½ tsp. salt	3 tblsp. melted butter
⅛ tsp. pepper	2 tblsp. grated Parmesan cheese

Combine mustard, Worcestershire sauce, onion, lemon juice, Tabasco, salt, pepper and salad dressing. Stir in bacon and eggs; mix well. Spread one side of each bread slice with egg salad. Stack slices back into loaf shape on a greased baking sheet. To hold, press a 3″ strip of foil around the loaf, lengthwise. Bake in hot oven (450°) for 10 minutes. Brush top with butter; sprinkle with cheese. Bake 8 minutes longer or until golden brown. Serve on a platter (remove foil strip). Makes 10 to 12 servings.

GLAZED CRAB SANDWICHES

1 c. crab meat or 1 (7½ oz.) can
2 tblsp. chopped green onion
1 tblsp. lemon juice

2 tblsp. ketchup or chili sauce
6 slices toast
½ c. mayonnaise
¼ c. grated Cheddar cheese

Combine crab, onion, lemon juice and ketchup; mix well. Spread mixture on toast slices.

Frost top of each sandwich with mayonnaise and cheese, mixed together.

Run under broiler a few minutes or until crab mixture is heated and glazed by topping. Makes 6 sandwiches.

Variations: Put a thin slice of tomato on each slice of toast before adding crab mixture. Or top crab on each sandwich with 2 slices of avocado before adding the mayonnaise and cheese.

SAUCY CHICKEN-CHEESE SANDWICH

1 (10½ oz.) can condensed cream of chicken soup
⅓ c. milk
⅓ c. shredded sharp Cheddar cheese
1 (5 to 6 oz.) can chicken, cubed, or ⅔ c. cubed cooked chicken

1 (14½ oz.) can cut asparagus, drained
6 slices toast

Blend soup and milk in saucepan. Add cheese, chicken and asparagus. Heat until cheese is melted, stirring occasionally.

Serve over toast. Makes 6 servings.

Note: Add ¼ c. sliced pimiento-stuffed green olives for additional flavor and color.

PARMESAN ROLLS

½ c. butter
½ c. grated Parmesan cheese
½ tsp. onion salt
¼ tsp. paprika

1 tblsp. chopped parsley
(optional)
12 dinner rolls

Combine butter, cheese, onion salt, paprika and parsley.
Split rolls. Spread with butter mixture. Place on a baking sheet.
Bake in hot oven (425°) a few minutes until cheese melts. (Or
slip under hot broiler to melt cheese.) Serve hot. Makes 12 servings.

Variations: Use hard rolls or buns instead of soft rolls. Substitute
garlic salt for onion salt.

QUICK YEAST BREADS

MADE WITH ROLL MIX

If you like the yeasty flavor in coffee breads, here are recipes
you will use often. There's no kneading and little work. These
treats are so inviting you will want especially to share them with
family and friends around the kitchen table at mid-morning on a
wintry day. Cups of steaming coffee complement them. But also
serve them with chilled canned fruits for desserts that satisfy and
please.

APPLE KUCHEN

1 (13¾ oz.) pkg. hot roll mix
¾ c. warm (not hot) water
1 egg
1 tblsp. melted butter

3 c. peeled, sliced apples
(3 medium apples)
½ c. sugar
1½ tsp. cinnamon

Prepare roll mix with water and egg as directed on package.
Spread in greased pan (13×9×2″). Brush with butter. Arrange
apples in rows over dough, pressing in slightly. Sprinkle with sugar
and cinnamon, mixed.
Let rise until almost doubled, 30 to 45 minutes.
Bake in moderate oven (375°) until deep golden brown, 40 to
45 minutes. Makes 12 servings.

CHEESE BUNS

1 (13¾ oz.) pkg. hot roll mix   ⅔ c. shredded sharp Cheddar
1 c. warm (not hot) water   cheese
1 egg, unbeaten

Prepare roll mix with water as directed on package. Stir to dissolve yeast. Blend in egg and cheese. Add flour. Blend, then beat 50 strokes.

Drop dough into 18 well-greased muffin-pan cups. Let rise in warm place until light and almost doubled in bulk, 30 to 60 minutes.

Bake in moderate oven (375°) 15 to 20 minutes or until golden brown. Makes 18.

POPULAR PIZZA

1 pkg. active dry yeast   ½ tsp. salt
1¼ c. warm water (110 to   Pizza Filling (recipes follow)
   115°)
3½ to 4 c. sifted all purpose
   flour

Sprinkle yeast on warm water; stir to dissolve. Add 2 c. flour and salt. Beat thoroughly. Stir in remaining flour. Turn onto lightly floured board and knead until smooth and elastic, about 10 minutes.

Place in lightly greased bowl; turn dough over to grease top. Cover and let rise in warm place until doubled, about 30 minutes.

Turn onto board and knead just long enough to force out large bubbles. Divide in half. Roll each half to make an 11" circle. Stretch each circle to fit an oiled 12" pizza pan. Add filling.

Bake in very hot oven (450°) 20 to 25 minutes. Exchange position of pans on oven racks once during baking to brown pizzas the same. Makes 2 pizzas.

Note: If you do not have pizza pans, use baking sheets. Roll each half of dough into a 12×10" rectangle, or one that almost fills your baking sheet. Place on oiled baking sheets and build up edges slightly. Fill and bake like pizzas in round pizza pans.

PIZZA FILLINGS

Hamburger Filling

2 (8 oz.) cans pizza sauce
1 lb. ground beef

3 c. shredded mozzarella cheese

Spread pizza sauce over dough in pizza pans, using 1 can for each pizza.

Brown ground beef in skillet. Drain. Sprinkle one-half over each pizza. Then sprinkle cheese on top, using 1½ c. for each pizza.

Ham and Salami Filling

2 (8 oz.) cans pizza sauce
4 slices ham, cut in strips

6 slices salami, cut in strips
3 c. shredded mozzarella cheese

Spread pizza sauce over dough in pizza pans, using 1 can for each pizza.

Lay strips of ham and salami alternately over sauce. Top with cheese, using 1½ c. for each pizza.

Sausage Filling

2 (8 oz.) cans pizza sauce
1 lb. bulk pork sausage

3 c. shredded mozzarella cheese

Spread pizza sauce over dough in pizza pans, using 1 can for each pizza.

Brown pork sausage in skillet. Drain. Sprinkle one-half over each pizza. Top with cheese, using 1½ c. for each pizza.

Assorted Pizza Fillings Pizzas can be topped with pizza sausage, anchovies, mushrooms, sliced ripe olives, sardines or miniature frankfurters.

To Freeze Pizza Dough: When you divide the risen dough in half, roll each into an 11″ circle. Place in oiled pizza pan with double thickness of waxed paper between circles. (Or roll each half of dough into a 12×10″ rectangle, place on oiled baking sheet with waxed paper between rectangles.) Wrap and freeze. Keeps up to 1 week.

To Use Frozen Pizza Dough: Remove from freezer and let stand at room temperature 20 minutes. With fingers pull and stretch circles to cover pizza pans. (Or stretch rectangles of dough almost to edges of baking sheet and make small rim around edge.) Fill and bake as directed.

TOASTED ENGLISH MUFFINS—HOT AND BUTTERY English muffins are not always easy to locate in some of the smaller food stores. You need not deprive your family of them if they enjoy toasted muffins with strawberry jam or some other fruity spread. You can make them with packaged roll mix.

Bake a batch of these yeasty muffins some day when you have spare time. Cook and freeze them. Then you can split, toast and butter them in a jiffy when you're getting a special breakfast, lunch or supper. And if you have drop-in guests, you can toast the muffins and open the fruity spread while you make coffee.

The traditional method of splitting muffins for toasting cannot be surpassed. Break them apart with a fork. Then the surface you toast will be attractive and rough. You cannot get the same effect by cutting with a knife.

BUSY WOMAN'S ENGLISH MUFFINS

1 (13¾ oz.) pkg. hot roll mix   ¼ c. cornmeal
2 tblsp. light corn syrup

Prepare roll mix as directed on package, adding syrup with water.

Place dough on lightly floured board and knead a few strokes to make smooth, adding only enough flour to prevent hands from sticking to soft dough.

Roll about ½″ thick; cut in 3″ circles with floured cookie cutter.

Sprinkle half of cornmeal on greased cookie sheet. Place rounds of dough about 3″ apart on sheet. Scatter remaining cornmeal on dough. Cover loosely with waxed paper and let rise in a warm place until doubled in bulk, about 1 hour.

Lightly grease an electric skillet, set temperature at 340° and let heat. Cook 4 muffins at a time, about 10 minutes on each side. Split cooled muffins in half to serve, toast and butter. Makes 10 muffins.

Note: You can bake muffins on a lightly greased, hot griddle.

STRAWBERRY ROLLS

1 (13¾ oz.) pkg. hot roll mix
¾ c. warm (not hot) water
1 egg, unbeaten
1 c. strawberry preserves

1 c. flaked or shredded coconut
1 c. sifted confectioners sugar
4 to 5 tsp. milk

Prepare dough with mix, water and egg as directed on package. Roll out on well-floured surface to a 20×15″ rectangle. Spread with preserves. Sprinkle with coconut. Roll, starting with 20″ side, like jelly roll. Seal seam. Cut into 18 slices.

Place slices, cut side down, in 2 greased (9″) round pans. Let rise in warm place until almost doubled, 30 to 40 minutes.

Bake in moderate oven (375°) until golden brown, 30 to 45 minutes.

Mix confectioners sugar with milk until smooth and spread on rolls. Makes 18 rolls.

Variation: Substitute peach, apricot or pineapple preserves for strawberry.

BATTER BREADS ARE EASY Some busy, minute-conscious cooks omit loaf yeast breads from their baking schedules. The reason is apparent: there is no known way to make them rise fast.

But the batter breads are less time-consuming. You skip kneading and shaping and have no floured board to clean. And the kitchen has that same warm, yeasty aroma that invites everyone in.

The cook who bakes batter breads the first time may be alarmed that the dough is sticky. She needn't be—this is one of its characteristics. For success, be careful to spread the dough evenly in the pan and don't let it rise longer than necessary.

It's a good idea to slice batter breads slightly thicker than other breads. A serrated knife and a sawing motion give excellent results when the loaf is cool.

Try toasting and buttering batter breads for something especially good to eat.

One farm woman suggests, "If you are looking for a hobby, baking breads may be the answer. It will also give pleasure to family and friends."

OATMEAL BATTER BREAD

¾ c. boiling water
½ c. regular or quick-cooking
  rolled oats
3 tblsp. shortening
¼ c. light molasses
2 tsp. salt

1 pkg. active dry yeast
¼ c. warm water (105 to
  115°)
1 egg
2¾ c. flour

In large mixer bowl, stir together boiling water, rolled oats, shortening, molasses and salt. Cool to lukewarm.

Dissolve yeast in warm water. Add yeast, egg and half the flour to the lukewarm mixture. Beat 2 minutes on medium speed or 300 strokes by hand. Scrape sides and bottom of bowl frequently. Add remaining flour and stir with spoon until flour is blended thoroughly into dough.

Spread dough evenly in a greased loaf pan (8½×4½×2¾″). Smooth top of loaf with floured hand. Cover and let rise in warm place until batter reaches top of pan, about 1½ hours.

Bake in moderate oven (375°) 50 to 55 minutes. Remove from pan at once and brush top with butter. Cool on rack out of draft. Makes 1 loaf.

WHOLE WHEAT BATTER BREAD

1 pkg. active dry yeast
1¼ c. warm water (105 to
  115°)
2 tblsp. honey or brown sugar

1 c. unsifted whole wheat flour
2 c. white flour
2 tsp. salt
2 tblsp. soft shortening

Dissolve yeast in warm water. Add honey, half the white flour, salt and shortening. Beat 2 minutes on medium speed, or 300 vigorous strokes by hand, scraping sides and bottom of bowl frequently. Blend in remaining flours with spoon. Cover and let rise in a warm place until doubled, about 30 minutes.

Stir batter down and spread it evenly in a greased loaf pan (8½×4½×2¾″). Smooth top of loaf with floured hands. Let rise until batter reaches ½″ from top of pan, about 40 minutes.

Bake in moderate oven (375°) 45 to 50 minutes or until brown. Remove from pan at once, brush top with butter and cool on rack before cutting. Do not place in direct draft. Makes 1 loaf.

ONION/MUSTARD BUNS

1 pkg. active dry yeast	2 tblsp. instant minced onion
¼ c. warm water (105 to 115°)	2 tblsp. oil
	2 c. scalded milk
2 tblsp. sugar	6 c. sifted flour
1 tblsp. prepared mustard	1 egg, slightly beaten
1½ tsp. salt	2 tblsp. instant minced onion
½ tsp. pepper	¼ c. water

Dissolve yeast in water.

Combine sugar, mustard, salt, pepper, onion and oil in a large bowl. Stir in milk. Cool until lukewarm.

Add 2 c. flour, beating until smooth. Add yeast and egg. Stir in enough flour to make a soft dough.

Turn onto floured surface; knead until smooth, about 5 to 8 minutes. Place in greased bowl. Cover; let rise until doubled, about 1½ hours. Punch down. Divide dough into 2 equal parts. Let rest 10 minutes. Pat each portion of dough into a 9″ square. Cut each square into 9 portions. Tuck corners under to form buns. Flatten with palm of hand. Let rise until doubled, about 30 minutes.

Meanwhile, combine onion and water; allow to stand 5 minutes.

Brush rolls with a glaze using 1 beaten egg and 2 tblsp. water. Sprinkle with onion. Bake in moderate oven (375°) for 20 minutes or until golden brown. Makes 18 buns.

GERMAN TWISTS

1½ pkgs. active dry yeast	1 tsp. salt
¼ c. warm water (105 to 115°)	½ c. evaporated milk
½ c. boiling water	2 eggs, beaten
½ c. shortening	5 to 6 c. sifted flour
⅓ c. sugar	Granulated sugar

Dissolve yeast in warm water.

Combine boiling water and shortening; blend well. Add sugar and salt. Stir until lukewarm. Blend in yeast, milk and eggs. Gradually stir in enough flour to make a soft dough. Turn onto lightly floured surface. Knead until smooth and satiny (about 7 minutes). Place in lightly greased bowl; turn over to grease top. Cover. Let rise in a warm place until doubled, about 1 to 1½ hours.

Turn dough onto floured surface. Roll to ½″ thickness; cut into

$8 \times \frac{1}{2}''$ strips. Place fingers on ends of each strip and gently roll back and forth to form evenly shaped 12" sticks. Fold in half; cross ends of stick over each other to form twist. Pinch to secure ends well. Cover; let rise until doubled (about 30 minutes).

Fry in deep hot fat (375°). Drain on absorbent paper. Roll in sugar. Makes about 3 dozen.

GLAZED POTATO DOUGHNUTS

1 pkg. active dry yeast
¼ c. warm water (105 to 115°)
1 c. milk, scalded
¼ c. shortening
¼ c. sugar
1 tsp. salt

¾ c. mashed potatoes (instant may be used)
2 eggs, beaten
5 to 6 c. sifted flour
1 lb. confectioners sugar
6 tblsp. water
1 tblsp. vanilla

Dissolve yeast in warm water.

Combine milk, shortening, sugar and salt. Cool until lukewarm. Stir in yeast, potatoes and eggs. Gradually add enough flour to make soft dough. Turn onto floured surface; knead until smooth and satiny. Place in lightly greased bowl; turn over to grease top. Cover. Let rise in a warm place until doubled, 1 to 1½ hours.

Roll to ½" thickness; cut with 3" doughnut cutter. Cover; let rise until doubled (about 30 minutes).

Meanwhile, stir confectioners sugar, water and vanilla together.

Fry in deep hot fat (375°). Drain on absorbent paper. Drop hot doughnuts into glaze. Place on cooling rack until glaze is set. Makes about 3½ dozen.

CRANBERRY NUT BREAD

3 c. flour
1½ tblsp. baking powder
1 tsp. salt
1¼ c. sugar
1 c. milk
3 tblsp. melted butter or margarine

1 egg, beaten
½ c. chopped nuts
1½ c. frozen Cranberry Relish, partially thawed (see Index)

Sift together flour, baking powder, salt and sugar.

Combine milk, butter and egg; add to dry ingredients; beat until flour is just moistened.

Fold in nuts and relish. Pour into greased loaf pan (9¼ ×5¼ × 2¾"). Bake in moderate oven (350°) 1 hour and 15 minutes. Remove from pan to rack immediately. Makes 1 loaf.

MAKING, STORING AND USING BREAD CRUMBS Smart young cooks who like short cuts discover fast ways to fix bread crumbs to sprinkle over casseroles and to use in a hundred other dishes. There are about as many favorite ways as there are cooks. But freezer owners agree on one point: it's handy to keep a plastic bag or air-tight container of bread crumbs frozen to add to foods in a hurry.

Some busy homemakers say it pays to buy packaged bread crumbs at their food markets. Other women prefer to make their own. The electric blender makes quick work of this chore.

A farmer's wife explains how she fixes dry bread crumbs. "I really make the sparks (crumbs) fly," she says. "I use the Indian technique of rubbing two pieces of dry bread together over a paper bag, partly torn open, to catch the crumbs. It's mighty convenient when I'm trying to get the casserole in the oven before the men, coming in from the field, reach the house."

Some speedy cooks admit they don't bother to butter the crumbs. They just dot them, once they're atop the dish, with butter or margarine. Others follow this conventional method: melt ⅓ c. butter or margarine in a skillet, add 1 c. bread crumbs and stir constantly until crumbs are golden brown.

Busy women who plan ahead frequently stick to the traditional method: putting dry bread through the food chopper, using the fine blade. This is a chore they tuck into a day when there's a little free time. They store the crumbs in the freezer. And as one thoughtful woman added, "Be sure to tie a paper bag over the blade end of the chopper to catch the crumbs. Then you can pour them into a container in a jiffy—without spilling."

Whatever system you develop or adopt, be sure to use bread crumbs when the recipe so specifies. They add crunchy texture, attractive brown, and delightful flavor atop a casserole. They help sell the dish.

Section 4
Desserts

Most of the desserts in this section freeze beautifully. So even on short notice, you can be the hostess with the most exciting desserts in the neighborhood.

We predict you will have a difficult time choosing which sweet to try first. Why not set aside a rainy day and bake several of these goodies? Then wrap, seal securely, label and tuck into the freezer.

Will it be the Frozen Mincemeat or the Frozen Pumpkin or perhaps the Chocolate Lime Refrigerator Pie? All are simple to fix and are spectacular to look at, as well as to eat.

Special guests coming? Whip up the Frozen Mint Frosted Cake Loaf or try our famous Countryside Test Kitchen recipe for Frozen Fruit Cake. Men will reach for third helpings when you serve the spicy First Prize Applesauce Cake. (A handy tip for freezing cake: freeze in small portions for family use.)

You will want to make up and freeze several batches of the Raisin Griddle Cookie Dough to have on hand for a spur-of-the-moment dessert.

For lunch boxes and cookie jars, Soft Molasses Drops and Chewy Cranberry Squares will rate first on the list once you have served them to your family.

HOLIDAY CRANBERRY CAKE (recipe page 267), **CRANBERRY CHUTNEY** (recipe page 232) and **CRANBERRY TRENTON DESSERT** (recipe page 296) will add zing to your Thanksgiving and Christmas menus.

A gorgeous INFORMAL WEDDING CAKE to make at home (recipe page 267). Frosting is quickly and decoratively studded with miniature marsh-mallows. Flowers are cut from larger marshmallows, petals dipped in colored sugar.

Pies

HAWAIIAN PINEAPPLE PIE

1 (20 oz.) can crushed
  pineapple
1 (3 oz.) pkg. vanilla pudding
  and pie filling
⅛ tsp. salt

½ c. water
1 tblsp. butter or margarine
1 baked (9″) pie shell
½ c. heavy cream, whipped
⅓ c. flaked or shredded coconut

Drain pineapple, reserving juice. Combine pudding mix and salt in saucepan. Blend in water and pineapple juice. Cook over medium heat, stirring constantly, until mixture comes to a full boil. Stir in pineapple and butter. Cool.

Pour filling into pie shell. Spread whipped cream over the top. Sprinkle with coconut. Makes 1 (9″) pie.

BLACK WALNUT CHOCOLATE PIE

½ c. butter or margarine
¾ c. sugar
1 (1 oz.) square unsweetened
  chocolate, melted
1 tsp. vanilla

2 eggs
1 baked (8″) pie shell
½ c. dairy sour cream
⅓ c. black walnuts

Beat butter until creamy. Add sugar gradually and beat until fluffy.

Beat in chocolate and vanilla. Add eggs, one at a time, beating well after each addition. Beat for 2 minutes. Spread in pie shell. Chill ½ hour. Spread sour cream over top and sprinkle with walnuts. Makes 1 (8″) pie.

Note: Try slightly sweetened whipped cream instead of the sour cream.

OPEN-FACED PEACH PIE

2 (1 lb.) cans sliced peaches,
  well drained
1 unbaked (9″) pie shell
⅓ c. sugar
3 tblsp. cornstarch

¾ tsp. nutmeg
¼ tsp. salt
¾ c. heavy cream
¾ tsp. vanilla
Whipped cream

Arrange peach slices in pastry shell.

Combine sugar, cornstarch, ½ tsp. nutmeg, salt, cream and vanilla. Pour over peaches in shell; sprinkle with remaining nutmeg.

Bake in hot oven (400°) 30 minutes; reduce heat to moderate oven (350°) and bake 20 minutes. Serve with whipped cream. Makes 1 (9") pie.

Note: Extra good made with fresh peaches. Use ½ c. instead of ⅓ c. sugar.

BUTTERMILK PIE WITH CORNMEAL PASTRY

3 eggs, separated	¼ tsp. grated lemon rind
1 c. sugar	2 tblsp. lemon juice
1 tblsp. butter	1 unbaked (9") Cornmeal Pie
¼ c. flour	Shell (recipe follows)
2 c. buttermilk	6 tblsp. sugar

Beat egg yolks, adding 1 c. of sugar gradually, blending well. Cut butter into flour; add buttermilk, lemon rind and juice; fold in yolks.

Pour into pastry-lined pan. Bake in hot oven (425°) 10 minutes; reduce heat to moderate (350°), and bake 20 to 25 minutes longer. Cool.

Beat egg whites until frothy; gradually add 6 tblsp. sugar; beat until stiff and glossy. Pile lightly over cooled filling. Bake in moderate oven (350°) 12 to 15 minutes. Makes 1 (9") pie.

Cornmeal Pie Shell

1 c. sifted flour	⅓ c. finely shredded Cheddar
½ tsp. salt	cheese
½ c. cornmeal	¼ c. water
½ c. shortening	

Sifted together flour and salt in bowl. Stir in cornmeal. Cut in shortening until mixture looks like fine crumbs. Stir in cheese. Sprinkle water over mixture, a little at a time, mixing lightly with fork. Shape into a ball; flatten on lightly floured surface. Roll to about ⅛" thickness. Line 9" pie pan with pastry; trim and flute edge. Fill and bake as directed.

FROZEN MINCEMEAT PIE

1 qt. vanilla ice cream, slightly
  softened
1½ c. ready-to-use mincemeat
1 baked (9") pie shell

¼ c. chopped nuts
Maraschino cherries, well
  drained

Beat together ice cream and mincemeat. Spread into pie shell.
Sprinkle with nuts and maraschino cherries, cut in halves.

Freeze until solid, about 4 hours. If kept longer, place in plastic
bag. Serve frozen. Makes 1 (9") pie.

FROZEN PUMPKIN PIE

1 qt. vanilla ice cream, slightly
  softened
1 c. canned pumpkin
⅓ c. sugar
½ tsp. salt

1 tsp. cinnamon
½ tsp. ginger
½ tsp. ground cloves
1 baked (9") pie shell
¼ c. chopped walnuts

Beat together ice cream, pumpkin, sugar, salt, cinnamon, ginger
and cloves with electric beater until well blended.

Pour into pie shell. Sprinkle with nuts. Freeze until firm. If pie is
kept longer, store in a plastic bag. Serve frozen. Makes 1 (9") pie.

DATE NUT PIE

12 soda crackers, crushed
½ c. chopped walnuts
12 dates, chopped
3 egg whites

½ tsp. baking powder
¾ c. sugar
½ tsp. vanilla
1 pt. vanilla ice cream

Combine crackers, nuts and dates. Beat egg whites until frothy;
add baking powder. Continue beating, adding sugar gradually, until
mixture forms stiff peaks. Beat in vanilla.

Fold cracker mixture into egg whites. Spoon into greased 9" pie
pan.

Bake in moderate oven (325°) 25 to 30 minutes. Fill with
spoonfuls of vanilla ice cream just before serving. Makes 1 (9")
pie.

OVERNIGHT CHERRY PIE

18 graham crackers, crushed
½ c. sugar
⅓ c. melted butter
1 c. heavy cream, whipped

2 c. miniature marshmallows
1 (1 lb. 6 oz.) can cherry pie
filling

Combine graham cracker crumbs, sugar and melted butter. Reserve 2 tblsp. mixture. Press remainder into 9" pie pan. Chill. (Chills quickly in freezer.)

Combine whipped cream and marshmallows. Spread half of mixture in bottom of crumb-lined pie pan. Top with cherry pie filling. Cover with remaining whipped cream mixture. Sprinkle with reserved crumbs. Chill overnight. Makes 1 (9") pie.

Note: You can buy graham cracker crumbs in handy (13½ oz.) bags—enough to make 3 pie crusts.

CHOCOLATE AND CREAM PIE

1 c. milk
½ lb. marshmallows (30 to 32)
⅛ tsp. salt
1 tsp. vanilla
1 c. heavy cream
2 (1 oz.) squares unsweetened
chocolate, grated

½ c. chopped walnuts or
pecans
1 baked (9") pie shell
¼ c. flaked or shredded
coconut

Heat milk in double boiler. Add marshmallows, stirring occasionally, until marshmallows are melted. Chill until partly congealed. Add salt and vanilla.

Whip cream until stiff. Fold cream, grated chocolate and nuts into marshmallow mixture.

Pour into pie shell. Sprinkle top with coconut. Chill until serving time. Makes 1 (9") pie.

CHOCOLATE-BAR PIE

20 marshmallows
4 (⅞ oz.) chocolate-almond
bars
1 (1 oz.) square unsweetened
chocolate

⅔ c. milk
1 c. heavy cream, whipped
1 baked (8") pie shell

Combine marshmallows, chocolate bars, chocolate and milk in top of double boiler. Heat over hot, not boiling, water until melted. Cool. Fold in whipped cream. Pour into pie shell. Chill 2 hours. Makes 1 (8") pie.

CHOCOLATE LIME REFRIGERATOR PIE

1¼ c. chocolate cookie crumbs
⅓ c. melted butter
1 (15 oz.) can sweetened
   condensed milk

½ c. lime juice
1 tsp. grated lime rind
   (optional)
1 c. heavy cream, whipped

Combine cookie crumbs and butter. Reserve 2 tblsp. crumb mixture. Press remaining crumb mixture on sides and bottom of greased 8" pie pan. Chill. (You can chill it quickly in freezer.)

Combine condensed (not evaporated) milk, lime juice and lime rind. Stir until mixture thickens. Fold in half the whipped cream. Pour into pan lined with cookie crumbs.

Spread remaining whipped cream over the top. Sprinkle with 2 tblsp. cookie crumb mixture. Chill. Makes 1 (8") pie.

REFRIGERATOR PUMPKIN PIE

1 (15 oz.) can sweetened
   condensed milk
⅓ c. lemon juice
1 (1 lb. 13 oz.) can pumpkin
3½ tsp. pumpkin-pie spice

½ tsp. salt
1 baked (9") pie shell
½ c. heavy cream, whipped
2 tblsp. chopped nuts

Combine condensed (not evaporated) milk and lemon juice; stir until mixture thickens. Stir in pumpkin, spice and salt. Lightly spoon into pie shell.

Chill in refrigerator until firm, about 4 hours. Spread whipped cream over the top. Sprinkle with nuts. Makes 1 (9") pie.

Variation: Top with Whipped Maple Topping instead of whipped cream. Drizzle 2 tblsp. maple or maple-blended syrup on ½ c. heavy cream, whipped. Carefully fold in the syrup.

HOT WATER PASTRY

⅓ c. boiling water
⅔ c. shortening

2 c. sifted flour
¾ tsp. salt

Pour water over shortening; beat with spoon until creamy. Cool. Sift flour and salt into the shortening mixture; mix with a fork.

Wrap the soft dough in waxed paper and chill before rolling. Makes enough for 1 (8") two-crust pie.

PASTRY FOR ONE-CRUST PIE

1 c. sifted flour	⅓ c. lard
½ tsp. salt	2 tblsp. water

Mix sifted flour and salt; cut in lard with pastry blender. Sprinkle on the water and mix with a fork until all the flour is moistened. Gather the dough together and press firmly into a ball. Makes enough pastry for 1 (8" or 9") one-crust pie.

Variation: Substitute ⅓ c. plus 1 tblsp. hydrogenated fat for the lard.

Pastry for 9" Two-crust Pie   Double recipe for Pastry for One-crust Pie.

Pastry for 8" Two-crust Pie   Use 1 c. flour, ⅔ tsp. salt, ½ c. lard (or ½ c. plus 1 tblsp. hydrogenated shortening) and ¼ c. water.

Pink Pastry   Add 3 or 4 drops red food color to water when making Pastry for One-crust Pie.

Freezing Pie Shells   Freeze pie shells baked or unbaked. They will keep satisfactorily 6 months. Freeze unbaked pastry in circles with a double fold of sheet-wrapping material, or one layer of foil or saran between. To use, remove pastry circle from freezer and fit into pans as soon as the dough can be manipulated. Quick-freeze baked shells in pie pans; remove from freezer and package.

Cakes

FROZEN MINT-FROSTED CAKE LOAF

1 (15 oz.) pkg. angel food cake mix	1 c. heavy cream, whipped
	3 tblsp. confectioners sugar
1 qt. brick strawberry ice cream	¼ tsp. peppermint extract
	4 to 6 drops green food color

Bake cake according to package directions in 2 (9×5×3") loaf pans. Cool.

Split 1 loaf into 3 lengthwise slices (freeze other loaf for use later). Cut ice cream into 7 equal slices.

Cover bottom cake layer with 3½ slices ice cream; top with middle cake layer; cover with remaining ice cream; top with third cake layer.

Blend whipped cream, sugar, extract and food color; use to frost sides and top of cake.

Let cake set a few minutes after you frost it; freeze uncovered until firm. Remove from freezer; wrap and return to freezer. Will keep about 8 weeks. Makes 8 servings.

Variation: Substitute chocolate ice cream for the strawberry.

LADY BALTIMORE CAKE

1 (1 lb. 3 oz.) pkg. white cake mix
1 (14 oz.) pkg. white frosting mix
¼ tsp. almond extract

¼ c. chopped dates
½ c. chopped seeded raisins
12 candied cherries, chopped
½ c. chopped pecans

Mix and bake cake as directed on package in two 8" round or square layers. Cool.

Prepare frosting as directed on package, adding almond extract. Combine ¾ c. frosting with fruits and nuts; spread between layers. Frost top and side of cake with remaining frosting. Makes 1 (8") layer cake.

Variation: Substitute well-drained maraschino cherries for candied cherries. Use syrup from cherries as part of liquid in frosting to tint a delicate pink. Or, tint frosting with red food color.

LORD BALTIMORE CAKE

1 (1 lb. 3 oz.) pkg. yellow cake mix
1 (14 oz.) pkg. white frosting mix
¼ tsp. lemon or orange extract

¼ c. blanched chopped almonds
¼ c. chopped pecans
½ c. dry macaroon crumbs
12 candied cherries, chopped

Mix and bake cake as directed on package in two 8" round layers. Cool.

Prepare frosting as directed on package, adding extract.

Toast nuts and crumbs in moderate oven (350°) 5 minutes.

Blend nuts, crumbs and cherries into 1 c. frosting; spread between layers.

Frost top and side of cake with remaining frosting. Decorate side of cake with strips of candied cherries and nuts. Makes 1 (8") layer cake.

UPSIDE-DOWN CHOCOLATE CAKE

2 c. miniature marshmallows
1 c. brown sugar
½ c. cocoa
2 c. hot water

1 (1 lb. 3 oz.) pkg. devil's food cake mix
1 c. chopped walnuts

Place marshmallows in bottom of greased 13×9×2" pan. Combine sugar, cocoa and hot water. Pour over marshmallows.

Spoon cake batter, made as directed on package, over marshmallow mixture. Top with walnuts.

Bake in moderate oven (350°) 45 to 50 minutes. Remove from oven. Turn out of pan. Cut in rectangles. Makes 1 (13×9×2") cake.

Note: Especially luscious topped with vanilla ice cream or whipped cream.

CHOCOLATE MOUND CAKE

1 (1 lb. 3 oz.) pkg. devil's food cake mix
1 recipe Coconut Topping (recipe follows)

1 (14 oz.) pkg. fluffy white frosting mix
Chocolate syrup

Prepare cake mix as directed on package. Bake in 2 (8") layers.

Top each cooled layer with Coconut Topping and broil as directed in recipe.

Prepare frosting mix as directed on package. Put layers together with frosting and frost sides. Leave top unfrosted with coconut showing.

Dip tip of teaspoon in chocolate syrup and swirl lightly through frosting for decorative effect. Makes 1 (8") layer cake.

COCONUT TOPPING

1 egg white	1⅓ c. flaked or shredded
⅓ c. sugar	coconut

Combine unbeaten egg white, sugar and coconut.

Place cake layers on baking sheets. Spread coconut mixture on them, using care to spread out to edges all around.

Place one layer at a time in broiler 6″ to 8″ from heat source and broil until bubbly and golden in color, about 2 to 3 minutes. Makes enough topping for 2 (8″) round layers.

Note: Broil each layer separately so you can watch easily, for the broiling is a fast process.

Fast-fix Petits Fours   Prepare batter with 1 (1 lb. 3 oz.) pkg. white cake mix as directed on package. Pour into greased and floured 15½×10½×1″ jelly roll pan. Bake in moderate oven (350°) about 25 minutes. Cool and frost in pan. Use your favorite confectioners sugar frosting. Cut cake in small squares or diamonds and top each one with a tiny candy, using candies of different colors.

FROZEN FRUIT CAKE

2 c. milk	2 c. vanilla wafers or
½ c. sugar	macaroon crumbs
¼ c. flour	½ c. candied red cherries,
¼ tsp. salt	halved
2 eggs, beaten	¼ c. candied mixed fruits
1 tsp. vanilla	1 c. broken pecans
1 c. light raisins	1 c. heavy cream, whipped

Scald milk in top of double boiler.

Mix together sugar, flour, salt, and add to milk all at once. Cook over hot water about 3 minutes until smooth and medium thick, stirring constantly.

Pour cooked mixture over beaten eggs and return to double boiler. Cook until thick, about 3 minutes, stirring constantly. Add vanilla. Cool.

Stir raisins, crumbs, and fruits and nuts into mixture.

Fold cream into mixture. Pour into 1½ qt. loaf pan, bottom

greased and lined with waxed paper. Cool, wrap and freeze. Makes 8 servings.

Note: To decorate top of fruit cake, arrange a few whole nut meats and candied red and green cherries on waxed paper in bottom of mold before pouring in batter.

EASY-DOES-IT FRUIT CAKE

¾ c. evaporated milk
½ c. frozen orange juice
    concentrate, thawed
3 c. miniature marshmallows
1⅓ lbs. graham crackers,
    crushed into fine crumbs
1 tsp. cinnamon
1 tsp. ground cloves

1 tsp. allspice
½ tsp. salt
1 c. chopped dates
1 c. seedless raisins
1 c. chopped nuts
2 c. chopped mixed candied
    fruits

Combine evaporated milk, orange juice concentrate and marshmallows. Let stand while you prepare other ingredients.

Combine cracker crumbs, spices and salt in large bowl. Add dates, raisins, nuts and candied fruits. Stir into orange juice mixture until crumbs are moist.

Press mixture firmly into 2 waxed paper-lined 9×5×3" loaf pans. Store in refrigerator at least 2 days before serving. Slice thin. Makes 2 loaves.

Note: Cake, well wrapped, will keep several weeks in refrigerator.

FRUIT CAKE DELICIOUS

1½ c. sifted flour
1½ c. sugar
1 tsp. baking powder
1 tsp. salt
2 lbs. pitted dates (do not
    chop)

2 lbs. shelled walnuts
1 lb. shelled Brazil nuts
1 (8 oz.) bottle maraschino
    cherries, drained
5 large eggs, beaten
1 tsp. vanilla

In large bowl, sift together flour, sugar, baking powder and salt. Add dates, nuts and cherries.

Combine eggs and vanilla. Mix into flour-nut mixture.

Spoon into 3 greased 8½×4½×2½" loaf pans.

Bake in moderate oven (325°) 1 hour. Cool thoroughly before slicing or freezing. Makes 3 (8½×4½×2½") loaves.

HOLIDAY CRANBERRY CAKE

1 (1 lb. 3 oz.) pkg. lemon
   cake mix
1 (3 oz.) pkg. cream cheese,
   softened
¾ c. milk
4 eggs

1¼ c. ground cranberries
½ c. ground walnuts
¼ c. sugar
1 tsp. mace (optional)
Confectioners sugar (optional)

Blend cake mix, cream cheese and milk; beat with mixer 2 minutes at medium speed. Add eggs; blend and beat for two additional minutes.

Thoroughly combine cranberries, walnuts, sugar and mace; fold into cake batter. Pour into a well-greased and floured 10″ tube or bundt pan. Bake in moderate oven (350°) for 1 hour or until done. Cool 5 minutes. Remove from pan. Cool on wire rack. Dust with confectioners sugar if you wish. Makes 1 (10″) cake.

INFORMAL WEDDING CAKE

2 (1 lb. 3 oz.) pkgs. white
   cake mix
2 recipes Fluffy White
   Frosting (recipe follows)

Marshmallow Flowers (recipe
   follows)

Prepare 3-tier cake pan set (9×1½″, 7¼×1½″, and 5×1½″) by lining bottoms with plain paper.

Prepare one package of cake mix as directed on package. Pour ½ c. batter into small pan, 1 c. batter into next-size pan and remaining batter into large pan. Spread batter evenly in pans. Tap pans sharply on table top to remove air pockets.

Bake small and medium layers in moderate oven (350°) about 20 minutes, the large layer, 30 minutes. Cool on rack 5 minutes and remove from pans. Brush crumbs from sides of cake while still warm.

Prepare batter from the second package of cake mix in the same manner.

Prepare one recipe of frosting. When layers are cool, put layers of same size together with frosting and coat the sides and tops with a thin layer of frosting to seal the crumbs. Stack layers on each other; hold in place with thin skewers. Let stand until set. Meanwhile, make Marshmallow Flowers.

Prepare another recipe of Fluffy White Frosting. Remove skewers from cake; frost entire cake, starting at bottom tier and working up. Apply thickly around bottom tier. Draw small spatula over frosting to smooth it. Then make ridges by pulling spatula in upward strokes all around. (If frosting seems to be crusting over quickly, do a small section at a time.) Pile frosting on bottom ledge and swirl around cake. Continue working up on the cake as directed for bottom tier. Pile and swirl frosting on top of cake.

Place miniature marshmallows in ridges in frosting as shown in picture, pressing firmly into frosting. Arrange Marshmallow Flowers on top of cake and around edge of plate for decoration. Makes 40 servings.

Note: Bake layers ahead; freeze.

FLUFFY WHITE FROSTING

2 egg whites, unbeaten	2 tsp. light corn syrup
1½ c. sugar	Dash salt
⅓ c. water	1 tsp. vanilla

Place egg whites, sugar, water, corn syrup and salt in top of double boiler. Beat 1 minute with electric mixer or rotary beater.

Cook over boiling water, beating all the time, until mixture stands in stiff peaks—about 7 minutes.

Remove from heat. Transfer mixture to mixing bowl; add vanilla and beat until of good spreading consistency.

Marshmallow Flowers Cut large marshmallows horizontally into 5 pieces, using kitchen scissors dipped in water. Attach these pieces as petals to a miniature marshmallow, used as a center. Dust fingers with confectioners sugar if pieces stick to fingers. Dip finished flower in colored sugar crystals.

CAKE FOR HIGH ALTITUDES The recipe for Quick Cake was developed for use in altitudes of 4000 to 6000 feet. We give the changes to make if you live in altitudes of 3000 to 4000 feet and above 6000 feet. Frost the cake as you like. Chocolate and coconut frostings are two favorites.

QUICK CAKE FOR HIGH ALTITUDES

2 c. sifted cake flour
1¼ tsp. baking powder
¾ tsp. salt
1 c. plus 2 tblsp. sugar
½ c. vegetable shortening,
  at room temperature

¾ c. milk
1 tsp. vanilla
2 eggs, unbeaten

Sift together flour, baking powder, salt and sugar.

Stir shortening just to soften. Sift in dry ingredients. Add milk and vanilla; mix until flour is dampened. Beat 2 minutes at medium speed of electric mixer or 300 vigorous strokes by hand.

Add eggs. Beat 1 minute longer with mixer or 150 strokes by hand.

Pour batter into 2 greased 8″ layer pans. Bake in a moderate oven (375°) 25 to 30 minutes. Makes 1 (8″) layer cake.

Baking Variations: Bake 30 to 35 minutes in a greased 9×9×2″ pan, 25 to 30 minutes in a 13×9×2″ greased pan, and 20 to 25 minutes in 2½ dozen greased medium muffin tins.

Ingredient Variations: Substitute butter or margarine for vegetable shortening. Use 1 c. minus 2 tblsp. milk and 1¼ c. sugar. Add ¾ c. of milk and vanilla to dry ingredients and the remaining milk with the eggs.

Altitude Variations: For altitudes of 3000 to 4000 feet, increase baking powder to 1¾ tsp. For altitudes above 6000 feet, decrease baking powder to 1 tsp. and sugar by 2 tblsp.

A reliable recipe for a 2-egg cake is at a premium in any busy woman's file. That's why we include one for this cake that gives excellent results in lower altitudes.

QUICK CAKE FOR LOWER ALTITUDES

1¾ c. sifted cake flour
2¼ tsp. baking powder
½ tsp. salt
½ c. shortening

1 c. plus 2 tblsp. sugar
2 eggs, unbeaten
¾ c. milk
1 tsp. vanilla

Sift flour, baking powder and salt together. Cream shortening thoroughly. Add sugar gradually and cream together until light and fluffy. Add eggs, one at a time, beating well after each addition. Then add flour alternately with milk, beating after each addition until smooth. Stir in vanilla.

Pour batter into 2 greased 8″ layer pans. Bake in moderate oven (375°) 25 to 30 minutes. Makes 1 (8″) layer cake.

CHERRY CRUMB CAKE

1 c. sugar	½ c. butter
2 c. sifted flour	1 egg
2 tsp. baking powder	1 (1 lb. 6 oz.) can cherry pie
½ tsp. salt	filling

Mix sugar and flour, sifted with baking powder and salt. Cut in the butter, add the egg and mix to make crumbs.

Place half of the crumb mixture in the bottom of a greased 13×9×2″ pan. Pour over it, distributing evenly, the cherries. Top with remaining crumbs.

Bake in moderate oven (350°) 30 minutes. Serve with whipped cream, ice cream or plain. Makes 1 (13×9×2″) cake.

Variations: Use peach, blueberry or other canned pie fillings instead of cherries. Add a touch of pumpkin-pie spice or cinnamon to the top crumbs.

High altitude adjustment
Above 3500 feet altitude: Increase baking temperature to 375° and bake 30 to 35 minutes or until delicately browned.

CRUMB CAKE

2 c. sifted flour	½ tsp. nutmeg
1½ c. brown sugar, firmly packed	¼ tsp. ground cloves
	¾ c. plus 2 tblsp. buttermilk
½ c. butter or margarine	or sour milk
1 tsp. baking soda	2 eggs
1 tsp. salt	½ c. chopped walnuts
1 tsp. cinnamon	

Mix flour and brown sugar (free from lumps) with pastry blender. Then cut in butter until dry mixture is evenly coated. Remove ¾ c. of this mixture and reserve for later use.

Stir soda, salt, cinnamon, nutmeg and cloves into remaining mixture. Add ¾ c. buttermilk and beat 2 minutes on medium speed of mixer.

Add remaining buttermilk and eggs; beat 1 more minute. Pour batter into greased and floured 13×9×2″ pan.

Add walnuts to the ¾ c. sugar mixture. Sprinkle evenly over the batter.

Bake in moderate oven (350°) 25 to 30 minutes. Makes 1 (13× 9×2″) cake.

High altitude adjustment

For all altitudes above 3500 feet: Increase baking temperature to 375° and bake 30 to 35 minutes. From 3500 to 5000 feet altitude: Use ingredients as listed in Crumb Cake recipe.

Above 5000 feet altitude: Use 1¼ c. brown sugar and 1 c. buttermilk.

BUTTERSCOTCH CRUNCH CAKE

⅓ c. butter or margarine
½ c. graham cracker crumbs
¼ c. chopped nuts
½ c. butterscotch morsels
⅓ c. shortening
1⅓ c. sifted flour

1 c. sugar
2 tsp. baking powder
½ tsp. salt
⅔ c. milk
1 tsp. vanilla
1 egg

Melt butter in 9×9×2″ pan. Sprinkle evenly with crumbs and nuts combined, then with morsels.

In a bowl, stir shortening to soften. Sift in flour, sugar, baking powder and salt. Add milk and vanilla; beat 2 minutes, medium speed on mixer. Add egg and beat 1 more minute.

Pour batter over crumb mixture and spread evenly. Bake in moderate oven (350°) 40 to 45 minutes.

Remove from oven and let stand 3 or 4 minutes. Then invert on plate and let stand a minute before removing pan. Cut in squares and serve warm with whipped cream. Or serve cold. Makes 1 (9″) square cake.

High altitude adjustment

For all altitudes above 3500 feet: Increase baking temperature to 375° and bake 35 to 40 minutes.

From 3500 to 6000 feet altitude: Use 1½ tsp. baking powder and ¾ c. milk.

Above 6000 feet altitude: Use 1¼ tsp. baking powder and 1 c. minus 2 tblsp. milk.

CHERRY CROWN CAKE

2 (8") yellow cake layers
2 tblsp. butter or margarine
¼ c. brown sugar, firmly packed
2 tblsp. heavy cream, or sour cream

16 maraschino cherries, drained and halved
1 recipe Glossy Fudge Frosting (see Index)

Place one layer on baking sheet.

Melt butter, stir in brown sugar and cream and add cherries. Spread mixture on cake layer, spreading out to edges all around.

Place cake in broiler 6" to 8" from heat and broil until bubbly all over and golden brown, 2 to 3 minutes. Use this for the top layer of cake.

Put layers together and frost sides of cake with Glossy Fudge Frosting. Leave top of cake unfrosted with the cherries showing. Makes 1 (8") layer cake.

CINNAMON COFFEE SQUARES

3 c. sifted flour
2 tsp. baking powder
2 tsp. cinnamon
½ tsp. baking soda
½ tsp. salt
1 c. butter

2 c. brown sugar, firmly packed
2 eggs
1 c. hot coffee
Icing (recipe follows)

Sift together flour, baking powder, cinnamon, baking soda and salt.

Cream together butter, sugar and eggs until fluffy. Alternately add dry ingredients and coffee, beating well after each addition.

Pour into a greased 13×9×2" cake pan. Bake in moderate oven (350°) for 35 minutes or until cake tests done.

Cool. Frost and cut into squares. Makes 1 (13×9") cake.

Icing

2 c. sifted confectioners sugar	Dash salt
⅓ c. soft butter	2 tblsp. milk
1½ tsp. vanilla	

Combine all ingredients; blend until smooth.

MARSHMALLOW-BANANA BARS

1½ c. sifted flour	1 tblsp. water
1 tsp. baking powder	1 tsp. vanilla
½ c. shortening	1⅓ c. mashed bananas
1 c. sugar	1 (7 oz.) jar marshmallow
1 egg	creme
1 tsp. baking soda	Vanilla Icing (recipe follows)

Sift together flour and baking powder.

Cream shortening and sugar. Add egg; beat well. Dissolve baking soda in water. Add to creamed mixture. Add vanilla. Add dry ingredients alternately with bananas, beating well after each addition.

Spread into a greased 15×9″ jelly roll pan. Bake in moderate oven (350°) for 25 to 30 minutes or until cake tests done. Remove from oven. Drop spoonfuls of marshmallow creme on bars. Let stand 2 minutes. Spread gently over surface of cake. Cool, frost with Vanilla Icing. Makes 1 (15×9″) cake.

Vanilla Icing

2 c. sifted confectioners sugar	1 tsp. vanilla
1 tblsp. butter	Yellow food coloring
2 tblsp. milk	

Combine confectioners sugar, butter, milk and vanilla. Beat until smooth. Add a few drops yellow food coloring.

BROWN SUGAR POUND CAKE

1 c. butter	½ tsp. salt
½ c. shortening	1 tsp. baking powder
1 lb. light brown sugar	1 c. milk
1 c. sugar	1 tsp. vanilla
5 eggs	1 c. chopped walnuts
3 c. sifted flour	Walnut Glaze (recipe follows)

Beat butter and shortening together; gradually add the sugars, creaming until mixture is light and fluffy. Beat in eggs one at a time.

Sift together dry ingredients and add alternately with milk and vanilla to the creamed mixture. Stir in nuts.

Pour batter into greased and floured 10″ tube pan. Bake in moderate oven (350°) 1 hour and 15 minutes, or until done when tested with a straw. Cool 10 minutes, then remove from pan. Pour Walnut Glaze over hot cake. Makes 1 (10″) cake.

Walnut Glaze

1 c. sifted confectioners sugar	½ tsp. vanilla
2 tblsp. soft butter	½ c. chopped walnuts
6 tblsp. light cream	

Combine confectioners sugar, butter, cream and vanilla. Blend well. Add walnuts.

SPICY PRUNE CAKE

1 c. vegetable oil	1 tsp. nutmeg
1½ c. sugar	1 tsp. allspice
3 eggs	1 c. cooked and mashed
2 c. sifted flour	prunes
½ tsp. salt	1 c. buttermilk
1 tsp. baking powder	1 c. chopped pecans
1 tsp. baking soda	Caramel Glaze (recipe follows)
1 tsp. cinnamon	

Cream oil and sugar. Beat in eggs one at a time.

Sift together dry ingredients. Add alternately to creamed mixture with prunes and buttermilk. Stir in pecans.

Pour into greased and floured 13×9×2″ pan. Bake in moderate oven (350°) for 35 minutes. Put pan on rack. Pour hot Caramel Glaze over cake immediately. Makes 1 (13×9×2″) cake.

Caramel Glaze

1 c. sugar	1 tblsp. light corn syrup
½ c. buttermilk	½ tsp. baking soda
½ c. butter	½ tsp. vanilla

Combine all ingredients in a medium saucepan. Bring to a rolling boil over low heat and boil 10 minutes, stirring occasionally.

FIRST PRIZE APPLESAUCE CAKE

4 c. sifted flour	2 c. sugar
4 tsp. soda	3 c. unsweetened applesauce,
1¼ tsp. salt	heated
2 tsp. cinnamon	½ c. raisins
½ tsp. nutmeg	½ c. chopped walnuts
½ tsp. cloves	Caramel Frosting (recipe
2 tblsp. cocoa	follows)
1 c. vegetable oil	

Sift together flour, soda, salt, cinnamon, nutmeg, cloves and cocoa.
In a large mixing bowl combine vegetable oil and sugar. Beat until
well blended. Stir in hot applesauce, blending thoroughly. Add dry
ingredients, blending well. Stir in raisins and walnuts. Turn batter
into 2 well-greased and floured 9×9×2″ cake pans. Bake in hot
oven (400°) for 15 minutes; then reduce oven temperature to 375°
and bake about 15 minutes longer. Remove to racks. Let stand in
pans 5 minutes. Remove from pans. Cool on rack. Fill and frost
with Caramel Frosting. Makes 1 (9″) square layer cake.

Caramel Frosting

½ c. butter	¼ tsp. salt
1 c. dark brown sugar,	¼ c. milk
firmly packed	2 c. sifted confectioners sugar

Melt butter in a medium saucepan over low heat. Stir in brown
sugar and salt. Bring to a boil over medium heat; boil hard for 2
minutes, stirring constantly. Remove from heat. Stir in milk. Return
saucepan to heat; bring to a full boil. Remove from heat, cool to
lukewarm. Stir in confectioners sugar, beating until smooth.

GRAND CHAMPION SPONGE CAKE

1¼ c. sifted flour	½ c. sugar
1 c. sugar	6 egg yolks
½ tsp. baking powder	¼ c. water
½ tsp. salt	1 tsp. vanilla
6 egg whites	Creamy Pineapple Frosting
1 tsp. cream of tartar	(recipe follows)

Sift together flour, 1 c. sugar, baking powder and salt.
In a large mixing bowl, beat egg whites until frothy. Add cream

of tartar. Gradually beat in ½ c. sugar, a little at a time; beat until whites form stiff, not dry peaks.

In a small bowl, combine egg yolks, water, vanilla and sifted dry ingredients. Beat at medium high speed for 4 minutes or until mixture is light and fluffy. Fold yolk mixture gently, but thoroughly into the beaten egg whites. Turn into an ungreased 10″ tube pan. Bake in moderate oven (350°) for about 45 minutes. Invert pan to cool. Frost with Creamy Pineapple Frosting. Makes 1 (10″) cake.

Creamy Pineapple Frosting

¼ c. butter
¼ c. shortening
3 c. sifted confectioners sugar
1 (8½ oz.) can crushed
   pineapple, drained

½ tsp. grated lemon rind
¼ tsp. vanilla
⅛ tsp. salt

Cream together butter and shortening. Gradually add confectioners sugar; beat until light and fluffy. Blend in pineapple, lemon rind, vanilla and salt. Beat until smooth.

BLUE RIBBON BANANA CAKE

¾ c. shortening
1½ c. sugar
2 eggs
1 c. mashed bananas
½ tsp. salt
2 c. sifted cake flour
1 tsp. soda
1 tsp. baking powder

½ c. buttermilk
1 tsp. vanilla
½ c. chopped pecans
1 c. flaked coconut
Creamy Nut Filling (recipe
   follows)
White Snow Frosting (recipe
   follows)

Cream together shortening and sugar until fluffy. Add eggs; beat 2 minutes at medium speed. Add mashed bananas. Beat 2 minutes.

Sift together dry ingredients. Add to creamed mixture along with buttermilk and vanilla. Beat 2 minutes. Stir in nuts.

Turn into 2 greased and floured 9″ layer pans. Sprinkle ½ c. coconut on each layer. Bake in a moderate oven (375°) 25 to 30 minutes. Remove from pan. Cool layers, coconut side up, on rack.

Place first layer, coconut side down, and spread with Creamy Nut Filling. Top with second layer, coconut side up. Swirl White Snow Frosting around sides and about 1″ around top edge, leaving center unfrosted. Makes 1 (9″) layer cake.

Creamy Nut Filling

½ c. sugar
2 tblsp. flour
½ c. light cream
2 tblsp. butter

½ c. chopped pecans
1 tsp. vanilla
¼ tsp. salt

Combine sugar and flour in a medium heavy saucepan. Gradually stir in cream. Add butter. Cook, stirring constantly, until thickened. Stir in pecans, vanilla and salt. Cool.

White Snow Frosting

¼ c. butter
¼ c. shortening
1 egg white

½ tsp. coconut extract
½ tsp. vanilla
2 c. sifted confectioners sugar

Cream together butter, shortening, egg white, coconut extract and vanilla until well blended. Gradually add confectioners sugar, beating until light and fluffy.

SUPERIOR FROSTINGS WITH SYRUP Sometimes it's a simple, quick trick that works magic in the kitchen. That's exactly what Basic Sugar Syrup does with frostings. Try our Glossy Fudge Frosting and Peanut Butter Frosting and see if you don't agree.

Keep a jar of the syrup handy in the refrigerator. Also use it to sweeten beverages. And when you have an elegant cake that deserves an out-of-the-world frosting, or a plain one that needs a glamorous coverlet, put the syrup to work for you.

BASIC SUGAR SYRUP

2 c. sugar
1 c. water

Boil sugar and water together 1 minute. Pour into jar. Cool, cover and store in the refrigerator. Makes approximately 2 cups.

Note: Frostings made with Basic Sugar Syrup in higher altitudes (above 3500 feet) take longer and more beating than in lower altitudes to become thick enough to stay on the cake.

GLOSSY FUDGE FROSTING

2 tblsp. butter or margarine   ⅓ c. Basic Sugar Syrup
1 (6 oz.) pkg. semi-sweet
  chocolate pieces

Melt butter over hot (not boiling) water. Remove from heat before the water boils.

Add chocolate pieces to butter over hot water and stir until melted, blended and thick.

Add Basic Sugar Syrup gradually, stirring after each addition until blended. Mixture will become glossy and smooth.

Remove from hot water and cool until of spreading consistency. Spread thinly over cake. Apply quickly by pouring a small amount at a time on top of cake; as it runs down on sides, spread with spatula. Frost top of cake last. Makes frosting for 2 (8″) layers, or 1 (13×9×2″) cake.

CHOCOLATE-BUTTERSCOTCH FROSTING

1 (6 oz.) pkg. butterscotch   ½ c. Basic Sugar Syrup
  morsels
1 (1 oz.) square unsweetened
  chocolate

Melt butterscotch morsels and chocolate over hot, not boiling, water.

Add Basic Sugar Syrup gradually to butterscotch-chocolate mixture, stirring until blended after each addition. (Mixture becomes glossy and smooth.)

Remove from hot water and cool until of spreading consistency. In warm weather, it may be necessary to set pan in iced water to cool quickly. Enough frosting for 2 (8″) cake layers or 1 (13×9×2″) cake.

Cake Trim Make cake as directed on mix package. Frost with fluffy white frosting made from packaged mix. To decorate, pour a few drops of food color into saucer. Dip a piece of white sewing thread in color, keeping ends dry by holding one in each hand. Hold wet thread tight and press design on frosted cake. You can smear lines a little with a spatula if desired. Make a spoke design on round cake and squares or diamonds on a square or rectangular cake.

PEANUT BUTTER FROSTING

¾ c. chunk-style peanut butter
¾ c. Basic Sugar Syrup

Whip peanut butter with mixer (or wooden spoon). Add syrup gradually, beating all the time. Makes enough frosting for tops and sides of 2 (8″ or 9″) cake layers.

A COUNTRY COOK SAYS: When you make a confectioners sugar frosting for a cake, stir up more than you need. Store the extra amount in an air-tight container in refrigerator. Next time you take a 13×9×2″ cake from the oven, put a big spoonful of the cold frosting on it while hot. As frosting starts to melt, begin the spreading. Spread it over the entire cake. When the cake cools, it will wear a lovely, glossy glaze.

Cookies

HONEY COOKIE BARS

⅔ c. sifted flour
½ tsp. baking powder
¼ tsp. salt
½ c. sugar
½ c. honey
½ c. shortening

1 egg
½ c. shredded coconut
½ c. crumbled shredded-wheat
cereal
1 c. quick-cooking rolled oats
1 tsp. vanilla

Sift flour, baking powder and salt into mixing bowl. Add remaining ingredients and beat thoroughly. Spread mixture in greased 9×9×2″ pan.

Bake in moderate oven (350°) until lightly browned, 30 to 35 minutes. Cut in squares. Makes 3 dozen (1½″) bars.

MINCEMEAT BARS

1 (11.4 oz.) pkg. butterscotch
refrigerator cookies
½ c. mincemeat

¼ c. brown sugar, firmly
packed

Crumble ⅔ roll of cookie dough into a (8×8×2″) pan. Pat down evenly to cover bottom of pan. Spread with mincemeat.

Crumble remaining dough into bowl and mix well with brown sugar. Sprinkle this mixture evenly over mincemeat.

Bake in moderate oven (350°) 30 to 35 minutes. Makes 32 (1×2″) bars.

DATE LOGS

¾ c. sifted flour
1 c. sugar
1 tsp. baking powder
¼ tsp. salt

1 c. chopped dates
1 c. chopped walnuts
3 eggs, well beaten

Sift together flour, sugar, baking powder and salt. Stir in dates, nuts and eggs.

Pour into greased 9″ square pan.

Bake in moderate oven (325°) 35 to 40 minutes. Cool and cut into 48 bars or strips. Roll in confectioners sugar.

Note: You can bake cookies at your convenience several weeks before Christmas. Package them in freezer containers with tight-fitting lids, label, date and freeze.

7-LAYER BARS

¼ c. butter or margarine
1 c. graham cracker crumbs
1 c. shredded coconut
1 (6 oz.) pkg. semi-sweet chocolate pieces
1 (6 oz.) pkg. butterscotch flavor pieces

1 (15 oz.) can sweetened condensed milk (do not substitute)
1 c. chopped nuts

Melt butter in 13×9×2″ baking pan. Sprinkle crumbs evenly over butter (tap sides of pan to distribute crumbs). Sprinkle on coconut, chocolate and butterscotch pieces.

Pour sweetened condensed (not evaporated) milk evenly over top. Sprinkle on nuts and press lightly into pan.

Bake in moderate oven (350°) for 30 minutes. Cool in pan. Cut into 40 (1×2″) bars.

CHEWY CRANBERRY SQUARES

¾ c. sugar
6 tblsp. butter
2 eggs
1½ tblsp. lemon juice
1½ c. sifted flour

1½ tsp. baking powder
½ tsp. salt
1 c. chopped nuts
¾ c. jellied cranberry sauce,
cut in ¼" cubes

Cream sugar and butter until light. Add eggs and lemon juice; beat until smooth and creamy.

Sift together flour, baking powder and salt. Stir into creamed mixture. Gently fold in nuts and cranberry cubes. Pour batter into a greased 13×9×2" pan. Bake in moderate oven (350°) for 25 to 30 minutes. Cut into squares while still warm. Makes 24 bars.

FRUITCAKE SQUARES

6 tblsp. butter or margarine
1½ c. graham cracker crumbs
1 c. shredded coconut
2 c. cut-up mixed candied
fruit

1 c. dates
1 c. coarsely chopped nuts
1 (15 oz.) can sweetened
condensed milk

Melt butter in 15½×10½×1" jelly roll pan. Sprinkle on crumbs (tap sides of the pan to distribute crumbs evenly). Sprinkle on coconut. Distribute candied fruit as evenly as possible over coconut.

Cut dates into a small amount of flour so they won't stick together. Distribute dates over candied fruit.

Sprinkle on nuts. Press mixture lightly with hands to level it in pan. Pour sweetened condensed (not evaporated) milk evenly over top.

Bake in moderate oven (350°) for 25 to 30 minutes. Cool completely before cutting. Remove from pan. Makes about 54 (1½") squares.

TOFFEE STICKS

¾ c. softened butter or
margarine
½ c. brown sugar, firmly
packed
1 egg yolk
1 tsp. vanilla
¼ tsp. salt
1½ c. sifted flour

2 tblsp. vegetable shortening
1 (6 oz.) pkg. butterscotch
flavor pieces
¼ c. light corn syrup
1 tblsp. water
¼ tsp. salt
Toasted, slivered almonds

Blend together softened butter, brown sugar, egg yolk, vanilla and salt. Stir in flour. Spread mixture in 13×9×2" baking pan.

Bake in moderate oven (350°) for 20 minutes or until nicely browned. Cool slightly.

Combine shortening, butterscotch pieces, corn syrup, water and salt in a saucepan. Heat and stir until sauce is smooth. Spread over top of baked dough. Sprinkle on almonds. Allow topping to set. Cut into 48 (1×2") sticks.

OVEN-BAKED SCONES

2 c. sifted flour	1 egg, beaten
1 tsp. salt	⅓ c. milk
3 tsp. baking powder	¾ c. raisins
½ c. sugar	
½ c. shortening	

Sift flour with salt, baking powder and sugar. Cut in shortening until mixture resembles meal.

Combine egg and milk. Add with raisins to flour mixture; stir just enough to mix well.

Turn out on floured board. Knead lightly. Divide into thirds. Roll each piece into a 6" circle. Cut each circle into 4 wedges.

Place on greased baking sheet. Brush tops with milk and sprinkle with sugar.

Bake in hot oven (425°) 12 to 15 minutes. Serve warm. Makes 1 dozen.

MEXICAN CHOCOLATE CRINKLES

¾ c. soft shortening	1¾ c. sifted flour
1 c. sugar	2 tsp. baking soda
1 egg	¼ tsp. salt
¼ c. light corn syrup	1 tsp. cinnamon
2 (1 oz.) squares unsweetened chocolate, melted	¼ c. sugar (for dipping)

Cream together shortening, sugar and egg. Stir in syrup and melted chocolate.

Sift flour, soda, salt and cinnamon into creamed mixture and stir to make stiff dough.

Shape dough into balls about the size of walnuts and roll in sugar.

Place on ungreased baking sheet about 3" apart. Bake in moderate oven (350°) 15 minutes. Cookies will flatten and crinkle.

Let stand a few minutes before removing to wire racks. Makes 3 dozen (3") cookies.

ORANGE-COCONUT CRISPS

2 eggs	2½ c. sifted flour
⅔ c. salad oil	2 tsp. baking powder
1 c. sugar	½ tsp. salt
¼ c. frozen orange juice concentrate, thawed	1 c. grated coconut

Beat eggs with fork until well blended. Stir in oil. Blend in sugar until mixture thickens. Stir in orange juice.

Sift together flour, baking powder and salt; add with coconut to egg mixture. Stir until well blended.

Drop by teaspoonfuls about 2" apart on ungreased baking sheet. Stamp each cookie flat with bottom of drinking glass dipped in sugar. (Lightly oil glass, then dip in sugar. Continue dipping in sugar for each cookie.)

Bake in hot oven (400°) 8 to 10 minutes. Remove immediately from baking sheet. Makes 3 dozen (3") cookies.

Note: Balls of cookie dough, rolled in sugar, may be packaged and frozen for future use. To bake: remove as many balls as desired from package, place on baking sheet and let stand about 30 minutes at room temperature. Bake as directed.

OATMEAL-GUMDROP COOKIES

2 eggs	2 tsp. baking powder
⅔ c. salad oil	½ tsp. salt
¾ c. sugar	1¼ c. quick-cooking rolled oats
¼ c. molasses	½ c. gumdrops, cut in small
1½ c. sifted flour	pieces

Beat eggs with fork until blended. Stir in oil. Blend in sugar until mixture thickens. Stir in molasses.

Sift together flour, baking powder and salt; add to egg mixture with rolled oats and gumdrops. Stir until well blended.

Drop by teaspoonfuls about 2" apart on greased baking sheet. Stamp each cookie flat with bottom of drinking glass, dipped in oil and then in sugar. Continue dipping in sugar for each cookie.

Bake in hot oven (400°) 8 to 10 minutes. Remove immediately from baking sheet. Makes about 3½ dozen (3") cookies.

DOUBLE TREAT COOKIES

2½ c. sifted flour
2 tsp. baking soda
½ tsp. salt
1 c. shortening
1 c. sugar
1 c. brown sugar, firmly packed

2 eggs
1 tsp. vanilla
1 c. peanut butter
1 c. chopped, salted peanuts
1 (6 oz.) pkg. chocolate chips

Sift together flour, baking soda and salt.

Beat together shortening, sugars, eggs and vanilla until fluffy. Blend in peanut butter. Add dry ingredients. Stir in peanuts and chocolate chips.

Shape into small balls; place on ungreased baking sheet. Flatten with a glass dipped in sugar.

Bake in moderate oven (350°) for 8 minutes or until brown. Makes 7 dozen (3") cookies.

COCONUT-NUTMEG COOKIES

1 (1 lb. 3 oz.) pkg. yellow or white cake mix
½ c. soft butter
1 egg

2 tblsp. water
¼ tsp. nutmeg
1 c. flaked coconut

Combine cake mix, butter, egg, water and nutmeg. Beat at medium speed for 1½ minutes or until well blended. Stir in coconut.

Drop by teaspoonfuls on lightly greased baking sheet. Bake in moderate oven (350°) 12 to 15 minutes or until lightly brown. Makes 3½ dozen (2¼") cookies.

SOFT MOLASSES DROPS

¾ c. butter
1½ c. brown sugar
3 eggs
1 tsp. vanilla

2 tblsp. molasses
1 tsp. baking soda
3 c. sifted flour
1 c. raisins

Cream butter and sugar until light and fluffy. Add eggs and vanilla; beat well.

Combine molasses and baking soda. Add to creamed mixture. Gradually stir in flour. Add raisins.

Drop by teaspoonfuls onto greased baking sheet. Bake in moderate oven (350°) for 8 minutes or until brown. Makes about 6 dozen.

WAFERS MADE WITH PIE CRUST

SESAME-SEED WAFERS

2 sticks pie-crust mix	¾ c. sugar
3 tblsp. sesame seeds	½ tsp. vanilla
1 egg	

Crumble pie-crust mix into bowl. Add sesame seeds.

Beat egg in another bowl; add sugar and vanilla. Mix well.

Add egg mixture to pie crust mixture; stir with fork until well blended (dough will be soft).

Turn dough out on waxed paper and form a roll 1½" in diameter between layers of the paper. Chill dough thoroughly.

Slice dough thin and place on ungreased baking sheet. Bake in hot oven (400°) 8 to 10 minutes. Makes 4 dozen cookies.

Note: Roll of cookie dough may be frozen for future use. When ready to bake, allow dough to stand at room temperature 15 to 20 minutes before slicing.

MOCHA WAFERS

2 sticks pie-crust mix	2 tblsp. instant coffee
1 egg	1 tsp. baking powder
¾ c. sugar	¼ tsp. almond extract

Crumble pie-crust mix into bowl.

Beat egg in another bowl; add remaining ingredients and mix well.

Add egg mixture to pie crust; stir with a fork until well blended. (Dough will be soft.)

Turn dough out on waxed paper. Form a roll 1½" in diameter between layers of waxed paper. Chill dough thoroughly.

Slice thin and place on ungreased baking sheet. Bake in hot oven (400°) 8 to 10 minutes. Makes 4 dozen cookies.

Variation: To make Black-Walnut Wafers, omit instant coffee and almond extract; add ½ c. finely chopped black walnuts to crumbled pie crust before adding egg and sugar.

Note: Roll of dough may be frozen. Follow directions for freezing and baking of Sesame Seed Wafers.

Freezing Cookies: Frozen baked cookies will keep a year if packaged properly; unbaked ones about 6 months. Most frozen unbaked cookies need to be partly thawed before baking.

GRIDDLE COOKIES—BACK IN STYLE Grandmother used to bake cookies on the griddle to avoid heating the oven in midsummer. Children stopping in her kitchen, hopeful of a handout, remember how good the warm cookies were with glasses of cold lemonade or bowls of ice cream. No childhood eating experience could be more memorable. So it's good news that the cookies again are coming off griddles to please people of all ages.

Give freezers the thanks. Today's cooks roll and cut the dough and stack the circles with foil between like hamburger patties. As they are wrapped in packages and frozen, it's easy to bring the desired number out. Bake them in your electric skillet—at the table, if that's convenient.

RAISIN GRIDDLE COOKIES

3½ c. sifted flour	1 tsp. nutmeg
1 c. sugar	1 c. shortening
1½ tsp. baking powder	1 egg
1 tsp. salt	½ c. milk
½ tsp. baking soda	1¼ c. raisins

Sift dry ingredients together into bowl. Cut in shortening until mixture is mealy.

Beat egg, add milk and blend. Add egg mixture and raisins to flour mixture. Stir until all the ingredients are moistened and dough holds together.

Roll on lightly floured board to ¼″ thickness. Cut with 2″ round cookie cutter.

Heat griddle until a few drops of water dance on it. (Do not overheat griddle.) Oil griddle lightly and place cookies on it. As the bottoms brown, the tops become puffy. Then turn and brown on other side. Serve warm. Makes about 4 dozen cookies.

Variation: To make Lemon Griddle Cookies, omit raisins and add 1 tsp. grated lemon rind.

Freezing Short-cut: Pack unbaked cookies in freezer containers with pieces of foil between them; freeze. Then a few cookies may be removed from the freezer any time you want warm cookies. Let them thaw at room temperature 15 to 20 minutes. Bake on griddle as directed.

Other Desserts

BLUEBERRY DESSERT ROLL

2 c. biscuit mix
½ c. milk
1 c. fresh blueberries or
   frozen blueberries, thawed

½ c. brown sugar
2 tblsp. butter or margarine,
   melted

Combine biscuit mix and milk as directed on package. Roll into rectangle ½" thick.

Sprinkle blueberries and brown sugar over dough, leaving 1" dough uncovered around edges. Roll like jelly roll. Seal lengthwise seam of dough tightly by pressing with fingers. Seal ends well and fold under.

Place roll, seam side down, in greased 9×5×3" loaf pan. With scissors make 4 small openings in top to permit escape of steam. Brush with melted butter.

Bake in hot oven (400°) 30 minutes. Slice with sharp knife and serve roll-ups with cream. Makes 6 servings.

Note: You may sprinkle 1 tblsp. lemon juice over berries.

SNOWY GLAZED APPLE SQUARES

2½ c. sifted flour
½ tsp. salt
1 c. shortening
2 eggs, separated
Milk
1½ c. crushed corn flakes

8 medium-size tart apples,
   pared and sliced (about
   5 c.)
1 c. sugar
1½ tsp. cinnamon
Glaze (directions below)

Combine flour and salt in bowl. Cut in shortening. In a measuring cup, beat egg yolks with enough milk to make ⅔ c. Add to mixture; toss lightly.

Divide dough almost in half. Roll larger portion to fit a 15×9″ jelly roll pan. Sprinkle with corn flakes. Spread apples over flakes. Combine sugar and cinnamon; sprinkle over apples. Roll out remaining dough. Place on top; seal edges.

Beat egg whites until foamy; spread on crust. Bake in moderate oven (350°) for 1 hour or until golden brown. Cool slightly. Makes 24 (2½″) squares.

Glaze

1¼ c. sifted confectioners sugar   ½ tsp. vanilla
3 tblsp. water

Combine all ingredients; stir until well blended.

GOLDEN TREASURE PIE

2 (8½ oz.) cans crushed   ¼ c. sifted flour
  pineapple, undrained   1 c. cottage cheese
½ c. sugar   1 tsp. vanilla
2 tblsp. cornstarch   ½ tsp. salt
2 tblsp. water   2 eggs, slightly beaten
⅔ c. sugar   1¼ c. milk
1 tblsp. butter   Unbaked 10″ pie shell

Combine pineapple, sugar, cornstarch and water in small saucepan. Bring to a boil; cook one minute, stirring constantly. Cool.

Blend sugar and butter. Add flour, cheese, vanilla and salt; beat until smooth. Slowly add eggs, then milk to cheese mixture, beating constantly.

Pour pineapple into crust, spreading evenly. Gently pour custard over pineapple, being careful not to disturb first layer. Bake in hot oven (450°) for 15 minutes, then reduce heat to 325° and bake 45 minutes longer. Makes 8 to 10 servings.

CREAMY CHEESECAKE

3 c. cottage cheese, drained   ¾ c. sifted flour
5 eggs, slightly beaten   1½ c. milk
¼ tsp. salt   Tangy Jam Sauce (recipe
1 tsp. vanilla   follows)
¼ tsp. almond flavoring   Whipped cream
1 c. sugar

RAISIN GRIDDLE COOKIES (recipe page 286), full of raisins, are unforgettable. Today's busy cooks freeze the cutout dough stacked like hamburger patties to bake when needed. Excellent with coffee or ice cream.

Snack Packs—A superb selection of tasty nibbles that can be made and frozen. When guests arrive unexpectedly—just take a batch from the freezer and pop into the oven. Recipes for CORNMEAL/BEAN TARTS (page 299), PIZZA FRANKS (page 300), CHICKEN TURNOVERS (page 301), DEVILED HAM TWISTS (page 301), TUNA TOPPERS (page 302), SAVORY HAM (page 302), CHEESE AND BEEF POTPOURRI (page 302).

Press cottage cheese through sieve (or blend with 1 c. of the milk in blender until smooth). Add eggs, salt, vanilla and almond flavoring to cheese; blend thoroughly.

Combine sugar and flour; slowly blend into cheese mixture. Add milk. Pour into buttered 9×9×2″ cake pan. Set dish in pan of water. Bake in moderate oven (350°) for 1 hour or until knife inserted halfway between side and center comes out clean. (Surface may be pale.) Cool. Cut in squares and serve with Tangy Jam Sauce and whipped cream.

Tangy Jam Sauce

½ c. strawberry jam   ¼ tsp. vanilla
½ tsp. lemon juice

Combine all ingredients; blend thoroughly.

RASPBERRY SWIRL

¾ c. graham cracker crumbs   1 c. sugar
3 tblsp. butter, melted   ⅛ tsp. salt
2 tblsp. sugar   1 c. heavy cream
3 eggs, separated   1 (10 oz.) pkg. frozen
1 (8 oz.) pkg. cream cheese   raspberries, partially thawed

Combine thoroughly crumbs, melted butter and 2 tblsp. sugar. Lightly press mixture into well-greased 11×7×1½″ pan. Bake in moderate oven (375°) about 8 minutes. Cool thoroughly.

Beat egg yolks until thick. Add cream cheese, sugar and salt; beat until smooth and light.

Beat egg whites until stiff peaks form. Whip cream until stiff and thoroughly fold with egg whites into cheese mixture.

In a mixer or blender, crush raspberries to a pulp. Gently swirl half of fruit pulp through cheese filling and spread mixture into crust. Spoon remaining purée over top; swirl with a knife. Freeze, then cover and return to freezer. Makes 6 to 8 servings.

VANILLA ALMOND CRUNCH

1 (4 oz.) pkg. slivered almonds   ½ c. flaked coconut
¼ c. butter, melted   ⅛ tsp. salt
1 c. crushed rice cereal   1 qt. vanilla ice cream,
    squares   softened
½ c. light brown sugar

Toast almonds in the melted butter. Remove half of almonds from butter and set aside.

Combine crushed cereal, brown sugar, coconut and salt with remaining almonds and butter. Pat mixture gently into 13×9×2" pan. Bake in moderate oven (375°) 5 minutes. Cool.

Spread ice cream over cooled crust. Decorate top with reserved almonds. Makes 10 servings.

VELVETY LIME SQUARES

1 (3 oz.) can flaked coconut
½ c. vanilla wafer crumbs
2 tblsp. butter, melted
2 tblsp. sugar
2 (3 oz.) pkgs. lime flavor
    gelatin
2 c. boiling water

1 (6 oz.) can frozen limeade
    concentrate
1 qt. plus 1 pt. vanilla ice
    cream, softened
⅛ tsp. salt
Few drops green food coloring
Pecan halves

Carefully toast ½ c. coconut in moderate oven (375°) until lightly browned, about 5 minutes. Set aside.

Combine remaining coconut, crumbs, butter, sugar. Lightly press into 11×7×1½" pan and bake in moderate oven (375°) 6 to 7 minutes. Cool.

Dissolve gelatin in boiling water. Add limeade, ice cream and salt; stir until dissolved. Add a few drops of green food coloring. Pour into crust. Top with reserved toasted coconut and garnish with pecans, if you wish. Freeze until firm. Cover tightly. Return to freezer.

Remove dessert from freezer 20 minutes before cutting. Makes 6 to 8 servings.

FROZEN LEMON TORTE

1 c. finely crushed gingersnaps
2 tblsp. sugar
3 tblsp. butter or margarine
2 egg yolks
1 (15 oz.) can sweetened
    condensed milk

½ c. lemon juice
1 tblsp. grated lemon rind
2 egg whites, stiffly beaten

Combine cookie crumbs, sugar and butter. Reserve 3 tblsp. of mixture. Press remainder in bottom of buttered refrigerator tray. Chill in freezer section while you make filling.

Beat egg yolks well; stir in sweetened condensed (not evaporated) milk. Add lemon juice and rind and stir until thick. Fold egg whites into mixture.

Pour into crumb-lined tray. Top with remaining crumbs. Freeze at least 4 to 6 hours. Makes 6 servings.

SURPRISE STRAWBERRY SHERBET

1 pt. fresh strawberries, sliced	1½ c. buttermilk
¼ c. sugar	½ c. sugar
1 envelope unflavored gelatin	2 tblsp. lemon juice
⅓ c. strawberry juice	

Combine strawberries and the ¼ c. sugar and mash well. Let stand 10 minutes then strain off ⅓ c. juice. Set aside remaining crushed berries.

Soften gelatin in ⅓ c. of the strawberry juice. Dissolve over hot water. Add to buttermilk along with the remaining crushed berries, sugar and lemon juice, stirring well to dissolve sugar.

Pour into two refrigerator trays. Freeze until mushy. Beat in mixing bowl until smooth. Return to refrigerator trays. Freeze until firm. Garnish with whole berries. Makes 6 to 8 servings.

MINCEMEAT BROWN BETTY

2 c. coarse dry bread crumbs	¼ tsp. salt
4 apples, sliced in eighths	3 tblsp. lemon juice (1 lemon)
1 c. prepared mincemeat	¼ c. water
½ c. sugar	2 tblsp. butter or margarine
¼ tsp. cinnamon	

Put ⅓ of crumbs into bottom of buttered 1½ to 2 qt. casserole; cover with half of apples and half of mincemeat.

Mix sugar, cinnamon and salt together; sprinkle half over mincemeat.

Add layer of crumbs; then one of apples and mincemeat; sprinkle with remaining sugar mixture.

Top with remaining crumbs; pour lemon juice and water over all; dot with butter.

Cover; bake in moderate oven (350°) 20 minutes; uncover; bake 15 minutes longer. Serve hot or cold with plain or whipped cream. Makes 5 servings.

PEACHES IN LEMON SAUCE

1 (1 lb. 4 oz.) can peach halves or slices	½ c. syrup (from peaches)
	1 tblsp. sugar
1 egg	Dash salt
2 tblsp. lemonade concentrate	1 (3 oz.) pkg. cream cheese

Drain syrup from fruit; reserve. Spoon fruit into individual dessert dishes.

Beat egg in top of double boiler. Add lemonade concentrate (don't add water), ½ c. reserved syrup, sugar and salt. Beat well.

Place over boiling water; cook until thick and smooth, stirring occasionally, about 6 to 8 minutes.

Add cream cheese. Beat with a rotary beater until smooth. Serve warm or cool over peach halves. Gingersnap cookies are good accompaniment, although any desired crisp cookie may be served. Makes 6 servings.

PIE-PAN ICE CREAM DESSERTS The Kansas woman who created these desserts in her country kitchen called them ice-cream pies. The ice cream makes the pie shell—you need no pastry. First you freeze the shell. Then you add the fillings and return "pies" to the freezer. It's a scrumptious dessert to have on hand for quick use.

Ice Cream "Pie" Shell Line an 8″ pie pan with 1 pt. vanilla ice cream. Or use ice cream of any flavor you desire. For a more generous "crust," use 1½ pts. ice cream. Cut it in 1½″ slices; lay on bottom of pan to cover. Cut remaining slices in half; arrange around pan to make rim. Fill spaces with ice cream where needed. With tip of spoon smooth "crust." Freeze until firm before adding filling.

CRANBERRY-NUT "PIE"

2 c. fresh or frozen cranberries	½ c. chopped nuts
1 c. sugar	1 (8″) frozen vanilla ice cream
1 c. heavy cream, whipped	"pie" shell

Put cranberries through food chopper, using fine blade. Add sugar; let stand overnight.

Whip cream. Mix cranberries and nuts. Fold into whipped cream. Pour into ice cream shell. Freeze. Makes 1 (8") pie.

CHOCOLATE-PEPPERMINT PIE

1 tblsp. cocoa	1 tsp. vanilla
½ c. sugar	2 c. heavy cream, whipped
1 (4 oz.) pkg. chocolate	2 (8") frozen peppermint-stick
pudding mix	ice cream shells

Combine cocoa and sugar. Add to pudding mix and prepare as directed on package. Cool; fold in vanilla.

Fold cream into chocolate mixture. Pour into 2 peppermint-stick ice cream shells. Freeze. Makes 2 (8") pies.

BROWNIE PUDDING

1 (1 lb.) pkg. brownie mix	¾ c. brown sugar
1 or 2 eggs	¼ c. cocoa
½ c. chopped nuts	1¾ c. hot water

Mix batter according to directions for cakelike brownies, adding eggs and nuts as directed. Pour into greased 9×9×1½" pan.

Mix together brown sugar and cocoa. Sprinkle over top of batter. Gently pour hot water over sugar mixture. (When baked, this topping makes a small amount of chocolate sauce in bottom of pan.)

Bake in moderate oven (350°) 45 to 55 minutes until cake layer tests done. Serve warm or cold. Spoon into serving dishes. Serve with light cream or whipped cream. Makes 6 to 9 servings.

CHRISTMAS CRANBERRY ICE

1 qt. cranberries	¼ c. lemon juice
4 c. water	½ c. orange juice
2 c. sugar	

Cook cranberries in 2 c. water 8 to 10 minutes, or until skins are broken. Rub through fine sieve for smooth pulp.

Stir in remaining ingredients. Pour into refrigerator trays or loaf pan. Freeze until firm, 2 or 3 hours (stir 2 or 3 times). Makes 8 servings.

Note: Serve the pretty red ice in sherbet glasses as an accompaniment for turkey, chicken or other meat. Or decorate fruit salads with spoonfuls of it. And although the colorful ice is on the tart side, try it for dessert with coconut cake or cookies.

CRANBERRY SHERBET

1 (1 lb.) can jellied cranberry sauce	2 tsp. grated orange rind
¼ c. sugar	⅓ c. orange juice
	1 c. heavy cream, whipped

Mash cranberry sauce with fork; add sugar, orange rind and juice. Freeze in refrigerator tray until almost firm.

Beat with electric mixer or rotary beater until smooth; fold in whipped cream. Return to tray and freeze until firm. Makes 6 servings.

LEMON MIST

2 pkgs. unflavored gelatin	½ c. lemon juice
½ c. cold water	1 tsp. grated lemon rind
1 c. boiling water	2 egg whites
½ c. sugar	Sunshine Sauce (recipe
¼ tsp. salt	follows)

Sprinkle gelatin over cold water to soften. Add boiling water, sugar and salt, stirring until dissolved. Stir in lemon juice and rind. Chill until syrupy. Beat until frothy. Add unbeaten egg whites (always select eggs that have no cracks when they are to be used raw). Continue beating until mixture is light, fluffy and begins to mound, about 10 minutes. Pour into serving dish. Chill until set. Serve with Sunshine Sauce. Makes 8 servings.

Sunshine Sauce

⅓ c. sugar	2 egg yolks
⅛ tsp. salt	1 egg
½ c. water	½ c. light cream
2 tblsp. lemon juice	

Combine sugar, salt, water and lemon juice in the top of a double boiler; add egg yolks and egg. Beat just enough to blend. Place over gently simmering water and beat constantly with a rotary beater until mixture thickens, about 8 to 10 minutes. Cool.

Beat cooled lemon mixture until smooth. Stir in cream. Makes 2 c. sauce.

RASPBERRY/RICE SURPRISE

1 c. uncooked rice	2 tblsp. honey
3 c. boiling water	¼ tsp. almond extract
¾ tsp. salt	1 c. heavy cream, whipped
½ c. sugar	Berry Sauce (recipe follows)

Cook rice in salted water until tender and fluffy. Blend in sugar, honey and almond extract. Chill. Fold in whipped cream.

Berry Sauce

1 tblsp. cornstarch	2 c. raspberries
½ c. sugar	1 tblsp. lemon juice
¼ c. water	

Mix cornstarch and sugar. Add cold water and stir until smooth. Add the raspberries and lemon juice. Bring to boil; reduce heat; simmer 5 minutes. Chill. Top each serving of rice with Berry Sauce. Makes 6 servings.

PINEAPPLE-MARSHMALLOW PARFAIT

1 (1 lb. 4½ oz.) can crushed pineapple	½ c. chopped nuts
1½ c. miniature marshmallows	⅓ c. grated or flaked coconut
1 c. heavy cream, whipped	Maraschino cherries

Combine undrained pineapple and marshmallows. Refrigerate overnight, or at least 6 hours.

At serving time, fold in whipped cream, nuts and coconut. Serve in parfait glasses or dessert dishes. Garnish with cherries. Makes 6 to 8 servings.

FROSTED SHORTCAKES

30 graham crackers	1 c. heavy cream, whipped
¾ c. raspberry jam	1 tblsp. sugar

Stack graham crackers 5 high with jam spread between. Frost top and sides of each stack with cream with sugar added.

Chill 6 hours or overnight. Makes 6 servings.

DESSERT SANDWICHES

½ c. cold milk
1 (2 oz.) pkg. dessert topping
    mix
½ tsp. vanilla

Red or green food color
⅛ tsp. peppermint extract
1 (8¼ oz.) pkg. chocolate
    wafers

Combine milk with dessert topping and vanilla. Whip as directed on package. Tint a delicate pink or green with a few drops of food color. Add flavoring.

Frost crisp chocolate wafers with mixture. Top with chocolate wafers, sandwich style. Freeze several hours or days. Makes 15 (2¼″) sandwiches.

CRANBERRY TRENTON DESSERT

3 c. chopped cranberries
3 c. chopped tart apples
1 tblsp. cornstarch
⅓ c. light brown sugar,
    firmly packed
¾ c. sugar
1 tsp. salt
1 tsp. vanilla

1 c. oatmeal
½ c. light brown sugar,
    firmly packed
⅓ c. sifted flour
2 tblsp. crushed corn flakes
¼ c. butter
½ c. chopped nuts

Combine cranberries, apples, cornstarch, ⅓ c. brown sugar, granulated sugar, ½ tsp. of the salt and vanilla. Pour into a buttered 7×11×2″ baking dish.

Mix together oatmeal, the ½ c. brown sugar, flour, corn flakes and the remaining ½ tsp. salt. Cut in butter until mixture is crumbly; stir in nuts. Sprinkle evenly over top of cranberry mixture. Bake in moderate oven (350°) for 35 to 40 minutes. Top with whipped cream if you wish. Makes 10 servings.

CREAM PUFF HEART

1 c. water
½ c. butter
1 c. sifted flour
4 eggs

Cream Filling (recipe follows)
1 (10 oz.) pkg. frozen
    strawberries, drained
Confectioners sugar

Fold a 9×8½″ piece of paper in half lengthwise. Sketch half of a heart on it; cut out. Open paper to full heart; trace with pencil on baking sheet. Grease sheet lightly.

Heat water and butter to boiling; reduce heat. Add flour. Stir vigorously over low heat until mixture forms a ball (about 1 minute). Remove from heat.

Beat in eggs, one at a time, beating until smooth after each addition. Drop mixture by spoonfuls, with sides touching, onto heart outline on greased baking sheet.

Bake in hot oven (400°) for 45 minutes. Cool on rack. Cut off top. Fill shell with Cream Filling; top with strawberries. Replace top. Dust with confectioners sugar. Serve at once. Makes 8 servings.

Cream Filling

1 (3¼ oz.) pkg. vanilla pudding   1 c. heavy cream, whipped
   and pie filling   1 tsp. vanilla
1½ c. milk

Combine pudding and milk in a medium saucepan. Cook, stirring constantly, over medium heat until it comes to a full rolling boil. Remove from heat. Cover surface of pudding with waxed paper; cool. Fold whipped cream and vanilla into cooled pudding.

Section 5
Snacks, Nibbles
and Beverages

If you keep a small "company corner" in your freezer and refrigerator, unexpected guests need never put you in a dither.

For those spur-of-the-moment occasions we present a scrumptious assortment of goodies that we predict will become part of your entertaining repertoire.

Look for the tantalizing collection of delicacies called Snack Packs. An interesting variety of hot nibbles . . . tiny chicken turnovers subtly spiced with curry; baby franks wrapped in pizza-flavored dough for a new idea . . . light golden Deviled Ham Twists—all are bite-size, puffy and delicious.

TOMATO JUICE IN PUNCH BOWL

A country hostess who likes to entertain many friends at a time often serves tomato juice in her punch bowl. "It keeps everyone in the living room out of the way while I arrange the food on the buffet," she says, adding, "I usually freeze a ring of ice for a garnish."

Here is how she fixes it a few days before her party. She uses a ring mold that fits into the punch bowl. On the bottom of it she arranges thin lemon, cucumber and radish slices, pours on ¾" cold water and puts it in the freezer. When frozen, she fills the mold about three-fourths full of water and returns it to the freezer.

To turn out the decorative ring in the punch bowl, she quickly dips the bottom of the mold in warm water. She pours on the chilled tomato juice, seasoned as the spirit moves. The gala ring floats in the red juice, festive side up.

SNACK PACKS Tasty nibbles give a lift to any gathering, and it's easy to produce a tempting assortment of snacks if you do them ahead and freeze them ready-to-bake or thaw in variety packs. You'll always be ready for guests.

For Hot Snack Packs Select 2 to 4 of the following snacks per tray: Bean Tarts, Pizza Franks, Chicken Turnovers and the Deviled Ham Twists. Prepare according to recipe directions which follow.

Place assorted unbaked snacks close together in a $7\frac{1}{4} \times 11\frac{1}{4}''$ disposable aluminum foil pan or pizza pan. Freeze until firm; next cover closely with a plastic wrap, then with aluminum foil. Seal foil to edges of each tray securely with freezer tape. Then tape all the snack trays in a neat stack for convenient storage in your freezer.

To serve hot snack assortments, remove foil and plastic coverings and bake unthawed in a hot oven (400°) for 13 to 15 minutes, until the snacks are nicely browned and puffed.

CORNMEAL/BEAN TARTS

Filling

1 (15½ oz.) can refried beans
¾ c. shredded Provolone
  cheese (or other sharp
  cheese)
2 tsp. garlic salt

2 tblsp. red chili sauce
1½ tsp. crushed dried red
  pepper
¼ tsp. chili powder
2 tblsp. butter

Combine ingredients in top of double boiler; heat until cheese melts. Spoon into cornmeal tarts.

Pastry

2 c. sifted flour
1 tsp. salt
1 c. cornmeal
⅓ c. shortening

⅔ c. finely shredded Cheddar
  cheese
⅔ c. water

Sift flour and salt; stir in cornmeal. Cut in shortening until mixture resembles fine crumbs. Stir in grated cheese. Sprinkle water over mixture, tossing lightly with a fork until pastry is uniformly dampened. Roll to about ⅛" thickness on lightly floured surface. Cut with 2" biscuit cutter. Press pastry circles into tiny tart cups, ruffling edges. For larger bean tarts, use small muffin-cup pans. Bake unfilled in hot oven (400°) for 13 minutes. Makes 2½ dozen.

PIZZA FRANKS

2¼ c. sifted flour	½ tsp. oregano leaves
4 tsp. baking powder	⅓ c. shortening
½ tsp. cream of tartar	⅓ c. milk
¼ tsp. garlic salt	⅓ c. tomato paste
¼ tsp. onion salt	1 egg, unbeaten
1 tblsp. sugar	1 lb. frankfurters, cut in ½"
¼ c. Parmesan cheese	pieces
¼ tsp. basil leaves	

Sift together flour, baking powder, cream of tartar, garlic salt, onion salt and sugar. Stir in cheese, basil, and oregano; cut shortening into flour mixture to make coarse crumbs. Add milk, tomato paste and egg; stir with fork until dough follows fork around the bowl.

Knead on floured board five or six times. Roll dough ½" thick. Cut into 1" rounds (we used a doughnut hole cutter). Press dough around franks to form cups. Makes 8 dozen.

CHICKEN TURNOVERS

1 tblsp. chopped onion	1 tsp. curry powder
¼ c. diced green olives	¼ tsp. salt
1 (3 oz.) can mushroom pieces	1½ c. ground cooked chicken
(reserve liquid)	1 (9½ oz.) pkg. pie crust mix,
1 tblsp. butter	prepared according to
1 tsp. flour	package

Sauté onion, olives, and mushroom pieces in butter. Stir in flour, curry powder and salt, then mushroom broth. Simmer 1 minute; add chicken. Place a teaspoonful of mixture in center of 3" pastry circle. Fold pastry over, dampen edges and seal with a fork or handle-end of a table knife. Makes 2½ dozen.

SPICED FRUIT COCKTAIL

2 (1 lb. 1 oz.) cans fruit for salad or fruit cocktail	2 tblsp. lemon juice
	1 (6" piece) stick cinnamon
1 (1 lb. 1 oz.) can light cherries	1 tsp. whole cloves
	⅛ tsp. salt

Drain syrup from fruit into saucepan. Add lemon juice, cinnamon and cloves (tied in cheesecloth bag) and salt. Boil 5 minutes. Remove spices. Pour over fruit. Chill several hours or overnight.

Serve in sherbet glasses. Garnish each serving with a sprig of mint. Makes 6 servings.

MARSHMALLOW POPCORN BALLS

1 c. popcorn	¼ c. butter or margarine
1 tsp. salt	½ lb. marshmallows

Pop corn; sprinkle with salt.

Melt butter in skillet. Cut marshmallows in quarters. Alternate layers of popcorn and marshmallows in skillet.

Cover; heat slowly until marshmallows are partially melted. Mix well; form into balls. Makes 9 (2") popcorn balls.

Cheese Popcorn To freshly popped, hot, salted popcorn add ¼ c. melted butter and ⅓ c. shredded or grated Parmesan cheese. Toss to mix.

DATE-MARSHMALLOW BALLS

1½ c. chopped dates	3½ c. graham cracker crumbs
1¼ c. chopped nuts	1 (6½ oz.) pkg. fluffy white frosting mix
2 c. miniature marshmallows	

Combine dates, 1 c. nuts, marshmallows and 2½ c. graham cracker crumbs. Mix thoroughly.

Prepare frosting mix as directed on package. Add to the date mixture and mix until completely moistened.

Combine ¼ c. nuts and 1 c. graham cracker crumbs in small bowl.

Form date mixture in 1½" balls. Roll in graham cracker crumbs and nuts. Store in covered container at least 12 hours to mellow. Makes 36 balls.

POPSICLES

1 (3 oz.) pkg. orange flavor
   gelatin
1 (⅝ oz.) pkg. grape flavor
   drink powder

1 c. sugar
2 c. boiling water
1¾ c. cold water

Dissolve gelatin, drink powder and sugar in boiling water. Stir in cold water. Freeze in ice-cube tray. (You may insert wooden sticks or picnic spoons in mixture when partly frozen.) Makes 18 cubes.

Variation: Substitute other flavors of gelatin and drink powder for the orange and grape ones.

Index